D1626598

British Avant-Garde Theatre

British Avant-Garde Theatre

Claire Warden

palgrave
macmillan

First published 2012 by
PALGRAVE MACMILLAN

Palgrave Macmillan in the UK is an imprint of Macmillan Publishers Limited, registered in England, company number 785998, of Houndmills, Basingstoke, Hampshire RG21 6XS.

Palgrave Macmillan in the US is a division of St Martin's Press LLC, 175 Fifth Avenue, New York, NY 10010.

Palgrave Macmillan is the global academic imprint of the above companies and has companies and representatives throughout the world.

Palgrave® and Macmillan® are registered trademarks in the United States, the United Kingdom, Europe and other countries.

ISBN 978–0–230–28578–1

This book is printed on paper suitable for recycling and made from fully managed and sustained forest sources. Logging, pulping and manufacturing processes are expected to conform to the environmental regulations of the country of origin.

A catalogue record for this book is available from the British Library.

A catalog record for this book is available from the Library of Congress.

10 9 8 7 6 5 4 3 2 1
21 20 19 18 17 16 15 14 13 12

Printed and bound in Great Britain by
CPI Antony Rowe, Chippenham and Eastbourne

To my Granny Margaret

Contents

List of Illustrations   ix

Acknowledgements   x

A Note about Illustrations   xi

Introduction: A British Theatrical Avant-Garde   1

1 Structure: The Fragmented and the Episodic   22
Performing current affairs: the Living Newspaper   25
Expressionism and *Stationendrama*   31
Montage and cinematic editing   40
Variety theatre and popular entertainment   46
'Time, gentlemen, please': naturalism and beyond   48
Questioning conclusions   53

2 Staging: Platforms and Constructions   55
Former theatrical traditions and the contemporary
   political space   57
'Precursors of great promise'   61
Using the platform   63
Construction and projection   66
New lighting innovations   71
The new stage: cages and prisons   75
Limited experiment?   82

3 Language: Disturbing Words   85
Poetry in theatre: a British tradition   86
Poetry, drama and linguistic style   91
Towards a political poetic   97
The poetics of declamation   104
Dialect, accent and vernacular speech   106
Non-communicative language   109
Speaking to an audience   112

4   Character: The Screaming Man and the Talking Feet   **115**
Ancient modes reinterpreted   116
Isolation: psychoanalytical science and the
    fragmented mind   120
Modern humanity: the nameless, the dead and the
    non-human   127
Animals, mannequins and robots: new characters for
    the modern stage   134
Redeeming the human   140

5   Crossing Genres: Movement and Music   **147**
Crossing genres: music, dance and the dramatic form   148
Dance, movement and the modern world   152
Dalcroze's eurhythmics to Meyerhold's biomechanics   154
Modern dance: Theatre Workshop's experiments
    with Laban   158
The Dance of Death: the influence of ballet   162
Rhythms, beats and drumming   168
'Incidental' theatrical music   171
The creation of critical dialogues   174

Conclusion: A British Theatrical Avant-Garde?   **176**

Notes   183

Bibliography   195

Index   210

List of Illustrations

1 Overcoming the forces of inertia 1
2 The heavy pulse of the masses 22
3 Space bounded 55
4 Trap me in my words 85
5 Marionette 115
6 A lace of rigging 147
7 Hung in the sky of the mind 176

Acknowledgements

Thanks to the faculty members, students and postgraduates of the University of Lincoln, the University of Edinburgh, Queen Margaret University and the Institute for Advanced Studies in Humanities, Edinburgh. There were so many conversations, emails and comments that helped me as I considered my ideas. Particular thanks to Roger Savage and Olga Taxidou: without the humorous scribbles of the former and the patient guidance of the latter, this book would never have been written. I also continue to appreciate the support of Ann Gray, Mark O'Thomas and John Bull, and Beth Fletcher who has produced some incredibly innovative visual responses to the plays. Thanks to all at Palgrave, particularly Ben Doyle and Paula Kennedy, and to all the archivists and librarians I have worked with, all of whom have been uncommonly kind and helpful. There are numerous other people whose knowledge and advice I have greatly benefited from in the course of writing *British Avant-Garde Theatre*. Thanks go to many eminent scholars whose words of guidance and helpful suggestions can be seen throughout this book. Any errors contained within these pages remain, nonetheless, entirely of my own making.

Final thanks to my family and friends in Stockport, Edinburgh, Lincoln and further afield. They have offered constant support throughout this process. Love and thanks to Mum, Dad, Sal and affiliated family, and the Warden/Young clan, especially Dave and Ailsa. And thanks particularly to David for your proofreading, your never-ending good humour and your unwavering belief that one day I would get a proper job!

A Note about Illustrations

While writing this book I came across a range of images that have proven useful to give some sense of original production. However, when deciding on the illustrations I concluded that commissioning original pictorial responses to the plays was more in keeping with the overall intention of the project. Beth Fletcher (www.bethfletcher. co.uk) has produced some incredibly vibrant designs and I offer my sincere thanks to her for capturing my own fairly vague initial vision. My hope is that this book will reinvigorate the archive, providing new raw material for contemporary performance. The British theatrical avant-garde, as I posit it, is defined by relationships between artists, directors, actors, dancers and writers, and I wanted to capture some of that interdisciplinary excitement in this book. The collaboration process has been extremely fruitful and exciting, creating new perspectives on old plays. I hope the new artwork will provide inspirational, contemporary ways into the historical canon.

Introduction: A British Theatrical Avant-Garde

Figure 1   Overcoming the forces of inertia (© the artist Beth Fletcher)

An autumn evening of 1934 saw the first UK performances of T. S. Eliot's *Sweeney Agonistes* at Group Theatre's headquarters, 9 Great Newport Street.[1] An esteemed crowd made its way to this outpost of artistic creativity, tucked away in a Westminster side street. According to Robert Medley, who made the masks for this production, 'a distinguished and elite audience climbed the precipitous and unsavoury stairs to see it at the time, amongst whom was W. B. Yeats (whom I was personally detailed to help up the stairs) and Virginia Woolf, brought by Eliot and a party of friends' (Medley 1983, p. 151). Indeed, Woolf referred to this event in her diary entry of Monday 12 November:

> Home with the car all acrid & yellow & red with chrysanthemums. And put them in water – a long job – & so to hear Sweeney Agonistes at the Group Theatre; an upper attic or studio: I sat by Tom: an audience, containing Ottoline & Hope & Raymond.[2] The acting made more sense than the reading but I doubt that Tom has enough of a body & brain to bring off a whole play: certainly he conveys an emotion, an atmosphere: which is more than most: something peculiar to himself; sordid, emotional, intense – a kind of Crippen, in a mask: modernity & poetry locked together. I liked the egg speech.
>
> (Woolf 1982, p. 260)

In this liminal space, Woolf, Yeats and friends were treated to a play that, as this diary entry suggests, both captured a sense of the Zeitgeist and created confusion in equal measure. Bertolt Brecht also saw *Sweeney Agonistes* and apparently told director Rupert Doone that it was 'the best thing he had seen for a long time and by far the best thing in London' (Sidnell 1984, p. 103).[3]

In the October of the following year Group Theatre performed *Sweeney Agonistes* again in a double bill with W. H. Auden's *The Dance of Death* (Sidnell 1984, p. 284). The juxtaposition of these two plays must have been a remarkable if somewhat perplexing affair, connecting Eliot's experimental poetic drama with Auden's innovative, politically conscious play. Visually and audibly this must have been an extraordinary theatrical experience, a performance fusion that challenged spectators on aesthetic and thematic levels. In the audience was Benjamin Britten, who later composed the music for a number of Group Theatre plays. In his diary he noted that he went to 'see Rubert [sic] Doone's ... production of T. S. Eliot's Sweeney Agonistes and W. H. Auden's Dance of Death. Both very exhilarating and interesting shows' (Evans 2009, p. 281). For Britten then, and presumably for Woolf, Brecht and others, these plays produced a sense of visceral excitement and intellectual engagement; both these responses remained central to many early to mid-twentieth-century experiments. More broadly these 1935 performances illustrated Eliot's direct association with 'the Auden generation' (Hynes 1976): that is, Stephen Spender, Christopher Isherwood and Louis MacNeice. From here, as we shall see, one can follow a theatrical family tree and find Unity Theatre and Theatre Workshop, as well as figures such as Montagu Slater, Terence Gray and Basil Dean. Moving across national boundaries and continuing to follow associative threads we find, of course, Brecht, but also Ernst Toller, Kurt Jooss and Sergei Diaghilev.

During these early decades of the twentieth century there were particular theatrical productions, like Group Theatre's versions of *Sweeney Agonistes* and *The Dance of Death* that, due to their content, formal techniques and challenge to taste or tradition, caused a stir. In order to understand the scale, scope and influence of these performances I aim to create a workable, versatile category – a British theatrical avant-garde – focusing in the main on a particular historical period between approximately 1914 and 1956, an epoch of great change culturally, socially and politically. This category is not a claim for homogeneity or a reductive method of enforcing uniform ways of understanding the theatre of this period; rather it enables us to create dialogues, vibrant parallels between different performances, crossing typical boundaries of nation, class and genre. These performances were theatrical renderings of this modern era, artistic representations of the confusions and uncertainties. In *Theatre, Performance and the Historical Avant-Garde,* Günter Berghaus maintains that, though such change has always been an inevitable aspect of human experience, the early part of the twentieth century was subject to a 'feeling of cataclysmic commotion' (2005, p. 26). Out of this (and indeed parallel to this) overwhelming 'feeling' came cultural changes. New forms, movements and techniques arose, directly connected to this 'feeling' in the modern world. There was a sense of rupture and change, affecting many different areas of life from politics and international relations to the economy and the societal structure.

This leads us to the inherent problem in the creation of a British avant-garde – the multiplicity of definition. The term 'avant-garde' has been interpreted in so many ways that it has become almost impossibly loaded. The troublesome relationship between the terms 'avant-garde' and 'modernist' and recent revisions have left us with a bewildering collection of, often conflicting, concepts. There seems to be no definitive understanding, no unchallenged interpretation. Can the avant-garde be understood in terms of originality or as a moment in a genealogy? Are avant-gardists always political whereas modernists more concerned with aesthetics? Can one even make such a terse distinction between the modernist and the avant-garde? Is the avant-garde actually, as Georg Lukács suggested, 'a subjectivist war on reality and all its works' (Jameson 2007, p. 40) and thereby meaningless, formless and without substance?

There are no easy answers here. Partly extricating my argument from these debates, the objective is to create a functional method specifically designed to explore an avant-garde that is both *British* and *theatrical,* that is local and performance-based. In order to do this we will return to some earlier definitions of the term to consider three important semantic elements that will lead to the construction of this category. Firstly, it is connected with leading, with providing an example for others to follow. Henri Saint-Simon, one of the first to connect this term, previously associated with military strategy, with cultural endeavour, called on the 'scientists and artists and those of you also who devote something of your energies and means to promoting enlightenment' to lead in these new ways of thinking (Saint-Simon 1952, p. 2). This is vital to the British theatrical avant-garde. All too frequently 1956 is perceived as the *annus mirabilis,* the year British theatre suddenly transformed itself, 'catching up' belatedly with things that had been going on in Continental Europe for decades. This is a highly reductive approach. Even if these later innovators were not consciously aware of a British historical avant-garde, it is an important paradigm; many of the most celebrated experiments of 1956 onwards were preceded and anticipated by the performances explored in this book. In presenting this connection, one begins to understand the British avant-garde as both a historical period, intrinsically implanted in a genealogy, and as a sensibility that moves beyond epoch. Of course, the very concept of leadership (especially in light of Saint-Simon's conclusions) might seem to imply an innate sense of elitism, of those 'with the eye of genius' (Saint-Simon 1952, p. 2) leading those without. However, transporting this to the British context, elitism here does not, by and large, suggest superiority or pomposity. There was an avant-garde elite in the sense that practitioners were trendsetters, but this elite was committed to destroying all elites,[4] thereby paving the way for future innovations. Rather than elitism, then, this concept of 'leadership' is an inherent aspect of the theatrical genealogy this book seeks to construct.

Secondly, and again returning to Saint-Simon, the principal aim of any avant-garde is to 'overcome the forces of inertia' (1952, p. 2). In the British context this aspiration was both artistic and, in the broadest sense of the term, political. One of the central connecting inducements of the British avant-garde was to challenge the established order and, as Wyndham Lewis had it in *BLAST*, 'destroy politeness, standardization and academic, that is civilized, vision' (Lewis 1914, p. 12). This direct questioning is a central tenet of any avant-garde and extends to aesthetics and belief systems. When practitioners do use historical stylistic practices, they are carefully chosen to assist the modern impetus rather than acting as impediments to progress. Any veneration of certain previous traditions does not inhibit a radical momentum.

Finally Saint-Simon maintained that 'the prosperity of France can only exist through the effects of the progress of the sciences, fine arts and professions' (1952, p. 73). This, in a British context (indeed, in any context), is perhaps overstating the point somewhat, but it would be correct to suggest that in the British avant-garde theatre, practitioners really believed that their art could assist in the transformation of society (or at least the conscious, engaged individual within society), whether by presenting a truthful representation on the stage, by challenging assumptions about taste or the nature of art, by drawing attention to the dexterity of the human body or the beauty of language, or by advocating a particular political opinion.

Thus, rather than attempt to compress the British avant-garde into previously constructed definitions that often do not adequately explain the local (and particularly the local *theatrical*) experience, a pliable understanding of the avant-garde as concerned with leading, challenging and changing (all inherently present within the military understanding of a 'vanguard') allows us to bring together disparate groups and figures and create a real sense of a British avant-garde. In recent years, breaking away from the assumption that there was no historical avant-garde in Britain, other scholars have appropriated the term 'avant-garde' in order to explore a distinctly British cultural experience, discussing British avant-garde sensibilities in poetry, in visual art and even in music. But there is not a real attempt to understand the theatre in similar ways.[5]

Historical avant-garde scholarship, as James Harding and John Rouse have noted, tends to display a noticeable 'antiperformative bias' (2006, p. 1), insofar as the theatre is often overlooked, or indeed read as literature, and nowhere is this more manifest than in a British context. While recognising the importance of the play text (indeed, as we will see the written text is a vital aspect of the British tradition) it is also crucial to resist the temptation to focus solely upon it. Due to a distinct lack of surviving material on the specific theatrical conditions, particularly from groups such as the Workers' Theatre Movement and its affiliates, it can become easy to base arguments on the written texts alone. However, as far as possible, I have attempted to break away from the primacy of the written text to construct a real *performative* history, looking at innovations and changes in staging, audience demography, the construction of a company, the use of the body, and audio and sonic elements. In using the term 'performative' I am also consciously tapping into influential critical work in this area. Like 'avant-garde', 'performative', in light of work by J. L. Austen and Judith Butler, has become an extraordinarily complex concept. And yet it remains useful and suitable in this context. It becomes particularly apposite when read through the recent ideas of Erika Fischer-Lichte:

> In contrast to the dominant principle of division and partitioning, the aesthetics of the performative emphasizes moments of transgression and transition. The border turns into a frontier and a threshold, which does not separate but connects.
>
> (2008, p. 204)

As she goes on to explain, 'frontiers' and 'thresholds' are, by their nature, gateways; we recognise them as moments of division but also as points to be crossed and re-crossed. This exposition, implicit in the term 'performative' is extremely useful to this understanding of a British avant-garde as based in discursive, creative, multi-way dialogues.

'British avant-garde theatre', however, is by no means a homogenous category. There are a number of inescapable contradictions and
uneasy parallels. Unlike the scene in Continental Europe, where discernible movements such as Surrealism, Dadaism or Expressionism
coexisted, overlapped or took up the avant-garde mantle from one
another, in Britain there seemed to be very few of these definable
categories, particularly in theatre. Rather than attempting to create arbitrary groupings, in this British context theatrical innovations can be read in terms of dialogues.[6] At times these dialogues
are self-evident: stage managers employed by a number of different
groups or playwrights working in collaboration. At other junctures
the dialogues are less explicit: perhaps two directors influenced by a
similar overseas movement or two companies using the same dance
techniques. Within the Saint-Simonian-based avant-garde definition
('leading, challenging and changing') these dialogues can actively be
explored without having to bring circumscribed '-isms' into play.

Constructing a methodological category does not require a comprehensive overview of twentieth-century theatre history. A number
of excellent books provide exhaustive descriptions of the history of
British theatre, and this is not my objective here. The plays mentioned in this book are representative examples of a particular, and
I would say admirable, kind of activity. By drawing attention to that
field of activity, by creating such a model, other playwrights, companies and movements may, in time, sit alongside those mentioned
here, and these useful and fascinating dialogues can then grow and
develop. This category is ever shifting, constantly being transformed
as other nodes are added. This sort of analysis challenges the notion
of archival research as solely or largely a work of resurrection and
preservation. Certainly there is a focus on the former, but it is rein-
vigoration rather than preservation that is the catalyst for this study.
This process comes about as disparate groups and ideas are brought
together in relationship and imagined in light of performance rather
than as the abiding, fixed products of an archaeological dig.

Dates are, though useful, a guide only, and, indeed, one of the central objectives here is to connect this historical period (1914–56) with
the past and the future. It was a crucial contention in one of the most
influential critiques of the avant-garde, Renato Poggioli's *The Theory
of the Avant-Garde,* in which he pointed to a 'historical synthesis of
avant-gardism [which] will begin with its prehistory' (1968, p. 226).

For Poggioli this meant a sustained study of *Sturm und Drang* and Romanticism. In this British theatrical context it leads to a focus on melodrama, music hall, poetic drama and symbolism, all movements that in some way provide a 'pre-history'. Concurrently, and inextricably connected with the notion of 'leading' already outlined, the innovations mentioned here also remain influential in the contemporary theatre. And, in addition, many remain *potentially* influential as modern practitioners search for new methods of creating theatre in our twenty-first-century context. The historical avant-garde can be understood as a particular period but, more than this, an avant-garde sensibility moves across history connecting a variety of diverse traditions from different eras together.

The term 'avant-garde', awkward as it is, is rarely applied to Britain, partly because avant-gardism is often seen as 'foreign', the preserve of the large number of refugees who fled to Britain during this particularly turbulent period. Toller, Laban, Jooss and Gropius all found refuge both politically and artistically in Britain, while prominent figures such as Copeau and Reinhardt brought their productions to London (Roose-Evans 1989, pp. 58, 65). Furthermore, there is also a semantic issue here, with the very term 'avant-garde' suggestive of a foreign invasion, a Continental European army descending on the British Isles bringing unfamiliar ideas and methods. So *British Avant-Garde Theatre* is a re-imagining of British theatrical history,[7] an attempt to resurrect 'other traditions', whether those connected with well-known poets/novelists (Auden, Isherwood, Spender and so on) or with more peripheral figures. But the re-evaluation takes place within the category of the 'avant-garde' thereby immediately bringing these 'other traditions' into alignment with these eminent figures of the European avant-garde, breaking through conventional categorisation (the poetic vs. the political) and bringing an immediate suggestion of artistic experimentalism to the argument.

Using the term 'avant-garde' rather than 'modernist', then, is a conscious decision. In attempting to break down the perceived tensions between the poetic and political traditions, 'avant-garde', as understood above, seemed the more useful term. Indeed it acts as a sort of linguistic *Verfremdungs-Effekt*, 'making strange' the canon of early twentieth-century British theatre. In recent scholarship there has been a renewed attempt to read 'modernist' and 'avant-garde' in dialogue rather than as terms in enmity, challenging the notions of 'modernism' as rather literary-focused and Anglophone and 'avant-gardism' as Continental, defined by experiment and antagonism. Perhaps most usefully, recent analyses have presented a case for a 'modernist avant-garde',[8] thereby disposing with the tension altogether, using 'modernist' as a synonym for 'historical'. This not only challenges the 'modernism versus avant-garde' debate, but actually brings the two terms together in a mutually beneficial relationship that seems to ground these innovations within a specific context while acknowledging their formal experimentation. For a study such as *British Avant-Garde Theatre,* this confluence of form and context is extremely profitable.

In conjunction with this, the book also seeks to bring together a number of figures and companies who have largely been studied separately. There are a good many books about specific companies, and a number of them are regularly cited in this volume. Studies such as Michael Sidnell's *Dances of Death: The Group Theatre in London in the Thirties,* Colin Chambers's *The Story of Unity Theatre,* Howard Goorney's *The Theatre Workshop Story* and, more recently, Robert Leach's *Theatre Workshop: Joan Littlewood and the Making of Modern British Theatre* all provide fascinating insights into the companies working in the first half of the twentieth century and beyond. But there hasn't yet been a text that has really tried to unite these groups under a single banner while maintaining a strong sense of diversity. This book aims to fill that gap.

While recognising the differences between the projects and intentions of the theatre companies mentioned, there are evident connecting points and parallels. However, initially it may seem that there are two distinct traditions – the poetic and the political. Certainly, there are two distinguishable genealogies involved: the university-educated poets and their affiliates composing theatrical poetry, and the working-class companies searching for a form that would further their political ideas. But there is a far greater sense of dialogue between them than might be imagined. In fact, it is a theme that Michael Billington takes up in his recent *State of the Nation*:

> And it is true that it is as hard to imagine Joan Littlewood directing *The Cocktail Party* as it is to contemplate T. S. Eliot enjoying a rough night with Theatre Workshop in Barrow-in-Furness. Yet,

although they were leagues apart stylistically and the poetic dramatists were eagerly embraced by the theatrical Establishment, these two strands of post-war theatre had more in common than one might suppose. Both were suspicious, to varying degrees, of the prevailing naturalism. And both viewed the new post-war Britain with a mixture of hope and disappointment born out of moral idealism. It was just that Joan and her gang wanted more red-blooded socialism and the poetic dramatists more Christianity.

(2007, p. 26)

Billington recognises the differences between these poetic and the political traditions but, at the same time, is decidedly aware of the similarities. While *State of the Nation* discusses the post-war scene, Billington's conclusion is equally as applicable in a pre-war context. Deciphering these connections is also a central intention for Peter Billingham in his analysis of other lesser known theatre groups, *Theatres of Conscience: 1939–53*. He conveniently articulates my own intentions in this book:

Whilst I do not want to stretch inappropriate connections between such a diverse range of theatre from The Gate through to the Red Megaphones, there was, amongst these non-commercial companies amongst which the Unity would eventually be included, a commitment to perform plays in repertoire that were of high artistic value, but which would not find a platform with the hegemony of commercial theatre.

(Billingham 2002, p. 10)

Both Billington's and Billingham's verdicts clearly reveal the difficulty and value of constructing parallels between such diverse companies. They are careful to maintain this important and inescapable diversity while noting the exciting parallels that may be uncovered if this barrier between the poetic and the political is regarded as permeable.

In fact, there are a number of ways that this connection between the poetic and political can be made: the challenge to the audience, the use of the manifesto, the shared performers and directors. Certainly, all the performances examined here pose a challenge for any potential audience member. There are unusual images, intertextual references, non-linear stories, direct political declamation, complicated poetry and a contemporaneousness that means that these plays often only seem relevant for a short time. All these facets of performance have led to accusations of unpopularity and this may be partly the reason that a number of the plays mentioned here have largely dropped out of the canon. Many were unpopular at the time of performance and many remain unpopular with hindsight. In its numerous incarnations, the avant-garde has often been regarded as decidedly unpopular; as Ortega Y Gasset says, 'modern art, on the other hand [as opposed to Romanticism], will always have the masses against it. It is essentially unpopular; moreover it is antipopular' (1945, p. 5). Gasset revels in this antipopularity, creating an artistic movement that is decidedly elitist as 'the average citizen [is] a creature incapable of receiving the sacrament of art, blind and deaf to pure beauty' (1945, p. 6). This is an attitude similarly prevalent in Marinetti's writings on theatre; the subtitle for his *Manifesto of Futurist Playwrights* is *'The pleasures of being booed'* (Marinetti 2008, p. 181). In the same piece, Marinetti goes on to say, 'we Futurists instruct authors **to despise the public'** [emphasis his] (ibid., p. 181). Gasset and Marinetti's conclusions may not sit well with us (nor would they have been appreciated by many of the playwrights and directors mentioned in this book), but they do point to a key issue: avant-garde theatre is generally perceived as difficult, as a challenge to fashions and habitually accepted conventions.

It is a concept developed in Poggioli's work when he points to two distinct categories – 'accidental unpopularity' and 'substantive unpopularity' (1968, p. 46). The issue is whether a given play is unpopular by intention or whether it just happens to be unpopular due to complex experiments in form or demanding thematic concerns. Either way, many of the plays I refer to have been regarded as 'unpopular'. Often this was due to the perceived success of any given performance. Isherwood perhaps described it best when reviewing *The Ascent of F6*, a play he wrote in collaboration with Auden in 1936:

> If *F6* didn't quite succeed as a whole, it at least pleased many people by the variousness of its parts.
>
> (Isherwood 1977, p. 200)

The experimental sense of plays such as *The Ascent of F6* meant that certain aspects worked successfully while other aspects failed to engage the audience; as cited at the start of this chapter, Woolf made a similar comment about *Sweeney Agonistes*. If the central premise of any avant-garde is experiment, then it could be presumed that there would be successes and failures. Theatre Workshop, too, suffered under accusations of unpopularity. As company member, Howard Goorney, recollected, '*Uranium 235* [a 1946 anti-nuclear play by Ewan MacColl], as far as the West End was concerned, was "avant-garde" theatre, and, as such, suspect and to be avoided' (Goorney 1981, p. 83).[9]

Another recurring motif is the manifesto, a form that had a distinct British history as 'in some sense, of course, London was the birthplace of the genre' (Puchner 2006, p.109). The manifesto is quite rightly associated with an avant-garde questioning of the position of the artist, the perpetual dialogue between art and life, and the purpose of art in the modern age.[10] The Vorticists, Group Theatre, Theatre Workshop, and Unity Theatre, amongst others, used the manifesto form to set out their agenda. Although the manifestos vary greatly in content, all contain a certain formidable passion. Group Theatre's 1934 manifesto asserted that the members 'are thus creating a theatre representative of the spirit of to-day' (Medley 1983, p. 146). The *Manifesto of Theatre Union* (later Theatre Workshop) called for a 'facing up to the problems of our time and ... intensifying our efforts to get at the essence of reality' (Goorney 1981, p. 25). Auden in his 1935 *Manifesto on the Theatre* concluded that, 'ideally there would be no spectators. In practice every member of the audience should feel like an understudy' (Auden 1986, p. 273). Perhaps more problematically (and I will address this later in the book) Lewis began *BLAST* with, 'long live the great art vortex sprung up in the centre of this town!' (1914, p. 7). Although the groups, companies and individual figures had different, at times conflicting, political views, the use of the manifesto form reveals a unifying sense of passion and intention. It is also emblematic of a perennial dialogue between the Continental European and the British scenes, for the manifesto was a vital mode for a range of avant-garde practitioners across the Channel, from the Dadaists to the Futurists.

In addition to noticeable similarities in intention (while, of course, noting the evident differences), a brief consideration of personnel reveals more concrete connections. One obvious, well-known example is the actress Sybil Thorndike. Early on she worked with Basil Dean at Miss Horniman's Gaiety Theatre, Manchester and with Edith Craig's Pioneer Players (Morley 1977, p. 62). In 1924 she also played Sonia in Ernst Toller's groundbreaking *Masses Man* (ibid., p. 156). Of her performance in this latter production *Sunday Times* theatre critic James Agate wrote 'the highest praise must be accorded to Miss Thorndike for her presentment of the Woman. She spoke exquisitely throughout' (1944, p. 133). But she also participated in Unity's theatre school, acting as a tutor alongside those other stalwarts of 1930s theatre, Andre van Gyseghem, Paul Robeson and Miles Malleson, amongst others (Chambers 1989, p. 137).

Indeed, many of the central figures within the British theatrical avant-garde actively collaborated on certain projects. Take playwright, Montagu Slater who wrote *New Way Wins*, taken from his original *Stay Down Miner*. It describes the experiences of Merthyr miners threatened with unemployment and was produced by Left Theatre in 1936. Concluding with Howel's court scene in which the Magistrate declares, 'your Christianity sounds suspiciously like Socialism, Howel' (Slater 1937, p. 63), it resembles, with some moments of avant-garde experimentalism, the politically engaged naturalism of Sean O'Casey's Dublin Plays. However, the music was written by Benjamin Britten who was an important figure in Group Theatre (White 1973, p. 3). In 1936 Britten was also writing musical scores for a number of other plays including MacNeice's translation of *Agamemnon* and Auden and Isherwood's *The Ascent of F6*. Indeed, Auden's relationship with Britten was recently documented in Alan Bennett's 2009 play, *The Habit of Art,* proving that these figures still influence and inspire the modern generation of theatre practitioners.[11] Montagu Slater eventually took on the role of librettist for Britten, contributing to such celebrated pieces as *Peter Grimes* (1945). But Slater was not Britten's only connection with Unity for he also worked with the poet Randall Swingler (who wrote the 1936 mass declamation, *Spain,* for the company) on pieces like *Advance Democracy* and *Ballad of Heroes* (both 1939) (Croft 2003, p. 290). Coming full circle, Auden also contributed to the libretto for the *Ballad of Heroes*. In addition, Britten also worked at the BBC with Theatre Workshop's Ewan MacColl marking another connection between companies, and between the poetic and the political traditions.[12] This is a single example, emblematic of the connections that can be made between British-born artists.

Of course, these links can also be made across national boundaries. German playwright, Ernst Toller, for example, marks a central connecting point for a whole range of individuals. He clearly had a following in Britain as a 'kind of cultural hero of the British Left' (Samuel, MacColl and Cosgrove 1985, p. 26) and there is evidence of performances of Toller's plays by the Independent Labour Party, the Workers' Theatre Movement and Unity, amongst others. Yet Toller's influence on British theatre is more complex than one might initially expect. Certainly, he was one of the most popular playwrights for left-wing politically engaged theatre companies and, in fact, in 1935 Toller produced a version of his *Draw the Fires* in Manchester, employing members of Theatre of Action (later Theatre Workshop) as miners. Although MacColl and Toller did not always see eye to eye, the former did regard *Draw the Fires* as an interesting text, superior to much of the contemporary theatre of the 1930s (Goorney 1981, p. 7). Yet Toller's influence was felt across the British theatrical avant-garde. Ashley Dukes, founder of the Mercury Theatre, met Toller in prison in 1922 and, though he remained unconvinced with his 'sentimental left-wing' politics, he did conclude that 'for a while [Toller] wrote marvellous things, and he touched expressionism with poetry' (Dukes 1942, p. 77). Dukes recollected that the Stage Society performed a version of Toller's *The Machine Wreckers* in 1923 under the direction of Nugent Monck, the influential founder of the Maddermarket Theatre in Norwich (ibid., p. 79). Auden and Isherwood, too, met Toller in Sintra when they were writing *The Ascent of F6* in 1935 (Isherwood 1977, p. 180). Auden's admiration for Toller was clear in his 1939 poem *In Memory of Ernst Toller* in which he cited 'the friends who are sad and the enemies who rejoice' (2007, p. 143). Furthermore, Stephen Spender also had some contact with this important theatrical figure. He remembered:

> Shortly before the war, the German poet Ernst Toller came to see me. He had some scheme he wanted to discuss, about an appeal through high functionaries to the conscience of the world on behalf of the Spanish Republicans.
>
> (Spender 1980, p. 258)

In 1939 Spender translated Toller's challenging anti-Nazi play, *Pastor Hall,* with Auden translating the songs (Toller 1939, p. 97). All of this reveals not only the distinct relationships built up within the British avant-garde, relationships that broke through political and social barriers, but also the aesthetic similarities across the theatrical spectrum. As the book progresses the artificial distinctions between, to poach Billington's phrase, the 'two strands' (the poetic and political), become more and more arbitrary.

In fact, this creation of workable dialogues (in personnel, intention and aesthetics) is vital to the efficacy of this book. As the Toller example illustrates, while constructing a narrative for a local avant-garde and connecting diverse British figures, dialogues are also actively occurring across geographical boundaries. 'Dialogue' is the preferred term here because of the inherent associations; dialogues require active conversations and are constantly in flux as new speech acts change the relationship between the speakers. In their attempt to break away from a Eurocentric avant-gardism, Harding and Rouse have constructed a new sense of discourse that may well be useful as we construct these dialogues:

> Above all, a return to the site of cultural exchange and contestation between cultures gives us a very different vision of the center-to-edge/edge-to-center relationship than that which heretofore has served as a paradigm for conceptualizing the avant-garde. The most crucial revision of that paradigm, gained in a step back to the site of cultural contestations, is the recognition of a plurality of edges devoid of an identifiable center, a plurality that the recti-linear center-to-edge/edge-to-center convention in scholarship on the avant-garde has obscured. In the simplest terms, that move necessitates that we reconceptualize our notion of the vanguard within a theory of borders, and that we supplant *the cutting edge* with *the rough edges* of contestation.
>
> (2006, p. 24)

It must, of course, be noted that Harding and Rouse's aim is to disclose non-Western avant-gardes, whereas the central objective of this text is to uncover an under-represented British avant-garde. However, their conclusions regarding centres and peripheries still apply. Rather than see this book as a British-centric text, it is instead an attempt to break down this centre-to-periphery model. Even in terming this book *British Avant-Garde Theatre* I have no intention of understanding 'British' as a homogenous category. The class divides which so often appear in this book defy this easy categorisation, as do, of course, the profound differences between regions both within England and, even more acutely, between England, Wales and Scotland. Breaking down this centre-to-periphery model still further, often Continental European techniques impacted upon the British scene; at times, British experiments influenced changes on the European mainland; more often than not (and this is probably the most interesting aspect of the argument) figures on both sides of the Channel were solving theatrical problems in similar ways without necessarily being conscious of one another; American movements also influenced the British scene while many of the central plays in this book received early performances in the US. Further, the socio-historical antagonism between Ireland and Britain brings another facet to the dialogue. I have very consciously resisted writing about British and Irish theatre as somehow analogous. Rather, Irish examples have been used in a similar way to their American and Continental European counterparts. Context is central to the themes and reception of all the plays mentioned in this book so Irish theatre is necessarily different from British drama in focus and intent (Levitas 2002, p. 7). In fact, with the inextricable connection between Irish theatre and Irish politics, often the cultural scene of this near neighbour stands in direct conflict with British imperialism. This commitment to presenting British and Irish theatre as distinct, at times contrasting, traditions has meant focusing primarily on just two Irish playwrights, W. B. Yeats and Sean O'Casey. As I will go on to prove, both these figures were highly influential in the British context and their plays provide useful parallels. So, without necessarily moving specifically away from a Western-centric model, the notions of centres and peripheries remain always already contested.

The framework of this book permits a sustained study of some of the most prevalent and interesting formal innovations of this British theatrical avant-garde. Thus, Chapter 1 looks at play structure, examining the break away from a linear consequential narrative form towards a versatile, highly fragmented system. It focuses on some of the most important and recurring forms and techniques – the

Living Newspaper, Expressionist *Stationendrama*, montage and variety theatre – before finally reassessing the place of naturalism in the British avant-garde. Chapter 2 focuses on matters of staging from the simplicity of the platform stage to the complex experiments in lighting. Influences from the medieval tradition, contemporaneous experiments and the political scene are all vital to this discussion of the omnipresent platform stage. This chapter also introduces some of the precursors to the British avant-garde, figures who were already leading the way. Chapter 3 analyses language in light of the poetic and the declamatory, two different signifying systems that existed concurrently in British avant-garde theatre. It also attempts to read language very specifically in light of performance, as dialogue on a stage rather than as words to be read. Towards the end there is some analysis of the audiences these languages attempted to reach. The creation of character is the focus of Chapter 4, looking at both the figure in isolation and the individual as part of an inclusive community. Initially this may seem an irreconcilable paradox, but the British theatrical avant-garde (like the historical avant-garde overseas) contains both in abundance. In conjunction, there is a close study of the complex politics of individual groups and the difference these convictions made to character construction and play choice. The final chapter looks at the impact of other genres on the British theatrical avant-garde, particularly music and dance. In a major move away from the strong British naturalist and 'well-made play' traditions, the performances examined in this chapter detail the vital importance of the 'sister arts' in the creation of an exciting, challenging theatre. The conclusion will bring us back to the notion of dialogue, reassessing it in light of the examples provided in the preceding chapters. This structure means that diverse traditions can be read in parallel, using aesthetic innovations as connecting points.

The book considers a number of companies and practitioners that could be read as participants in a British theatrical avant-garde. These are used as examples of a central premise and my hope is that dialogues will continue to grow as other innovations (and innovators) are unearthed. Largely, I have centred my argument on four major companies/movements: the Workers' Theatre Movement and its affiliate groups, Unity Theatre in its various regional guises, Group Theatre and its playwrights and Theatre Workshop, particular in its pre-Stratford East days.[13]

The Workers' Theatre Movement (hereafter WTM) had its origins in Tom Thomas's Hackney People's Players which became the starting point for an organisation that eventually included groups from across Britain. This founding company was established in 1926, becoming an affiliate of the WTM in 1928 (Samuel, MacColl and Cosgrove 1985, p. 81). In many ways it was the British version of similar societies in Germany and Russia, putting on short sketches and agitational performances for local, regional audiences. Given the disparate nature of these groups, the performances varied in content and, indeed, skill. Largely, though, the plays and sketches chosen by these groups rejected the tenets of naturalism in favour of a politically motivated agitprop. Declamation, platform stages and song defined these performances and many, such as *The Judge of all the Earth* (1928) and *Meerut* (1933), are quite aesthetically and politically accomplished. However, the WTM eventually lost impetus, partly due to the international turn towards 'socialist realism' and partly because of the changing socio-political mood; as the Thirties progressed unemployment affected fewer members of the population and, instead, focus shifted to the growth of fascism (Stourac and McCreery 1986, p. 246). This meant that new theatrical methods had to be found.

But from the death of the WTM came the emergence of Unity Theatre and, in fact, there is a direct line of descent through a former associate group of the WTM: Andre van Gyseghem's Rebel Players.[14] Unity was officially founded in 1936 and based at Britannia Street, King's Cross before moving to Goldington Street near St Pancras the following year. But, despite this London home and like the WTM before it, Unity was actually a conglomeration of theatre companies from across Britain. While retaining the Unity name, these groups had very distinct identities, focusing on local needs and issues. Unity continued on well after the Second World War and from it came a range of innovative performances from the 1939 political pantomime *Babes in the Wood* to Living Newspapers like *Busmen* (1938) and on to plays by Brecht and Odets. Its London home burnt down in the 1970s and the land was eventually sold (Chambers 1989, p. 398), but, even today, Unity Theatre in Liverpool traces its origins back to the original Unity Theatre.

As the Unity Theatre Movement made an impact across Britain, in Manchester Ewan MacColl and Joan Littlewood founded

Theatre Workshop. The origins of this company can be found in MacColl's 1931 agitprop group, the Red Megaphones, which brought declamatory sketches on to the streets of Manchester and Salford. Joan Littlewood's arrival in Manchester led to a fruitful collaboration and the founding of Theatre of Action (1934) later to become Theatre Union (1936) and, in 1945, Theatre Workshop (Leach 2007, pp. xiii–xiv). Like Unity, the company continued to perform long after the war, moving to Stratford East in 1953, and, of all the theatre companies discussed in this book, arguably made the greatest impact upon future generations of theatre makers. MacColl, who broke with the company after its move to London, was the principal playwright for a number of years, and his plays mark some of the most innovative contributions to the canon of British avant-garde theatre.

The origins of Group Theatre were not found in the experiments of the WTM and its affiliates, but rather in choreographer-director Rupert Doone's experiences with the Ballets Russes and in the poetic innovations of its associated writers: Auden, Isherwood, Eliot, MacNeice and Spender. The company was founded in 1932, beginning with a couple of small-scale productions and readings (Sidnell 1984, pp. 275–6). From these small beginnings grew a permanent theatre company, committed to experiment and training. Group Theatre produced some of the most innovative performances of the British avant-garde, combining the words of some of the most important poets of the early twentieth century with the methods of the Ballets Russes. In terms of personnel and aesthetics this was the group that provided the clearest link between Britain and Continental Europe. But its life span was short. Company designer, and Doone's partner, Robert Medley, suggested that Group Theatre were 'quintessentially a "thirties" phenomenon' (Medley 1983, p. 167) and the outbreak of war marked the formal end of Group Theatre's existence.

These four groups act as useful illustrative examples of a British theatrical avant-garde. That said, a number of other practitioners, companies and theatrical societies are placed alongside them; these include the Festival Theatre in Cambridge, the Mercury Theatre and the Pioneer Players amongst others. All of these companies and societies can be directly connected to our major groups through personnel, aesthetics or political intention. This conscious decision to restrict my inquiry may appear contrary. Given the importance of moving dialogues, such limits seem somewhat puzzling. Yet they are necessary in such a study. Actually, in actively limiting myself greater potential for dialogue is created, as other researchers and practitioners integrate their own areas of study into this argument. Again, in order to fully explore this intention, we can return to Fischer-Lichte's understanding of the 'performative', for, in many ways, 'British avant-garde theatre' is a performative category. She maintains that the aesthetic of the performative 'unflaggingly attempts to transcend historically established borders which have since become so ossified that they appear natural' (Fischer-Lichte 2008, p. 203). Inherent in her description is the idea of persistently moving across pre-conceived boundaries. 'Performative' is, by definition, versatile and multi-faceted. It is open-ended, dependent on reciprocal, shifting relationships between audience and actor, and the various elements of the *mise-en-scène*. While I have placed restrictions on this book for practical, temporal and spatial reasons, the model that it describes can be used to create new parallels. As this shifting category is explored further in relation to other companies and practitioners, additional dialogues will be uncovered that will change our understanding of 'British avant-garde theatre', drawing on newly unearthed traditions, movements and performances.

I have also included a number of Continental European and American performances as comparable pieces, focusing in the main on plays that have had particular impact in a British context and particularly those that sit alongside British plays in the companies' repertoire lists. A number of these plays from Britain and overseas remain troublesome study matter. Due to their inextricable connection with the socio-political situation of these decades they often feel somewhat dated. Responding immediately to international crises they are also, at times, a little juvenile. Yet it is their ephemeral nature and sense of urgency that makes them exciting and gives this theatre its dynamism. It does, however, bring certain logistical problems for a researcher: which version of the play should be cited here? How can a theatre historian respond to the gaps and omissions? How can we formulate an accurate picture of actual performance rather than presenting the written text as an historical artefact? Images (though often of poor quality) and descriptions of performances have been extremely helpful, as have the written accounts and manifesto-style narratives of the key practitioners and, while at times leading us to bemoan the lack of existing evidence, it is exactly this ephemerality that makes these plays, playwrights and companies so fascinating to study. Yet, much material does survive and, in keeping with Berghaus's conclusion that 'the historical avant-garde was never a homogenous phenomenon, but encompassed a wide range of artists who were opposed to the aesthetic and social conventions of the day' (2005, p. 40) the archive discloses a multifaceted, dynamic collection of dialogues.

1

Structure: The Fragmented and the Episodic

Figure 2   The heavy pulse of the masses (© the artist Beth Fletcher)

Aristotle famously declared that tragedy must contain six parts: spectacle, melody, diction, character, thought and plot (1969, p. 13). The last is of particular interest as we discuss the issue of structure in the British avant-garde. He went on to say that this plot 'must connect the various incidents in such a way that the whole will be disjoined and dislocated if any one of them is transposed or removed' (1969, p. 17). Though by no means universal, this sequential plot structure had become a predominant form in British theatre, engendered by the late nineteenth-century cult of the 'well-made play' and the London productions of plays from the Continent (particularly Ibsen)[1] and from Shaw (Irish but situationally British), but also by a new commitment to constructing British plays in their image and to creating a local naturalist tradition. Writers such as John Galsworthy explored this genre at length. His influential plays, *Strike* (1909) and *Justice* (1910) used a naturalistic dramatic medium to explore the problems and tensions of society. Further, the playwrights of the Manchester School, namely Stanley Houghton and Harold Brighouse, produced works that embodied Emile Zola's belief that 'either theatre will become modern and real or it will die' (Schumacher 1996, p. 70). Performed by the highly influential and pioneering repertory company, the Gaiety Theatre Manchester, under the direction of Miss Horniman, plays such as Houghton's *Hindle Wakes* (1912) and Brighouse's *Hobson's Choice* (1916) looked to the industrial northern landscape for inspiration.

As clearly identified in the introduction, the practitioners of the British avant-garde had a variety of different intentions and aesthetic projects. Yet, a commitment to directly challenging Aristotelian notions of 'order in the arrangement of its [the plot's] parts' is an important moment of unity (1969, p. 15). The plays are not plotless, but rather full of multiple, at times conflicting, plot fragments. It is, in fact, summed up in a highly metatheatrical speech from the Radio Announcer in Louis MacNeice's 1937 play *Out of the Picture*:

> Aristotle insisted on unity and dignity. Further, Aristotle liked to know where he was. He liked to know whether he was in a tragedy or a comedy. But in these plays of Tchekov and many other plays which have succeeded them, who is to say? One moment you are laughing at the foibles of the characters and the next moment you

find they have shot themselves. Terribly inconsequent: but, ladies and gentlemen, terribly true to life.

(1937, p. 29)

MacNeice's description helpfully identifies some of the central tenets of the argument here. Genre became a complex notion and audience members were suddenly plunged into a complicated world where the relationship between cause and effect, logic and action was questioned. As MacNeice suggested, the narrative structures of the theatre began to reflect the daily uncertainty of modern existence.

To a greater or lesser extent, all the practitioners and playwrights of the British theatrical avant-garde questioned the very structural basis of drama and, given such artistic solidarity, it may well be easy to claim homogeneity in this area. However, this would be a highly reductionist approach. Although many of the plays and performances display a striking sense of similarity in their structural elements and concerns, they were often influenced by (or can be juxtaposed with) a broad number of different traditions and innovations. The structures may initially appear almost indistinguishable, but the intentions, foci and thematic concerns differ quite dramatically. So, rather than unite these performances under a specific banner of 'fragmentation' or 'episodic sequences', I would urge a certain more open-ended sense of unity by claiming that all the plays of the British avant-garde challenged Aristotelian linearity. This idea of narrative interruption in its various guises is an important one in avant-garde scholarship and, indeed, central to theoretical interpretations of avant-gardism (Osbourne 1996, p. 150). Thus, the avant-garde itself is perceived not as a historical moment per se, but as an interruption to history. Interruption is both an attribute of avant-garde artistic forms and a means of defining the 'avant-garde' as a concept. And, given that this idea of interruption is so vital to our understandings of the modernist avant-garde, it seems a useful place to start our analysis in earnest; so this chapter will take this concept and read it through British avant-garde performance. Yet, as we will see, despite the similarities, the differences, contrasts and variations in approach persist. Christopher Innes suggests that, 'indeed, on the surface the avant garde as a whole seems united primarily in terms of what they are against' (1993, p. 1) and, in the case of performance structure, this certainly seems to be upheld.

Performing current affairs: the Living Newspaper

Confronting the contemporary was one of the central motivations across the British theatrical avant-garde. Often this self-consciously modern outlook had a particular polemic feel; playwrights and theatre companies were attempting to actively participate in a political project. This engagement took many different forms, from challenging the very notion of art to advocating radical political change. Raymond Williams suggests that, in spite of the multiple incarnations of the avant-garde, it has always 'been, in its own way, a politics. It has continued to shock and challenge' (Timms and Collier 1988, p. 319). Williams's supposition is useful because it points to 'politics' as a unifying principle with constantly shifting meanings. This intention to create a politically engaged theatre evidently affected form as well as content, and led to the development of a range of new (or at least adapted) structures. One such form was the Living Newspaper, a documentary genre that blurred the boundary between dramatic creation and factual accuracy. Its efficacy is reliant on the appropriation of these facts by the audience through the theatrical experience.

Its earliest incarnations were found in Russia and America, with the Blue Blouse groups (1923–8) and Federal Theatre Project (1935–9) respectively. There is evidence that the British scene was directly influenced by both traditions. In its earliest British incarnation amongst the agitprop groups, there was a conscious effort to align themselves with the Russian stage (Samuel, MacColl and Cosgrove 1985, p. 64); Peter Davison, for example, writing in a published version of Unity Theatre's Living Newspaper *Busmen* notes, 'the idea underlying the Living Newspaper can be traced back to the use of drama in the Soviet Union' (Unity 1984).

However, from the available evidence it seems that the two companies working most regularly, and most successfully, within this genre (Theatre Workshop and Unity Theatre) took their lead largely from their American compatriots. A contemporaneous review of *Busmen*, for example, introduced the play as 'an English parallel to the American theatrical experiment' (Drama Societies 1938) and in the published version, *Busmen* is presented alongside the American piece *One Third of a Nation* which Unity produced in 1943. Unity's experiments were based primarily in an American tradition and, indeed, there are clear connections to be made as Andre van Gyseghem and Herbert Marshall, two important figures for the development of Unity's aesthetic, attended performances of Living Newspapers while in America (Forsyth and Megson 2009, p. 52n).

From a Theatre Workshop perspective Ewan MacColl suggested he became aware of the Living Newspaper genre through regular contact with the Laboratory Theatre in New York (Woods May 1973a, p. 6.). Indeed, in 1934, as Theatre of Action, the company performed a version of the Laboratory Theatre's multi-narrative dramatisation of contemporaneous unemployment, *Newsboy*. So, again there are clear connections to be made here between the local scene and the innovations overseas. However, importantly, an undeniably British tradition developed, partly out of the experiments in Russia and America, and partly simply in response to specific local socio-political events. In fact the history of the Living Newspaper is one of trans-Atlantic dialogue; there are strong connections between Erwin Piscator and the documentary theatre traditions in America and 'consequently, one could interpret from this that a pattern was emerging in the evolution of documentary theatre: it was returning to its European sources' (Dawson 1999, p. 78). With the visits of Van Gyseghem and Marshall, this form was transported to Britain too. Here is a fruitful duplex in which the techniques cross the Atlantic and return back to Europe, the ideas moving back and forth in complex, ever-changing dialogues.

Unity Theatre's *Busmen* is a prime example of a British Living Newspaper, resembling American examples in its fragmented form while focusing on a distinctly British theme. Written and performed by Unity in 1938, it was based on the Coronation Bus Strike of 1937, examining the circumstances through the everyday experiences of busmen themselves. While the narrative focuses on a single issue and chronologically discusses the events of the 1930s through to March 1938, it is still constructed in a highly fragmented style (Chambers 1989, p. 144). Lists of statistics and voice-overs are juxtaposed with discussions in the House of Commons before going on to a number of fairly naturalistic scenes. These latter fragments are centred first on the everyday experiences of the busmen at work and then on the personal lives of these men (Unity 1984, pp. 5–10). The central reason for the busmen's complaints seem to be summed up by the Conductor in Scene 13:

> It's just that we want to be treated like human beings and less like a cross between a mule and a machine.
>
> (1984, p. 17)

This differentiation in the speeded up, modern urbanised environment is a recurring theme in the British theatrical avant-garde. The worker as animal or machine is found in many of the plays, pointing to the dehumanisation caused by modern working processes. The production was given a perceived authenticity by inviting busmen to participate in its formulation:

> The enormous interest taken in the 'Living Newspaper' by Busmen, the assistance given by them in attending rehearsals means that this play will prove of tremendous value in presenting the Busmen's case to the Public and makes it the most important production we have ever undertaken.
>
> (Unity 1936–1940)

For a company searching for a real working-class audience, such a connection between lived experience and the theatre must have appeared extremely attractive and exciting. Being able to bring real voices to the stage, to provide a platform for debate and reasoned argument meant that the Living Newspaper became a vital part of Unity Theatre's repertoire.

Whereas *Busmen* focused on an historical event, albeit from an extremely recent history, Theatre Union's *Last Edition* (Manchester 1940) revelled in its contemporaneous flexibility. Co-writer MacColl (then known as Jimmie Miller) remembered that, 'we kept changing the show and putting in new scenes every week' (MacColl 1973, p. 66). Here chronological linearity is rejected in favour of contemporary political efficacy, producing a play that, like *Newsboy*, broke through the typical stories of the bourgeois press. It is constructed in 'episodes', moving from unemployment in Britain to the Spanish Civil War to a gangster version of the Munich Pact.[2] Even more than *Newsboy*, which Theatre Workshop had performed some six years earlier, this play relies on the juxtaposition of disparate scenes. Although there seems to be very little noticeable connection between, say, the Gresford Pit disaster (the focus of one of the most effective episodes) and the Munich Pact, there is a central focus which permeates the text: the condition of the working class in Britain, and, specifically, 'the Northern men!' (Goorney and MacColl 1986, p. 22). Each episode reflects MacColl's intention to dramatise diverse events and personalise them, reading them through the experiences of emblematic working-class voices. So, the Spanish Civil War Episode concludes with a list of Salford/ Manchester men killed in the war. The Munich Pact Episode ends with 'this is war, war to the knife! This is war!' (ibid., p. 33) which feels like a rallying call, a warning and a direct challenge to a 1940s audience confronting war outside the theatre space. Moreover, given the flexible, episodic structure, the play could be adapted for specific audiences and could respond quickly to contemporary issues. It is the play's dialogue between perceived objective fact and subjective response that makes *Last Edition* so effective. Each episode demands a reaction, a personal and collective assessment of the evidence.

Living Newspapers are inherently controversial and provocative, and there is evidence to show that both these British examples caused small but significant ruptures. In a short article of April 1938, the author suggested that the Lord Chamberlain agreed to the performance of *Busmen* subject to changes being made:

> Cromer [the Lord Chamberlain] has insisted that actual names of organisations be changed to imaginary ones, that no living person be represented: as play [*sic*] is a documentary, based on real speeches & reports, this has meant a lot of rewriting.
>
> (Hickey 1938)

Last Edition, too, attracted attention when it was first performed. MacColl recollected that after five performances, the police stopped the run and, with Joan Littlewood, he was fined and arrested (Goorney and MacColl 1986, p. xlvii). This is corroborated in MacColl's MI5 files, released in 2006. No other productions of the British avant-garde led to such a police response. There was evidently something about this form that was perceived as dangerous and powerful. Derek Paget maintains that 'the documentary mode occupies a different position on the 'facts–truth axis' from most other drama, and it is this which makes it (potentially) dangerous to a hegemony under threat' (1990, p. 29). So it is the presentation of 'fact' as 'truth' that makes this form so controversial. This is not purely theatre as entertainment but theatre as challenging informant.

In many ways, in fact, it was a subversion of the way newspapers were put together, particularly those designed for the working class. In his highly influential analysis, *The Uses of Literacy* (originally 1957), Richard Hoggart discusses the proliferation of escapist publications which invite their working-class readership to 'the enjoyment of "fragmentation", to the "dolly-mixtures" pleasures of a constant diet of odd snippets, of unrelated scrappy facts, each with its sugary little kernel of "human interest"' (1960, p. 202). It is interesting that it is the *structure* of these publications as well as the thematic content that maddens Hoggart. The disconnected fragments prevent the reader from ever engaging fully. As he says, 'one doesn't read such papers; one 'looks' at them' (ibid., p. 203). While the Living Newspaper maintains this familiar fragmented structure, in general terms, each fragment is connected to a central theme which does not merely entertain but also educates and provokes. These British Living Newspapers stand in sharp contrast to the publication that is so memorably satirised in MacColl's later, similarly episodic, analysis of nuclear science *Uranium 235* (1946) with its 'tales of vice/tales of spice,/ juicy details, very nice' (Goorney and MacColl 1986, p. 79). This new theatrical mode is an active rejection (or rather, perhaps, reappropriation) of the 'dolly mixtures' structure that so piques Hoggart, and is an effective travesty of the newspapers that so much of the audience would have enjoyed.

So a burgeoning local Living Newspaper tradition can be clearly seen in the repertoire of Theatre Workshop and Unity Theatre. Its fragmented, non-chronological format leant itself to the discussion of contemporary politics, just as it had in Russia and America. In many ways this is a dramatic structure that confined itself to the experiments of the overtly political groups. However, it would be wholly incorrect to discount the Living Newspaper entirely within the so-called poetic tradition. Raymond Williams addresses this issue in *Drama from Ibsen to Brecht,* where he reads the three major Auden-Isherwood collaborative plays through this form:

Through conventions which corresponded to the techniques of com-mercial popular culture – the radio announcer, the loud-speaker, the pair of commentators, the headline, the slogan, the dance-tune – certain points about society could be forcibly made.

(p. 206)[3]

The connection is not a straightforward one, as Williams goes on to suggest, but it is certainly worth exploring.

The Ascent of F6 (1937), for example, presents the story of Michael Ransom, a mountaineer who is sent by his twin brother Sir James Ransom, and his powerful friends, to climb the Haunted Mountain. The local legend has it that the first white man to reach the top will be able to claim ownership over the whole country. Representing the general public, Mr and Mrs A's fascination with the quest is prompted by the regular radio and newspaper updates, which use Michael Ransom's journey as jingoistic propaganda. In fact, like a number of the Living Newspapers, the central objective here is to dissect the methods of the popular press, to analyse that tense relationship between 'truth' (either objectively given or subjectively constructed) and fiction. This is explicitly revealed in a discussion between Stagmantle (representative of the establishment newspapers) and James Ransom in the Colonial Office. Deliberating over the methods of ruling the Empire, James Ransom reflects, 'I only wished to remind you – not, alas, that any of us need reminding – how grossly a valued public servant can be maligned in the performance of a painful duty by the venom of the popular press' (Auden and Isherwood 1966, p. 20). Stagmantle's response is to recite a list of newspaper headlines, '*British General Butchers Unarmed Mob! Children Massacred in Mother's Arms! Murder Stains the Jack*', which James Ransom refers to as 'the nauseating clichés of gutter socialism' (ibid., p. 20). Newspapers can, like the Living Newspaper model of Theatre Workshop or Unity, break through the untruths propagated by the hegemony. But newspapers can also endorse the decisions of the government. This becomes clear as Mr and Mrs A cut maps and photographs out of their newspaper in order to follow Michael's quest. Pinning these to their wall the couple create a shrine to nationalistic pride, preventing them from looking critically at their own circumstances and challenging the powers that govern them (ibid., p. 40).

The quest they propose is an attempt to silence the press and maintain the status quo in the colonised state. It is based on myth, on the story of the Guardian Demon and, while this legend has a long history for the Ostnians, James Ransom mentions a 'sequel' that could be used as a propaganda tool (Auden and Isherwood 1966, p. 22). This updated story (that the first white man to reach the top will command all Sudoland) leads to Michael Ransom's journey. The 'fictional' story is further complicated when the Demon is revealed as a 'real' figure, not in a corporeal sense but as an imaginative projection of the individual (ibid., p. 57). The complex dialogue, then, between 'truth' and fiction, vital to documentary theatre, is just as evident here in the analysis of the modern media and modernised ancient myth. *The Ascent of F6,* rather like *Last Edition,* attempts to negotiate this tension, enabling the audience to question the intentions of the media and popular legend and the interested parties that exploit them.

Williams's suggestion is even more evident in *On the Frontier* (1938), a play that narrates the events leading up to an outbreak of war between Ostnia and Westland. It contains a striking interlude in which '*five male members of the chorus represent the typical readers of five English newspapers. They should be dressed according to their shades of political opinion*' (Auden and Isherwood 1966, p. 186). These opinions range from the conservative and 'violently reactionary' to 'liberal' to 'communist' (ibid., p. 186). This interlude enables the audience to see the explicit biases of the press. Responding to the same situations and events, the newspapers have conspicuously different perspectives. Again, just as with the Living Newspapers, this scene seems to be dealing with the complex issues of truth, objectivity and political agendas. Like *The Ascent of F6* before it, *On the Frontier* is described in explicitly journalistic terms; Julian Symons, writing in the February 1939 issue of *Life and Letters,* pointed to the political success of the play, suggesting that 'the fact that the play is topical, a piece of *reportage* instead of a myth, is a help' (Haffenden 1983, p. 286). Despite the formal and thematic differences, it becomes evident that these Auden-Isherwood collaborations can be satisfactorily compared to the Living Newspapers of Unity and Theatre Workshop. Without overstating the point, the perceived barrier between the poetic and political traditions in British theatre looks decidedly shaky.

Expressionism and *Stationendrama*

If the Living Newspaper was adapted and developed primarily by the overtly politically engaged theatre groups but had resonances elsewhere, the influence of Expressionism was much more general and far reaching. As mentioned in the introduction, Ernst Toller became a vital influence for Unity and Theatre Workshop, but also for playwrights such as Auden and Isherwood. Furthermore, a number of figures and companies adapted Expressionist techniques in a British context. The Cambridge Festival Theatre and the Gate Theatre London both looked to Expressionism rather than naturalism (Davies 1987, p. 90) while the WTM also employed the montage effects of Expressionism, embracing the movement's rejection of established, so-called bourgeois forms (Samuel, MacColl and Cosgrove 1985, p. 43). In addition, Doone's ideas with Group Theatre were partly derived from Expressionism as he sought to develop his own concept of 'fantastic realism' (Sidnell 1984, p. 132)[4] and MacColl recalled that during his early agit-prop work with the Red Megaphones, his primary influence was 'the German Expressionists more than anybody' (Woods May 1973a, p. 6). There were, of course, others who pointed to the vital importance of Expressionism in a British context, but what is particularly interesting about these examples is that, as a genre, Expressionism seemed to cross the perceived divide between the politically engaged groups and those from a poetic or dance-based background.

Indeed, plays associated with German Expressionism found their way into the repertoires of many theatre companies. Toller's plays, for example, were produced by companies such as Theatre of Action (later to become Theatre Workshop) who performed in a 1933 version of *Draw the Fires* in Manchester under the direction of Toller himself (Samuel, MacColl and Cosgrove 1985, p. 249),[5] and the People's Theatre, Newcastle, whose 1925–6 version of *Masses and Man* was 'a most interesting experiment which, on the whole, was very effective. The play drew good houses and was a success, and, once again, we were pioneers in Newcastle' (Veitch 1950, p. 74). Independent Labour Party (ILP) member Ashley Dukes[6] translated *The Machine Wreckers* in 1923, and the group produced a version of *Masses Man* the following year (Barker and Gale 2000, p. 175).

Toller was an indisputably vital figure for this emergent British avant-garde; yet, I suggest, British Expressionism (or at least, more accurately, experiments within the Expressionist mode), as with British documentary theatre, often looked more directly to America than to the European Continent.[7] Plays by Elmer Rice and Eugene O'Neill, for example, reappear in the repertoire lists of a number of societies and companies, including the WTM and Unity Theatre. Both of these playwrights can be associated with the notion of Expressionism, although, interestingly, they both maintained that the German Expressionist movement had very little influence on the development of their respective aesthetics (Walker 2005, pp. 153, 155).

While Expressionism is predominantly associated with Germany, there is a notable Irish tradition in the later plays of Sean O'Casey. At the founding of the Unity Theatre Club, which brought the independent Unity groups together, O'Casey gave the opening night message (1938):

> I hope the Unity Theatre Club will smash the myth that culture and the enjoyment of art are confined to what is sometimes called the better classes.
>
> (Chambers 1989, p. 112)

O'Casey's commitment to creating 'art' for the working class was shared by Unity. Although his Dublin plays are, to all intents and purposes, naturalistic melodrama with a distinctly political edge, his later plays are highly experimental in form (Simmons 1993, p. 23). This commitment to formal innovation can be seen in *A Star Turns Red,* produced by Unity in 1940, or even in the earlier *The Silver Tassie* (1928) and *Within the Gates* (1934). The language and episodic style of these plays are reminiscent of the dramatic composition of the German Expressionists.[8]

All this is to say, British avant-garde theatre was certainly influenced and moulded by overseas innovations. However, it is important to note that there was also a burgeoning local tradition that certainly paralleled the movements of Continental Europe and America but was also independent, simply responding directly to theatrical and contextual problems. I would echo Julia Walker's words in *Expressionism and Modernism in American Theatre*:

> While it is true that American and German expressionist dramas share many of these traits, it is not necessarily true that German expressionism was the only or even primary influence upon the development of the American form.
>
> (2005, p. 4)

One could make a similar observation of the British scene. The techniques of Expressionism influenced (or, in light of Walker's remarks, can be seen in) British innovations in a number of clear ways. Staging, the addition of music and dance, and the changes in language all, to a greater or lesser extent, owed something to the innovations of this movement and will be discussed in some detail later. Yet it is arguably in the structure of the plays that Expressionism can be most clearly discerned.

Like the Living Newspaper, the Expressionistic structure is highly fragmented, often divided up into 'episodes' or 'pictures'. Rather than following a linear plot, the plays associated with this movement are focused around a particular thematic concern (Sokel 1963, p. xv). Often this fragmented abstraction originates, in sharp contrast to the Living Newspaper-inspired pieces, in the notion of a spiritual quest. The use of the term *Stationendrama* to describe Expressionist structure suggests the re-enactment of ritual, a moving from one location to the next. Furthermore, the Expressionist form also imbibes a sense of visual art, often juxtaposing 'pictures'. This is unsurprising given the clear dialogue between art and theatre in the Expressionist movement. Painters like Oskar Kokoschka and Vassily Kandinsky also turned to playwriting and their theatrical works often reflect this connection. Kokoschka's *Murderer Hope of Womankind* (1907), for example, is generally regarded as one of the first Expressionist plays.[9] It connects with visual art from the off and retains this approach throughout. A clear example would be the Man's initial entrance, which is obviously visually illustrative, a kinetic tableau (Ritchie and Garten 1968, p. 25). While Kokoschka actively resisted the compartmentalising and classifying of his work (Keegan 1999, p. 40), this commitment to graphic, at times shocking, imagery clearly places him tentatively within notions of Expressionism. Kandinsky's *The Yellow Sound* (1912) also reveals the playwright's background in art. It is written in pictures, relying more on visual effect than a linear story. This is accentuated by the tempo of the piece. In Picture 3, for example, initially, 'everything remains motionless' until light brings some movement to the piece while in Picture 5 the dancer 'holds the pose for a few moments' (Kandinsky and Marc 1974, pp. 219, 222). Paintings/pictures are necessarily fragmentary, cut off from other visual images by framing devices. Using visual art as an artistic cornerstone for their brand of theatre inevitably led to a discernibly episodic structure.

Again like the Living Newspaper, the fragments of the Expressionist form sought to challenge theatrical antecedents, both ideologically and artistically. Fragmentation became an aesthetic project, testing the audience's understanding of the basics of theatre. However it also made a broader comment about the world. In this post-First World War era with its ongoing political threats, material inadequacies and fractures in the very structure of society, the Expressionist form (somewhat peculiarly given its level of abstraction) directly reflected the everyday lived experience.[10]

Such Expressionist fractured forms can be seen in a number of British plays, even as far back as a 1928 WTM play entitled *The Judge of All the Earth,* 'a one-act expressionistic morality play' (Stourac and McCreery 1986, p. 201).[11] However, I want to focus here on two contrasting plays in order to make a claim for a local Expressionist tradition that revelled in the disruption of form: Auden and Isherwood's *On the Frontier* and MacColl's *The Other Animals.* Both have been referred to as explicitly Expressionist; Michael Sidnell calls *On the Frontier* 'an Expressionistic montage' (1984, p. 244) while Ben Harker suggests that 'theatrically the play [*The Other Animals*] looked back to 1920s Expressionism' (Harker 2007, p. 86).

What is particularly interesting, given Expressionism's somewhat ambiguous relationship with politics, is that both plays are highly challenging, politically engaged pieces. Expressionism has always held a central position in debates about avant-gardism and political efficacy, particularly in the fiery condemnations of Georg Lukács (Jameson 2007, p. 40). Closer to home, however, in a 1933 article in the WTM bulletin, the author infers that 'expressionism is less a type of revolutionary and proletarian drama, than a type of decadent and pessimistic bourgeois drama' (Samuel, MacColl and Cosgrove 1985, p. 167). Yet, both these plays defy these notions. In many ways Toller acts as a guarantor, consciously or otherwise, for MacColl, Auden and Isherwood. From prison Toller reflected that 'the place of the proletarian poet is among the ranks of the workers. The proletarian needs poets whose speech he can understand and in whose speech throbs the heavy pulse of the masses, of the factories and of the inevitable grand towns' (1936, p. 41). This political fervour pervades Toller's canon. The song at the end of the fifth picture of *Masses Man* perhaps best illustrates Toller's commitment to political struggle and his dedication to leading the workers as a 'proletarian poet':

> Arise, ye Masses, seize the hour:
> The world needs turning upside down,
> We slaves shall grasp the reins of power.

> (2000, p. 171)

Though this moment of agitational unity is broken up by the Officers who take the revolutionary Sonia Irene (Woman) away, a powerful sense of solidarity has already been built up. It remains throughout the play, marking an attempt to break through the walls of the theatre space and directly contribute to the everyday ongoing campaign. Expressionism – at times accused of being apolitical or even fascistic – can be at the service of the left in its campaign for radical political change. While I do not want to claim Auden and Isherwood as 'proletarian poets', they, like MacColl (and Toller) certainly used Expressionistic methods as they created their brand of politically engaged theatre.

Like *The Ascent of F6*, *On the Frontier* presents the methods of a dictatorial state. It discusses the way governments repress their own people, making them components in a machine, and the propagation of international tension which encourages the people to commit to a jingoistic project rather than challenge those in power. Given its publication date (1938), it was a remarkably timely analysis of contemporary international relations that provided both a satirical take on governmental policy and a poignant discussion of the way hegemonic thought suppressed individual expression. From O'Casey's *The Silver Tassie* to Toller's *Transformation*, there are a broad range of Expressionistic plays that examine war to a greater or lesser extent. Exploring such timely themes necessitated a formally modern play and *On the Frontier* directly follows this pattern. Structurally and generically, this play is a highly complex piece. It begins with sung rhyming couplets which have an almost colloquial feel. The play then moves rapidly into a fairly naturalistic episode based in Valerian's study, through a long monologue on the structures of society and on to a short interlude in a prison which visually illustrates the suppressive response of the government (Auden and Isherwood 1966, pp. 111–29). And this sort of narrative variation continues through the play.

The connection between its formal experimentation and theme were summed up in a review of 29 October 1938 in the *Times Literary Supplement*:

> The piece is called a melodrama, but the horror of international events, surrounding the persons, is given an atmosphere of farce, and is perhaps the more horrible for that. Life is shown as a monstrous Kafka-like absurdity.
>
> (Haffenden 1983, p. 276)

The play becomes generically complicated simply because it is a 'drama so much absorbed with characteristic world events that the play hardly stays in the theatre at all' (ibid., p. 276). Melodramatic, farcical or absurdist, this play is constructed as an Expressionistic collation of fragments (Sidnell 1984, p. 244).

Four years previously Group Theatre had performed a version of T. S. Eliot's *Sweeney Agonistes*, a play in which fragmentariness comes to the fore. Sidnell's analysis again provides a clearer illustration of the relationship between the fragmented world and form. He suggests that 'Eliot's fragments were utterly contemporary in feeling and their very fragmentariness – which Doone emphasized by a series of blackouts – gave the effect of a preconceived Expressionist montage' (1984, p. 103). This is, of course, a noticeable precursor to *On the Frontier* where the fragmented form is inextricably connected with a commitment to exploring the contemporary. Why should these fragments be 'contemporary' in and of themselves? Well, they illustrate the very nature of modern experience. Across the historical avant-garde, and echoing perceptible changes in society's understanding of the world, modern artists were questioning the grand narratives of reason and belief (Berghaus 2005, pp. 32–3). As these grand narratives began to rupture, smaller, multitudinous fragments arose. Artistic form directly reflected this.

MacColl continued this marginal British Expressionist tradition with *The Other Animals*. Again it is a politically engaged piece, produced by Littlewood at Manchester Library Theatre in 1948 and later taken to the Edinburgh People's Festival (1949) (Leach 2006, p. 57). It is a play of dualisms: the dissident prisoner Robert Hanau and the image of the hegemony, the doctor Graubard; the beauty of freedom and truth, and the deformities of the authoritarian regime;

revolution and the stagnant status quo; an ever-increasing light and a gradually diminishing darkness. Like *On the Frontier*, it directly confronts the conventions of Aristotelian linearity. It is a play of self-contained fragments, from the initial incarceration of Robert Hanau to the depiction of a symbolic train which is transporting a group of characters who fail to comprehend the danger as they speed through history, refusing to challenge the capitalist hegemonic system that seems to continue apace with nothing and no-one to check it. Like Auden and Isherwood, in explicitly connecting his play with the Expressionist mode, MacColl was not required to remain in the same imaginative space or to present transition. The scenes can be almost wholly unrelated, connected only by the central theme: the enduring battle between progressive radicalism and repressive establishment.

Again the structure of *The Other Animals* reflects the fragmentation of the world in the mid-twentieth century. However, more critically, it displays the disintegration of the central character. This is a key aspect of the Expressionist movement. Kandinsky suggested that 'form is the outer expression of inner content' (Kolocotroni, Goldman and Taxidou 1998, p. 271), that the very structure of an artistic piece is determined by the subjective. This is certainly the image presented in *The Other Animals*. Robert Hanau is represented by two actors; Robert is able to escape the confines of the prison, moving between disparate scenes, while Hanau remains incarcerated. In conversation with Hanau, Robert refers to himself as 'that part,/ the divided self' (Goorney and MacColl 1986, p. 147). Hanau responds: 'you are a dream/ I am reality' (ibid., p. 147). This character rupture is reflected in the narrative which moves between recognisable, almost natural-istic scenes and imaginative episodes. So, rather than reflecting the undeniable fragmentation of the world per se, the structure of *The Other Animals* formally illustrates the mental state of its protagonist. There is a pronounced Expressionist tradition of structuring plays in light of the central figure. Toller's *Transformation*, for example, focuses on the experiences of the protagonist, Friedrich, as he attempts to understand the war and patriotism, and his confusion is reflected by the play's form. Like *The Yellow Sound*, it is also constructed in pictures. Certainly this is emblematic of Friedrich's state of mind, but it also enables Toller to juxtapose the imaginative and the 'real'. Again, the aim of the fragmented form is to blur the boundary between fact and fiction, to analyse notions of reality, truth and the subconscious.

The Expressionists also exhibited a renewed interest in the relationship between drama and music (Sokel 1963, p. xiv). This was mirrored in the British context with a number of cross-generic performances. Working outside mimetic structures meant that action and dialogue could be juxtaposed with dance sequences and musical interruptions. But Expressionist form itself was akin to a piece of music with a number of different, and at times contrasting, movements and a central theme to bring a certain sense of unity. Certainly MacColl's *The Other Animals* illustrates this preoccupation with musical form. Littlewood suggested that *The Other Animals* was inspired by Mahler's *Resurrection Symphony* (Littlewood 2003, p. 310).[12] MacColl alluded to this connection when responding to a critic's suggestion that *The Other Animals* was simply too difficult, too intentionally unpopular by saying that 'symphonies were listened to more than once, and that anyone who found it interesting but difficult could always see it again' (Goorney 1981, p. 68).

MacColl was not alone in looking to the formal attributes of music as he developed an experimental, fragmented form. Eliot, too, turned to musical structures as he created his dramatic works. In September 1921 Clive Bell suggested that 'like Stravinsky, he [Eliot] is as much a product of the Jazz movement as so good an artist can be of any' (Grant 1982, p. 117). *Sweeney Agonistes* is certainly emblematic of this interest in jazz.[13] While there seems to be a palimpsestic, fragmented musicality about the piece, there is also a running theme: an analysis of the modern world with all its contradictions. So, while jazz is defined by a certain fragmentariness, it also attempts to create something beyond this: a kind of multi-faceted, yet unified subject.

And these inter-generic relationships are crucial to understanding the objectives of Expressionism, pointing, as they do, to the inherently constructive nature of art. Certainly, Expressionism explores the fissures in society and in the individual psyche; however, it also enables the audience to understand the composition of art in its broadest sense. Rather than permitting the audience to escape into a recognisable story, Expressionism forces spectators to question the very methods of artistic composition. This is central to the move away from linear narrative. Fragmentation does not permit escapist empathy but exposes the fabricated edifice of the theatre, and so better enables the message of the play to be uncovered. Therefore in the very structure of Expressionism there is an intrinsic possibility of exposition. While there are Expressionist pieces that use this structural artificiality to create largely apolitical moments of abstraction, a latent political *possibility* remains.

Within theatre history studies there is often the suggestion that Expressionism had a negligible impact on the British stage, that it remained the preserve of the German refugees. Any local Expressionist movement that did occur was largely inconsequential; Breon Mitchell, for example, asserts that 'within the English theater proper only the verse plays of Auden and Isherwood displayed certain "Expressionist" features' (Weisstein 1973, p. 184). Leaving aside what is meant by 'English theater proper', I hope the preceding paragraphs question the assumptions that Expressionism exerted little effect in Britain or that any effect it did have was restricted to the poetic drama tradition. It is not, and does not become, a dominant mode; as Huntly Carter rightly concluded in 1925, 'the nature and value of expressionism are so surrounded by confusion in this country [England] that it has done no more, as yet, than make its bow' (1925, p. 112). Yet the 'bow' was significant, a vital uniting mode that moved across boundaries and engendered dialogue.

Montage and cinematic editing

In his book *European Avant-Garde: New Perspectives,* Dietrich Scheunemann connects the Expressionistic *Stationendrama* with another modern artistic genre: film.[14] Scheunemann examines the influential *From Morning to Midnight* (1912) by Georg Kaiser:

> A new dramatic structure which was to become a model for other expressionist writers, and which was immediately identified by contemporary critics as *cinematic*. It is the structure of *Stationendrama,* an episodic structure in which the dramatic action unfolds in a series of self-contained scenes.
>
> (2000, p. 38)

Like Toller, Kaiser was mentioned as an influence for a number of companies, including Theatre Workshop (Samuel, MacColl and Cosgrove 1985, p. 242) and Unity (Chambers 1989, p. 143). In fact, Ashley Dukes's translation of *From Morning to Midnight* was initially performed in London in 1920 (and 1926) (Dukes 1942, p. 63). As

Scheunemann suggests, this play imbued a strong sense of the cinematic and, further, the fragmented structure of cinema can be seen throughout the performances of the British avant-garde. The very structures and devices of the cinema reappeared in literature, painting and, indeed, theatre.[15] Unsurprisingly, given the connection on the level of performance, cinematic techniques became extremely important for a number of British theatre companies and playwrights.

There might initially appear to be an irreconcilable tension here. Whereas the theatre of the British avant-garde was concerned with the notion of 'challenging', cinema can be the most escapist of mediums, an opportunity for audiences to immerse themselves in an imaginary world of Hollywood romance or historical adventure. This sense of escapism (which is, of course, by no means automatically negative) was a source of concern for Eliot who, in 1923, referred to the cinema as a place 'where his [the working man's] mind is lulled by continuous senseless music and continuous action too rapid for the brain to act upon' (1966, p. 458). But, just as the Living Newspaper form subverted popular journalism, the theatrical cinematic montage was a direct appropriation of this escapist, non-engaged image. In fact, the aim of structuring theatre in a filmic manner was to create drama that directly challenged the audience rather than, in Eliot's terms, 'lulling the mind'.

Interest in cinema was growing steadily during the early decades of the twentieth century. Through the journal, *Close Up* (1927–33), a new way of understanding and describing the cinematic appeared. It became, 'a model for a certain type of writing about film – writing that was theoretically astute, politically incisive, critical of films that were simply entertainment' (Donald, Friedberg and Marcus 1998, p. 3). New ways of thinking about film directly addressed the concerns expressed by Eliot. Film societies appeared across Britain, once again challenging artificial barriers between the artistic and political scenes; for the sake of our argument, Group Theatre had an affiliated film group (Sidnell 1984, p. 169) and the Workers' Film Movement brought films from Russia and Germany to a working-class British public (Donald, Friedberg and Marcus 1998, p. 281). As cinema became an important art form, so it influenced the drama on the stage.

The playwrights and practitioners cited Sergei Eisenstein as a crucial influence. He became a significant figure in Britain, giving lectures here in 1929 (Marcus 2007, p. 270). These lectures were later published in *Close Up*. The journal's editor, Bryher, published her *Film Problems of Soviet Russia* in the same year. Huntly Carter, too, wrote *The New Spirit in the Theatre and Cinema of Soviet Russia* in 1924, updating it in 1929. Russian cinema, then, and particularly the innovations of Eisenstein, became increasingly prominent towards the end of the 1920s. And his cinematic structures became vital modes in theatre. Writing in *Close Up* in 1928, Eisenstein (along with his compatriots Pudovkin and Alexandrov) pointed to the importance of particular methods in the creation of film:

> Contemporary cinematography, operating as it does by means of visual images, produces a powerful impression on the spectator, and has earned for itself a place in the front rank of the arts. As we know, the fundamental (and only) means, by which cinematography has been able to attain such a high degree of effectiveness, is the *mounting* (or cutting).
>
> (Donald, Friedberg and Marcus 1998, p. 84)

It is this 'mounting' or 'cutting' that impacted the plays of the British avant-garde in pieces like Unity Theatre's *Busmen*, where it influenced set choices and narrative structure. Due to its cinematic qualities, it moves from scene to scene, providing different perspectives on the same story without the need for linear chronology or uninterrupted narrative flow. This structure was visually embodied by the set, which was split into areas. These areas were illuminated when required, again reflecting the methods of the cinema. Indeed, Chambers suggests that 'the influence of cinema was clear both in terms of montage and editing and in the search for realism and accuracy' (1989, p. 144).

The term 'montage' is inextricably connected to the cinematic; however, it can also be seen regularly in the writings of Bertolt Brecht.[16] Like the practitioners in the British avant-garde, Brecht was committed to questioning Aristotelian linear time; as the Dramaturg suggests in *The Messingkauf Dialogues*, he 'cuts his plays up into a series of little independent playlets so that the action progresses by jumps' (2002, p. 70). Brecht described his technique: 'what used to be an organic whole becomes an effect of montage' (2001, p. 249). His Epic theatre model defies logical linear progression, just as the British works in this section do.[17]

The relationship between Brecht and the British avant-garde play-wrights is particularly difficult to discern. Due to similarities in form it could be easy to claim a Brechtian influence, and at times there are obvious connections to be made. As we have seen, Brecht did attend Group Theatre productions during his stay in London and was impressed by the vitality and experimentation of the company. Medley did suggest, however, that 'Bert Brecht we met a couple of times in the mid-thirties, but neither Rupert [Doone] nor I saw any production of a Brecht play until long after' (1966, p. 159). In Group Theatre, Brecht's influence was felt more acutely by the playwrights than by the directors. Auden, certainly, had some correspondence with Brecht and even did some collaborative work after Auden's move to America which culminated in the 1946 Brecht/Auden version of John Webster's *Duchess of Malfi* (Osbourne 1980, p. 221: Brecht 1994, pp. 331–3). Auden also later translated a number of Brecht's plays.[18] Furthermore, in 1937 Brecht began to organise the Diderot Society. The aim was to create dialogue between like-minded practitioners across Europe. The list of names included figures such as Sergei Tretiakov and Erwin Piscator, but also Auden, Doone and Isherwood (Brecht 2001, p. 106n). In addition, and of particular interest when considering the influence of montage, Eisenstein's name was also included.

Also on the list was Léon Moussinac whose book, *The New Movement in Theatre* (1931), so influenced Theatre Workshop and which MacColl referred to as 'a veritable treasure-trove of concepts and ideas' (Goorney and MacColl 1986, p. xxxiv).[19] Moussinac's book is an inspirational visual collection of the most innovative productions of the day, full of engaging proclamations:

> The society of the whole world is being painfully rearranged; and the spiritual confusion created by these social, political and economic events is reflected in the arts with disconcerting obviousness. This is a period of drastic re-evaluation.
>
> (1931, p. 1)

Given Theatre Workshop's intentions, it is unsurprising that such a book was claimed as an inspiration.

In addition to Theatre Workshop's avid reading of Moussinac's book, Brecht was also claimed as an influence for the Manchester company. When MacColl and Littlewood became aware of Brecht is very difficult to determine. Almost certainly some connection was formed during the early to mid-1930s. MacColl recalled being sent a script from a 'YCLer in Leipzig ... a script by Bert Brecht and Hanns Eisler called *Auf den Strassen zu singen'* and later he claimed that he 'first knew about Brecht about 1933–4, and later served with him on an international committee of the theatre' (Woods May 1973a, p. 6). In an attempt to measure the veracity of these claims, Michael Verrier concludes that 'MacColl is virtually silent on the subject [of his relationship with Brecht] but Joan Littlewood believed that he met Brecht in the 1930s; and Doc Rowe, a leading authority on the *Radio Ballads*, recalls MacColl having shown him books presented to him by Brecht himself' (Russell and Atkinson 2004, p. 110). While it is difficult to be completely sure about the pre-Stratford East company's dialogue with Brechtian aesthetics, one can see a growing fascination with his work, with MacColl eventually taking the role of the Street Singer in Sam Wanamaker's version of *The Threepenny Opera* at the Aldwych theatre in 1956 and, a year earlier, under Littlewood's direction, came the British premier of *Mother Courage and her Children*. But this was not the first Brecht play to receive a British performance. In fact the earliest known Brechtian piece on the British stage was *Señora Carrar's Rifles*, produced by Unity Theatre in 1938 (Chambers 1989, p. 86). So, Brecht, then, is another European connecting point for the British avant-garde. Though the extent to which the British companies (and particularly playwrights) were influenced by him remains difficult to discern, there were certainly those engaging with Brechtian ideas in the first half of the twentieth century.

It remains a complex case; certainly Brecht may have been a potent influence over the British playwrights, yet simultaneously, there is a growing sense of a local Epic tradition; the thematic concerns led these playwrights to re-examine issues of form and they, invariably, created a montage effect. This becomes clearer if understood in light of Auden and Isherwood's 1936 *The Dog Beneath the Skin*.[20] The play's structure certainly resembles that of a Brecht play with frequent Chorus interruptions and the juxtaposition of seemingly disconnected scenes that are unified by a central theme: a quest for understanding. Like, say, Brecht's *The Threepenny Opera*, each scene could stand alone as an analytical tableau. However, again as in *The Threepenny Opera*, each scene also casts some light on the primary argument of the play.

Performed just two years before *On the Frontier, The Dog Beneath the Skin* (1936) similarly focuses on contemporary 1930s society. Though there are symbols of governmental control, this play is really a satirical analysis of bourgeois society. The central character, Alan, is sent off to find a missing aristocrat, Francis Crewe. He is accompanied by a dog who turns out to be Francis in disguise. Posing as a dog allows Francis to experience the world from a different perspective and he is horrified by what he sees. In the end Francis reveals the truth and leaves the village with Alan and a number of others. Like *The Ascent of F6* which Auden described as a 'cross between *Peer Gynt* and *Journey's End*' (1988b, p. 598), *The Dog Beneath the Skin* taps into the quest story, a mode with an established British tradition through legends like St George and the Dragon. In a distinctly Brechtian-esque style, the quest is a composite of various scenes. It is similar, for example, to the journey of the two Annies in Brecht's *The Seven Deadly Sins of the Petty Bourgeoisie* where they travel through the seven cities confronting each sin in turn. Interestingly, in 1958, Auden translated this play.

As Alan searches for Francis he travels to Ostnia where it is Execution Day. The King and Queen are vain emblems of the hegemony, maintaining power through a combination of crass insensitivity (like Marie Antoinette, the Queen offers the condemned women cake … with champagne) and brutal suppression (Auden and Isherwood 1968, p. 490). After leaving Ostnia (via the Red Light District) Alan finds himself a patient in a Westland lunatic asylum. Again, the focus is on the treatment of the people by the government, this time represented by a disembodied Voice who informs the 'lunatics', 'we love peace (I say in absolute confidence) more than any other country. Let us be ready and able to enforce it' (ibid., p. 73). Alan then discovers he is on a train where he meets the Financier who is described as 'the biggest crook in Europe' (ibid., p. 83).[21] While there is no traditional linearity here, there are, rather, a selection of self-contained scenes that, nevertheless, point to an important central issue: society is infused with injustice and tyranny and needs people to look again at the problems, to adopt a different perspective, a 'dog's-eye-view' (ibid., p. 172) as Francis would have it, and to make changes. As Sidnell indicates, the end suggests that an individual can change his own perspective, thereby concluding in a profoundly 'un-Brechtian' way (1984, p. 153). However, in its structure, obvious parallels can be seen.

So, again, here is the dialogue between the new Continental experiments and the individual local search for workable form. *The Dog Beneath the Skin* was certainly a play with a broad appeal with Group Theatre performing it first in 1936, and Merseyside Unity Theatre tackling it some four years later (Chambers 1989, p. 96). In spite of some reservations, MUT claimed it was a play that demanded a performance. In the programme, the Merseyside group maintained, 'the main plot serves chiefly, however, as a framework for scenes which satirise many of our contemporary follies and illnesses' (Dawson 1985, p. 2). Again it was the structure (and, evidently, the effect this had on the audience reception of theme) that attracted MUT. As a timely look at European politics and society, *The Dog Beneath the Skin* obviously appealed to both Group Theatre and Unity Theatre alike.

Variety theatre and popular entertainment

Though influenced by a great variety of figures and movements from Continental Europe and America, each play mentioned above represents a direct challenge to Aristotelian linearity. However, as so often in the British theatrical avant-garde, practitioners were also looking to local historical traditions. The variety theatre was one such model and, though it particularly influenced the use of music and dance in drama (and consequently we shall return to it later), it was also important as practitioners sought new structural systems. In fact, interest in this form crossed preconceived geographical and political boundaries. Marinetti appreciated the variety theatre mode as a direct challenge to linearity and logical narrative progression, saying, 'variety theater destroys all our preconceived notions about perspective, proportion, time, and space' (2008, p. 189). Sequential progression is questioned by this popular form.

One key British example of variety theatre inflected drama is Theatre Union's *Last Edition*. This was part of that vibrant Living Newspaper tradition originating on the Continent and in America, but MacColl and Littlewood also looked to British theatre history and 'the whole production was designed to resemble and radicalise the fast-moving variety-show format enjoyed by Miller [MacColl] and Littlewood' (Forsyth and Megson 2009, p. 33). So, *Last Edition* did not just come out of modern overseas innovations; rather, it was also part of an ongoing British institution, a form that would be recognisable (and therefore readily acceptable) for a wartime Manchester audience. This episodic variety theatre remained vital for Theatre Workshop's developing aesthetic and, of course, provided a template for the influential *Oh What a Lovely War* (1963).

Unity Theatre, too, were committed to reinvigorating the vibrant music hall traditions. *Get Cracking* (1942), for instance, was structured around a collection of songs, recitations and short sketches. In every way it resembles a popular variety theatre show, but rather than offering escapist entertainment, it, instead, was a direct response to the contemporaneous situation, namely the relationship between the Soviet Union and Britain. It is subtitled 'a revue in Unity's tradition of Musical Shows with a Political Point' (Unity 1942), using all of its composite parts to address the complexities of a modern world at war.

It might initially seem rather odd that practitioners so intent on discussing the contemporary might turn to a long-standing and rather escapist local tradition as they sought new forms. In order to understand it more fully, it may well be useful to return to Eliot's conclusion regarding cinema, where he rejected film as empty entertainment because of its form, its 'continuous action too rapid for the brain to act upon' (1966, p. 458). He compared this directly to the music hall where one could visit and be 'engaged in that collaboration of the audience with the artist which is necessary in all art and most obviously in dramatic art' (ibid., p. 458). This engagement is with individual fragments: a song, a sketch, a dance. According to Eliot, this does not create an escapist linear narrative, but small vignettes that demand a direct audience response. It is this rejection of linearity and commitment to creating a mutually empowering relationship between performer and audience that would have excited practitioners such as Littlewood. In 1963, under her direction, the variety show became a remarkable, poignant comment on the futility of war.

Alongside a renewed interest in the variety theatre mode were nods to other popular forms, such as jazz music and the popular press, but also slapstick comedy and caricature. It was part of a widespread avant-garde project, which combined high 'art' and low 'culture' together and in fact, directly challenged this easy demarcation. This was not an uncritical acceptance of all popular forms, nor a total rejection of traditional notions of art. However, it did lead to fruitful collusion that reassessed the popular and revivified art.[22] This relationship challenged cultural hierarchies and potentially made the theatre a more accessible space. It was part of two distinct impulses: the search for a vibrant form and a commitment to representing the modern on the stage.

'Time, gentlemen, please': naturalism and beyond

If fragmentation was at the heart of the British avant-garde, then where did this leave naturalism? Firstly, it is important to note that despite the experiments detailed above, the same theatre companies were often also producing quintessentially naturalistic plays. The works of typically naturalistic playwrights reappear time and again in the repertoires of some of the most experimental companies. Theatre Workshop, for instance, emerging from the same industrial landscape as Houghton and Brighouse, continued to point to the importance of Miss Horniman's innovative Gaiety Theatre. Even though the theatre became a cinema in the 1920s, company member Howard Goorney suggested, 'its influence on the cultural life of the city was still evident in the 1930s' (1981, p. 6). In fact, such was the Theatre Workshop's regard for the Gaiety's plays that it produced a version of *Hindle Wakes* in 1953 (Leach 2006, p. xv). Similarly, while the ILP was committed to bringing Toller's plays to the fore, there was also a distinct commitment to naturalism and 'while Shaw *was* one of the most popular writers (25 of his plays were produced), he was by no means the only writer looked to. In terms of popularity, Galsworthy and Chekhov were a close second, as were the plays of Miles Malleson (Barker and Gale 2000, p. 175). All four of these playwrights were most readily associated with an engaged naturalistic form. Unity Theatre, too, produced some formally experimental work but also (and perhaps more than any of the other theatre companies mentioned in this book) developed a keen naturalist tradition with new plays like Leonard Peck's *The Townsherd* (1949) and *The Circling Dove* by Leonard Irwin (1950) (Chambers 1989, pp. 305, 315).

Other plays such as Walter Greenwood's *Love on the Dole* (1934), *The Ragged Trousered Philanthropists* (1936) by Tom Thomas (also performed by Unity in a version by Bill Owen in 1949) and *In Time O' Strife* (1926) by Joe Corrie were all written in overtly working-class theatrical contexts in Manchester, London and Fife respectively. And, of course, D. H. Lawrence represented the mining community in plays such as *The Daughter-in-Law* (1912) and *A Collier's Friday Night*

(1934). Though different in intention and effect, these plays had at their heart a naturalistic representation of the industrial space and its inhabitants, and particularly examined the economic and social hierarchies of this modern landscape. There is no doubt that, at times, these plays slip into an indignant melodrama but, by and large, they contain the everyday dialogue and mimetic set design of naturalism. And this engaged naturalism continued to be a predominant form as the century progressed with plays like Ena Lamont Stewart's *Men Should Weep* (1947) and, of course, the later successes of John Osborne, Arnold Wesker and Shelagh Delaney.

This interest in the great classics of naturalism and in the creation of new naturalist plays is not wholly surprising, given the notions of challenge and change that lay at the heart of British avant-garde theatre. American designer and practitioner Mordecai Gorelik asserted that naturalism's 'birth was attended by controversy, [and] its existence has been marked by continuous dissent' (1947, p. 130). Gorelik embarked on European tours in 1922, 1935 and 1950, creating a further dialogue between America and Europe. His theatre experiments often adapted contemporaneous experiments, particularly from Continental Europe: Expressionism, Constructivism and metatheatre (Fletcher 2009, p. 2). But, despite his commitment to the avant-garde, Gorelik still recognised the importance and revolutionary intent of naturalism. It is a theme taken up by Raymond Williams, who posits a 'modernist naturalism' which was 'low and vulgar or filthy; it threatened the standards of decent society by subversion of indifference to accepted norms' (Timms and Collier 1988, p. 311). Naturalism has an undeniable radical and progressive history, reacting against the formulaic conventions of the 'well-made play' and melodrama, and the excesses of the Victorian spectacular. However, it would be accurate to say that the practitioners of the British avant-garde were largely more committed to developing forms that reacted *against* any sense of linearity; the case studies in this chapter reveal a direct counteraction to this once revolutionary form.

However, a new mode appeared that seemed to connect naturalism with the episodic. In order to explore this fragmented naturalism, I want to focus on three plays: J. B. Priestley's *Time and the Conways* (1937), Montagu Slater's *New Way Wins* (also 1937) and MacColl's *Landscape with Chimneys* (1951). All these plays have a basis in naturalism but do not restrict themselves to a linear model. Rather, variations, interruptions and discontinuities in form create a much more flexible praxis. Gorelik revealed the potentially beneficial relationship between naturalism and other forms, suggesting, 'epic principles can, quite definitely, be applied to other styles of theatre – Naturalism for instance – as a means of clarifying and strengthening other styles' (1947, p. 441). All three of these plays parallel Gorelik's conclusion.

Set initially in 1919, in the wake of the First World War, *Time and the Conways* then moves to 1937 before returning to 1919 in the final act. Although the characterisation and *mise-en-scène* would indicate that this play fits firmly into the genre of naturalism, the distinct break in linearity would suggest otherwise. This is coupled with a noticeable metatheatricality, from the initial game of charades to Mrs Conway's imagined play about her children in act three. Although it is an example of naturalistic dialogue and scene construction, it seems to challenge the stability of the naturalistic form. MacColl's *Landscape with Chimneys* is a very different play, focusing on the working-class[23] inhabitants of a single street in a city that strongly resembles MacColl's birthplace, Salford. Whereas *Time and the Conways* is responding to the Great War, *Landscape with Chimneys* begins as the soldiers return from the Second World War. Initially celebratory, this play becomes darker and more tragic as it progresses with governmental promises broken, personal tensions arising and industrial pressures becoming more acute. It ends with two moments of hope: the community coming together to protect Hugh, Clare and their newborn child against the police, and Ginger's idealistic political speech. Again the dialogue and character construction is reminiscent of Hauptmann's *The Weavers* or Galsworthy's *Strife*. However, once more the very identity of naturalism is called into question by MacColl's use of short dream sequences, music and episodic structure. Again, just as in *Time and the Conways*, the metatheatrical elements are vital, with the Stage Manager directly addressing the audience and interacting with the characters.

Although these plays both present an 'epic naturalism', they seem to be very different in focus and intention. However there is a key moment of exchange which connects directly to issues of structure: the constant movement of time. In his critical analysis, *Man and Time*, Priestley discussed the concept of time, both scientifically and artistically, as a dialogue between 'change and not-change, some things moving and others apparently keeping still, the stream flowing and its banks motionless' (1964, p. 64). For Priestley time became a complex, ever-shifting notion. In *Time and the Conways,* Kay reflects that 'there's a great devil in the universe and we call it Time' (1987, p. 60). Alan's response, 'No, Time's only a kind of dream' (ibid., p. 60), reveals this tension. Time can be both/either a repressive dictator and/or an intangible mirage.

Interestingly, a similarly dual-faceted image of time is present in *Landscape with Chimneys.* Certainly the thematic focus is different, but time as both dictator and as dream is a recurring motif. On the one hand life is timed by typical industrial noises: the 'factory hooter', the dock siren and the machines in action (MacColl 1951, pp. 28, 17, 30). It is a theme that MacColl confronted in his earlier Salford novel, *The Damnable Town,* in which he wrote, 'time is measured in periods of attendance on the machine and periods of preparation for attending the machine' (*c.*1940, p. 182). And MacColl was not alone in his discussion of industrialised time. In *New Way Wins* Slater dramatised the experience of a mining community. The miners' jobs are under threat and they take the decision to strike by staying down the pit at the end of their shift. Much of the play takes place in the mine, with the final scene moving to a courtroom. Like *Landscape with Chimneys*, it is largely naturalistic, but interrupts the linear structure with poetic elements, a brief chorus section and music. Time, again, is connected with the industrial:

> *Woman*: Time in the shape of a mine is three dead every day. It is a shape of time, one thousand and seventy-three in a year.
>
> (Slater 1947, p. 56)

Once more time is organised and perceived in a different way; it is a political construct rather than an apolitical given, a constant dictatorial power associated with capitalist hegemonic forces just as it is connected with notions of inescapable fate in *Time and the Conways*. In all three examples here, time is not on the side of the central characters; rather, it is a force to be fought.

Certainly *Landscape with Chimneys* presents a rhythmical industrial time but, again like *Time and the Conways*, time is also interrupted and presented as a fluid space reliant on imagination and subjective perception. This is clear in the dream sequences, from Shaunnessy's fanciful story about a beautiful girl he met in Venezuela to Swindels' pools win (MacColl 1951, pp. 45, 50). Young worker Jessie's movie star fantasy, 'where she is Cleopatra and the star of a thousand Hollywood epics', directly interrupts the monotony of the factory (ibid., p. 29). Yet time as dictator continually impedes the dreams. The Stage Manager's response to Jessie's fantasy is 'I'll give you two more minutes, which is more than the foreman would give you' (ibid.). In Priestley's terms, time as the 'great devil' and the 'kind of dream' are juxtaposed in a tense and unresolved conflict.

The structure of these plays, then, is directly connected to an explicit questioning of time: indeed, they are direct critiques of individual and corporate *experiences* of time. Priestley pointed to this in *Man and Time,* in which he suggested, 'we all share the time of watches and clocks; yet the passing of time is an individual thing, different in each situation' (1964, p. 277). While partially resembling Martin Heidegger's concept of *Dasein*, this proposition directly echoed J. W. Dunne's ideas which Priestley praised, saying 'those of us who are Time-haunted owe him an enormous debt' (ibid., p. 244). Dunne rejected a single-faceted scientific view of time:

> There was no help to be found in the conception of Time as a fourth dimension. For Time has always been treated by men of science as if it were a fourth dimension. What had to be shown was the possibility of *displacement* in the dimension.
>
> (1981, pp. 63–4)

In the theatre, this flexible notion of time is perhaps most vividly summed up by Toller in *Hoppla, We're Alive!* (1927) which focuses on the actions of a clock where 'the hands move first slowly, then more and more quickly' (2000, p. 24). Time is conspicuously visible, directly interrupting the plays. Again, this is visually illustrated in a play like Thornton Wilder's *Pullman Car Hiawatha* (1931), where the hours actually becomes characters, 'beautiful girls dressed like Elihu Vedder's *Pleaiades*' (1931, p. 11). So time is not linear and per-durable; rather, it is shifting, movable and imbued with politics and human consciousness. Even the idea of measured, scientific time (the clock) is questioned. Certainly these plays by Priestley, Slater and MacColl conform in some ways to the genre of naturalism, yet it is not a straightforward fit. The mutability of time is emblematic of the search for a sub-genre: a critical, flexible, non-linear naturalism.

These plays are useful examples of a naturalism infused with an avant-garde sense of experimentation. They parallel Brecht's notion, 'I myself can use both Aristotelian and non-Aristotelian theatre in certain productions' (2001, p. 135). From an American context, they can also be read alongside Tennessee Williams's *The Glass Menagerie* (1948) which, as a 'memory play' combined an avant-garde subjective response to set design and characterisation with naturalistic dialogue (Williams 2000, p. 235). They also mirror August Strindberg's formal experimentations. After sending a copy of *The Father* to Emile Zola in 1887, he received this reply:

> To be quite honest, I am somewhat uncomfortable with the short-cuts in your analysis. You know perhaps that I am not fond of abstraction.
>
> (Schumacher 1996, p. 303)

Strindberg[24] had produced a form grounded in naturalism yet, nevertheless, resisting unilateral mimesis. He addressed this, saying, 'to me falls the task of bridging the gap between naturalism and supra-naturalism by proclaiming that the latter is only a development of the former' (Styan 1997, p. 44). So, rather than dispose of naturalism entirely, it could form the basis for a new type of realism, infused with experimental techniques. This form would be better suited to discussing the constantly shifting modern world.

A type of flexible naturalism is the formal cornerstone for the three plays discussed above. Priestley, Slater and MacColl all saw the merit of naturalistic realism; with its recognisable characters and dialogue, it can provide a clear discussion forum for contemporary issues. However, in light of the changing complexity of modern society, the three playwrights created a more malleable form, based on naturalist foundations, that could more accurately deal with the epoch: a supra-naturalism.

Questioning conclusions

Despite the evident differences in these formal techniques, all the examples in this chapter negate the Aristotelian notions of linearity expounded in the introduction to this section. The fragmented compositions illustrate the growing complexities of the modern world and, consequentially, the confusion of the modern psyche. However, not-withstanding the contrasts, all the forms attempt to transform audience perception. Perhaps the strongest connecting point lies in the endings of these representative media; all the plays mentioned here question the very concept of conclusion. What, for example, 'ends' in the concluding part of Eliot's jazz-influenced *Sweeney Agonistes*? We are left with only doubt ('And perhaps you're alive/ And perhaps you're dead') and unanswered knocking that gives the impression that it continues well past the end of the play and on interminably into the distance (1969, p. 126). For the Living Newspaper, the aim was to use a documentary model to intervene in society outwith the theatre walls. The success of this mode lay in its ability to challenge and engage, to engender changes in society. Therefore, the conclusion should really become a starting point. In addition, montage (both from Brecht and Eisenstein) likewise sought to involve theatre in important contemporary issues. Many of the plays discussed above suggest that the play's ending is merely a moment of stepping over that boundary between the theatrical world and everyday actuality. The end of *Newsboy* perhaps reflects this best with the company uniting in the cry, 'TIME TO REVOLT! TIME TO REVOLT!' (Goorney and MacColl 1986, p. 20). This is not an ending in any conventional sense; rather it is a moment of unity for audience and actor, a final call to be taken out on to the streets of the city as a rallying cry.

Unlike the Living Newspaper or the Epic montage, the variety theatre had no innate political agenda per se. And yet, once again, the concept of ending was challenged as, due to the entirely flexible structure, juxtaposing self-contained episodes, there was no sense of growing tension leading to a finale. Expressionism, with its collocation of scenes/pictures, similarly challenged the finality of conclusions, revealed by Toller's proclamation at the start of *Transformation* that the prologue could also be thought of as an epilogue (2000, p. 57). So, the challenge to linearity that can be seen here was a direct questioning of our means of perception. The typical, and comfortably secure, beginning-to-end structure disintegrated. In a modern world of war, psychological confusion, changing societal structures, and growing political engagement, straightforward narrative structures seemed somewhat obsolete and the search for more flexible, functional forms became crucial.

2
Staging: Platforms and Constructions

Figure 3 Space bounded (© the artist Beth Fletcher)

As the previous chapter illustrated, during the course of the twentieth century, play narrative fragmented, imbued with a sense of fluidity and volatility. In fact the 'storytelling space', the stage itself, also underwent a radical re-envisioning. Rapid moving between fictionalised 'locations' and the juxtaposition of disparate images meant that a static, context-specific set became unworkable. The primary objective was now to create sets fit for purpose, in American designer Lee Simonson's[1] terms, 'to relate them to the needs of our own day' (1932, p. 10). For the practitioners of the British avant-garde, there were both aesthetic 'needs' and a search for a method of engagement with their 'own day' outside the theatre walls; there are, therefore, both artistic and political intentions, though it becomes increasingly difficult to differentiate between aesthetics and politics as the two become so inextricably linked. With the agitational message at the forefront of the modern theatrical experience, the platform stage became prominent, and was almost universally implemented by these experimental companies, regardless of specific political or artistic alignments. At this early stage in the argument, it must be noted that though these staging devices often look remarkably similar, the practitioners had a broad range of objectives in choosing such a sparse acting space. And while a platform-type device may have been the uniting feature, the realisation of these performances in actuality often differed. Using lighting effects, architectural symbols or visual art elements transformed the platform into a multi-faceted, multi-generic space. This diversity should be recognised at this point to avoid suggestions of uniform homogeneity.

The connection between painting and play structure has already been examined. But this link was, unsurprisingly, also important in the creation of scenic emblems. Indeed, the *mise-en-scène* of the Continental historical avant-garde was often determined by the relationship between visual artists and theatre directors. Meyerhold worked closely with the Constructivists, especially Lyubov Popova, who created the construction for Ferdnand Crommelynk's *The Magnanimous Cuckold* (1922). László Moholy-Nagy designed the set for Erwin Piscator's version of Upton Sinclair's *Prince Hagen* (1920) (Piscator 1980, p. 50) while Walter Gropius, a founder of the Bauhaus, drew up plans for the Piscator-Buhne, creating the idea of a 'stage instrument as impersonal, responsive and versatile as possible, so that the various directors are free to develop their various artistic concepts' (qtd. in ibid., p. 183). Relationships between theatres and visual artists can also be noted in the British context, with John Piper designing for Unity Theatre, Robert Medley creating scenes for Group Theatre and Barbara Niven's continuous affiliation with Theatre Workshop.[2] So, painting and sculpture (as a kinetic, performative mode rather than as a static backdrop) were vital to the British avant-garde's creation of acting space. And I think it is worth stressing the value of developing a visual way of examining British avant-garde theatre, recognising that though the poetry and politics are crucial to a complete understanding of this moment in theatre history, the visual construction of the stage is just as important. It is one aspect of a desired separation from anti-theatrical ways of understanding many of the plays mentioned here.

Former theatrical traditions and the contemporary political space

Although diverse, platform stages can be usefully seen as avant-garde devices, replicated in theatres across Europe and America, while also acknowledging that such 'placeless' space (Southern 1953, p. 106), where place can be inscribed and represented, is not a new construct. In fact, turning to such a method connected the modernist avant-garde with a particular history dating back to the ancient Greek theatre. In this tradition there was no pretence or illusion, and the stage became a presentational space, to be transformed into a specific place or indeed retain its placelessness. The British avant-garde playwrights, from Eliot to MacColl, often turned to Greek theatre as a foundational starting point. In many ways this was tapping into a modernist resurrection of Hellenic culture. Noticeably there was an academic reappraisal of the ancient Greeks, originating in Cambridge. Figures such as Francis Cornford, Gilbert Murray and Jane Harrison reread the Greek theatre as a 'web of practices' (Harrison 1927, p. xii). While their theories have been severely questioned (Ackerman 2002, p. 184), the Cambridge Ritualists were highly influential. Yeats certainly had connections with this group, while Granville-Barker produced Murray's translations of Euripides (1904–7). Eliot, too, admired the Cambridge Ritualists and claimed there are 'few books more fascinating than those of Miss Harrison, Mr Cornford or Mr Cooke when they burrow in the origins of Greek myths and rites' (1966, pp. 62–3). Yet, pre-empting later criticisms, Eliot tempered this praise by saying that, while Murray was an excellent classicist, he was a poor poet: 'it is because Professor Murray has no creative instinct that he leaves Euripides quite dead' (ibid., p. 64).[3] So there is a discernible connection between this sort of academic criticism and the intentions of the British theatrical avant-garde, where producing dramatic productions that reflect, connect with and change society was central. A reinvigorated Greek theatre became an important influence, particularly for Group Theatre and Theatre Workshop. It is perhaps best summed up by Joan Littlewood, who said, 'it was considered mere philandering to read latter-day classics, let alone modern plays, unless you'd acquired a thorough grounding in the ancients' (2003, p. 764).

The implementation of a placeless space also often marked a return to (or at least a reappropriation of) particular British traditions. For example, it is a key element in the Mummers play, where there is no theatrical paraphernalia used to create the stage (Cass and Roud 2002, p. 41); rather there is created 'space, nothing more' (Helm 1981, p. 6).[4] The Elizabethan and Jacobean stage, though more fixed than the mobile folk stage with the advent of the playhouses, also largely used a platform-style stage as its performance space. Peter Brook makes this connection between Elizabethan and modern performance methods, pointing to the 'true actor on a bare stage' which provides, in one sense, the mobility of a film (the empty stage able to give the impression of tracking and jumping in and out of screen), but also points to a much older form, that of the Shakespearian stage (1968, p. 87). Within working-class entertainment specifically, the platform had an even more pronounced tradition with the Penny Gaffs, transforming old buildings into stages, inscribing performance directly on to the industrial landscape (Davies 1987, p. 1). The platform-style stage has a long history in Britain, and, despite differences in intention and realisation, in all cases it resists the restrictive nature of specifically 'placed' sets, providing a sense of flexibility and mobility, and allowing the stage to be taken to potential audiences.

In fact this return to a platform stage was, for some, a direct reaction to the staging of the Victorian and Edwardian eras. The fashion for producing visually spectacular or explicitly 'realistic' sets meant that stage designs of this period could in many ways be equated to landscape painting. Largely, this was engendered by the disconnection of audience and stage. Over time the auditorium had split into two almost self-contained areas, separated by the ever-dominant proscenium (Booth 1991, p. 97). The search for static, visual beauty was particularly evident in the Victorian theatre of spectacle, which sought to bring 'stage art close to the art of painting' (Booth 1981, p. 16). The new characters of the British avant-garde, often representational, concerned with engaging with the contemporary in a direct manner rather than creating any sense of deception, could no longer function in this illusory, pictorial environment. In fact, Brook refers to this as Deadly Theatre with its 'red curtains, spotlights, blank verse, laughter, darkness … [which] are all confusedly superimposed in a messy image covered by one all-purpose word [theatre]' (1968, p. 9). The notion of 'deadly' is a useful one as it contrasts so markedly with the British theatrical avant-garde search for 'living' performance and therefore a 'living' stage.

But, as always, one must not generalise significant distinctions out of existence. Although the staging methods of, say, the Festival Theatre, Cambridge, and the WTM, for instance, may appear similar (they are both platforms of sorts), actually they were based on very different source material. What is interesting is that, in spite of the dissimilarities, the eventual stage sets noticeably resembled one another; again practitioners were solving theatrical (and, in some ways, ethical) problems in comparable ways, crossing that divide between the poetic and the political groups. The case studies that follow reveal a strong sense of heterogeneity while showing that interesting parallels can be drawn.

This new platform stage, as well as reacting against prevalent ideas of the previous generation and reappropriating more ancient dramatic modes, also tapped into a non-theatrical (at least in a conventional sense) tradition: the political spectacle. Rallies, for example, are often dominated by agitational speeches from a platform, and are highly performative in the Butlerian sense where '*performative*' suggests a 'dramatic and contingent construction of meaning' (Butler 1999, p. 177). The political spectacle/rally is a long-standing tradition, but came to the fore in new ways with the advent of the Industrial Revolution and the more politicised, urban class struggle. The early years of the twentieth century witnessed an ever-growing number of these events. The Suffragette movement, the General Strike of 1926, the Hunger Marches of the 1930s and the protests against fascism, particularly in light of the Spanish Civil War, meant that this was a period of political upheaval at home and in foreign policy. Political rallies became almost theatrical experiences with most of the central 'actors' presenting their 'scripts' on an outdoor platform stage.[5]

This political platform 'stage' tradition made its way into the theatrical realm through the ideas and performances of the WTM. At times it remained an outdoor device with companies such as the Salford-based Red Megaphones, which later morphed into Theatre Workshop, 'performing' sketches and songs in the open air. MacColl, as founder member of this early group, reflected that, in the early performances of this troupe, almost all presentations were given outside on the steps of the public baths or in front of the dock gates on Trafford Road (Goorney and MacColl 1986, p. xxiii).

Using the platform 'stage' as a declamatory outdoor space was a key development throughout Europe, marking a vital connection between British and Continental practitioners. The Blue Blouse troupes were, perhaps, the most influential of these European agit-prop groups, performing primarily in Russia and Germany in the 1920s (Bodek 1997: Leach 1994). They, like the Red Megaphones in Salford, performed sketches that could be adapted to a range of different spaces (Leach 1994, p. 172). The Blue Blouse platform stage appeared both indoors and outdoors, making its way from the streets to indoor spaces. For these troupes, the moving human figure became a crucial focus and, accordingly, the actor's body became an important site of meaning creation (Taxidou 2007, p. 198). The simplicity of the platform stage led to new developments in movement techniques as the body took precedence over the conventional trappings of the commercial stage. A number of British groups took their twentieth-century platform stage from this source, including the Salford Red Megaphones. MacColl recalled a meeting with a Comrade Ludmilla in which she explained the agit-prop tradition where 'they would appear on a street and do a very short political piece' (Samuel, MacColl and Cosgrove 1985, p. 228). The London-based Hackney People's Players, led by Tom Thomas, were also heavily influenced by groups linked with the Blue Blouse movement. Indeed, in 1931 Thomas and others from the London WTM groups visited the *Arbeiter Theater-Bund Deutschland*. They were struck by 'the flexibility of the shows' in which 'costumes and props had to be functional' (Stourac and McCreery 1986, pp. 208–9). The consequence of this visit for

Thomas was profound: 'from that point on we had a most tremend-ous growth, abandoning the closed theatre and going to where the people were, on the streets' (Samuel, MacColl and Cosgrove 1985, pp. 89–90). This agit-prop method of presentation became central to the general aesthetic of the WTM for a number of years. In a docu-ment entitled *The Basis and Development of the WTM* (1932), there is a specific call for a Blue Blouse-style platform stage:

> 'Agit-Prop' style [that] needs no elaborate stage, but an open platform. No scenery that is not easily carried about by hand; no make-up; and a minimum of costume. In a word, the propertyless class is developing the 'property'-less theatre.
>
> (ibid., p. 102)

Certainly, this was not primarily an aesthetic decision as such, but a conscious response to the need to take an agitational theatre to the people, a direct means of being able to connect the stage with the working class.

'Precursors of great promise'

However, it was not only the agit-prop based companies that utilised a bare stage; it can be seen throughout the canon of British avant-garde theatre. While, again, acknowledging the differences in objec-tive and inspiration here, there are some interesting connections to be made. Group Theatre's Robert Medley, for instance, reflected that 'Rupert [Doone]'s strength lay in his gift, developed in earlier years as a dancer, and carefully studied, for creating an atmosphere without cluttering the stage with irrelevant detail' (1983, p. 139). This idea of 'decluttering' is, in many ways, remarkably similar to the WTM's call for a 'property-less theatre'; both suggest a stripping back, a simplification. Certainly, there were profound differences in inten-tion between the agitational WTM and the more aesthetic-focused Group Theatre; yet the sense of ridding the stage of the conventional trappings of the theatre, either by maintaining the simplicity of the political platform or by developing an intentionally unadorned space, was central to both projects. The consequence for both tradi-tions was that a simple platform-style stage remained the prominent acting arena.

While both were reacting against contemporaneous staging methods, the bare stage was present even in the practitioners of the Victorian and Edwardian periods. Director Tyrone Guthrie mentioned two of these figures as theatrical revolutionaries: William Poel and Harley Granville-Barker. He suggested that 'Poel's productions were given on a bare stage; Barker, less austere, used very simple "stylized" indications' (Guthrie 1961, p. 183). Granville-Barker's aesthetic was of particular interest, given his call for a harmonious work of art, a search that, in one form or another, preoccupied many of the figures of the British avant-garde:

> Though there may be no fixed laws of construction, yet a play can have beauty of form ... It is a question of harmony mainly, of just proportions, significant emphasis, congruities and arresting contrasts, of an ultimate integrity.
>
> (Granville-Barker 1931, p. 158)

This 'harmony' did not require the clutter of a naturalist stage but could be presented, as Barker would have it, in 'just proportions'. Actually, Granville-Barker was a fascinatingly paradoxical figure given the difference between the simplistic plain sets of his Shakespearian productions and the more conventionally naturalistic sets of his own plays.

It is, however, the work of Edward Gordon Craig that has been most consequential for a twentieth-century local platform tradition. In *Scene* (1923), he reflected, 'a so-called real room is what we present on stage today ... real and yet quite dead – expressionless – unable to act ... so, then, to create a simplified stage is the first duty of a master of the drama' (Craig 1983, p. 51). Once again it is the living flexibility of this non-illusory stage that is so striking. In his stage visions, *The Steps* (1905), Craig presented a plain set of steps brought alive by figures and light. Craig described *The Steps 2* as the Second Mood:

> The steps have not changed, but they are, as it were, going to sleep, and at the very top of a flat and deep terrace we see many girls and boys jumping about like fireflies. And in the foreground, and farthest from them, I have made the earth respond to their movements. The earth is made to dance.
>
> (1983, p. 110)

The stage is, again, a living organism, able to respond to character, mood and theme. I suggest that Craig (alongside Poel and Granville Barker) was a *forerunner* of the British avant-garde; he prefigured and cast a long shadow over its staging techniques. Another antecedent of a local avant-garde, W. B. Yeats, was impacted by Craig's designs and indeed the two worked together between 1909 and 1912, the years leading up to what I am presenting as a potential British avant-garde (Dorn 1984, p. 13). Although he didn't always see eye to eye with Craig, Yeats's aesthetic was inflected with his ideas. This was particularly evident in the sets he created for the Abbey tours of 1913–14 with atmospheric colours and imaginative, symbolist space (Flannery 1972, p. 277).

Here was a living, malleable space, a flexible non-illusory stage which was both infinitely a place and infinitely 'placeless'. These staging concepts continued to interest Yeats, and this living platform remained crucial to the way he visually envisaged his plays. In fact, Karen Dorn connects all these reformers of the British stage together, reflecting that, 'Yeats followed closely the early productions of Poel, Craig and Granville Barker.[6] His own theatre was part of that movement' (1984, p. 65). A pre-avant garde 'movement', the distinct innovations of these four individuals paved the way for future, more agitational experiment.

Using the platform

The idea of a bare stage as both placeless and multi-place is particularly prevalent in British avant-garde productions. I suggest that there are two major aesthetic reasons for returning to the ancient tradition of platform-style staging and/or adapting Continental avant-garde methods. Firstly, the theatrical space partly liberated the imagination of the audience. Rather than the darkened, passive auditorium of the Victorian spectacular (Booth 1991, p. 12), this was a theatre that, in Brecht's terms, could 'give the incidents baldly so that the audience can think for itself. That's why I need a quick-witted audience that knows how to observe, and gets its enjoyment from setting its reason to work' (2001, p. 14). The blank stage compelled the audience members to reconstruct scene and place for themselves. In the plays this appeal to audience imagination is sometimes extremely overt. Auden and Isherwood's *The Dog Beneath the Skin* begins, 'we would show you at first an English village: You shall choose its location/ Wherever your heart directs you most longingly to look' (1968, p. 11). MacColl's *Landscape with Chimneys* begins in a similar manner with, 'imagine that this platform is a stage where eight tenths of the population of this sceptred isle live out their lives' (1951, p. 3). Rather than dictating to the audience, many of these productions actively sought audience imagination in order to create scene. This reliance on the audience's imagination rather than the trappings of the illusory stage did not, as might be expected, lead to the creation of fictions. Rather, by empowering the audience in this manner, a whole range of subjectively mediated 'realities' was engendered. The plays could gain an immediate relevance simply by enabling the audience to insert its own experience on to the staged production.

Jacques Copeau, another crucial figure in the development of a British avant-garde theatre, particularly in connection with Group Theatre, dissected this relationship between plain staging and the accuracy of the message:

> Our stage is such that it should be used without adding anything to it, no stairs, no moveable steps, no facile lighting effects; only the stage in all its truthfulness and implacability.
>
> (1990, p. 85)

Through the imagination of the audience, unencumbered by illusory elements, a real truthfulness of message could emerge. This could be a truth based on the subjective responses of the audience, and could, therefore, relate directly to the audience members' real lived experience. The importance of this for the agitational stage is clearly evident.

But, and secondly, it was not only the audience who benefited from staging developments; actors too found themselves in a very different space, one that would greatly assist them in the creation of a modern aesthetic, allow them to move freely (in space and time) and create a new sense of communication with the audience. Any platform stage lends itself to episodic structure and juxtaposition of the 'real' and 'imaginative', its placelessness allowing for complete flexibility in time and context. As well as providing a sense of unencumbered cognitive mobility, it also allows the actor, no longer restricted by the trappings of conventional theatre, to move freely.

Indeed, there were a number of examples of this indefinable, malleable space. In an Irish context, it was central in Yeats's aesthetic.

Rejecting the spectacular stage, Yeats advocated sets that really challenged the sensory perception of his audience (Flannery 1976, p. 239). Correspondingly, the set for *The Dreaming of the Bones* (1918) was, following Gordon Craig's innovations in a very personal way, '*any bare place in a room close to the wall. A screen, with a pattern of mountain and sky, can stand against the wall, or a curtain with a like pattern hang upon it, but the pattern must only symbolise or suggest*' (Yeats 1979, p. 125). It was on this platform, which is only ever *suggestive* of place that this powerful evocation of the Easter Rising took place.

The bare stage as suggestive of place and yet also placeless, symptomatic of a 'severance from Realism', became an equally important emblem for Terence Gray's Festival Theatre (Gray 1926, p. 49). Like Yeats, he had an Irish background and was keenly interested in Craig's innovations:

> Gray was the total uncritical disciple who wanted, above all else, to reproduce Craig's ideas at the Festival Theatre. Gray's personal contribution would be in the actual demonstration of Craig's theories in the living theatre.
>
> (Cornwall 2004, p. 106)

The Festival Theatre seems to be the first theatre in Britain to develop an actual, established, conventional stage space in this manner, widening the front of the acting area by removing the proscenium, adding a large flight of steps and creating a revolving stage (Dorn 1984, p. 79; Cornwall 2004, pp. 94–5). Gray's ideas were highly revolutionary, influenced by both Craig and Copeau (who gave a special matinee performance of *L'Illusion* at the Festival Theatre in 1928) amongst others (Cornwall 2004, p. 138). Copeau was of particular importance for Gray, due to his commitment to the unadorned stage and the centrality of the human figure:

> Give me real actors and, on a platform of plain rough-hewn boards, I will promise to produce real comedy.
>
> (Copeau 1990, p. 81)

Max Reinhardt, too, provided a template for stage development at the Festival Theatre with his cyclorama and revolving stage (Styan 1992, p. 4; Cornwall 2004, p. 70).

Gray's theatre was certainly not specifically coming from an agit-prop tradition and displayed a lack of real political agitation. Unlike Auden or Isherwood (or particularly a practitioner like MacColl), Gray was never political in the agitational, quasi-Marxist sense (Cornwall 2004, p. 45). Yet his distinction as being one of the first to develop theories of constructed, malleable staging in any real sense, and the list of productions attempted (the Festival Theatre saw productions of Eugene O'Neill and Pirandello's plays and he attempted to produce a range of other works from playwrights like Tretiakov, Toller and Wilde)[7] mean his innovations are vital to the construction of a British theatrical avant-garde. Even more important, in fact, was the influence Gray's theatre had. The Festival Theatre was a crucial foundation point for the eventual development of Group Theatre, with Doone playing an active role in the company in 1931. Indeed, Medley suggested that this was a real, formative experience for Doone (1966, p. 4). When Tyrone Guthrie took over the Festival Theatre he suggested that his 'aim was to be catholic, with a slight classical and conservative bias, because we felt that Cambridge had already had a good dose of *avant-garde* theatre from Terence Gray' (Guthrie 1961, p. 55) and it is this commitment to experiment in staging and, indeed, in play choice that marks Gray and his theatre as important for the current discussion.

Construction and projection

Although Unity Theatre's *Busmen*, with its Living Newspaper style, stood in marked contrast to Yeats's poetic drama and to Gray's productions, yet again the non-mimetic stage was vital to its success:

> The back of the stage was painted with a honeycomb of eight foot squares which corresponded to different levels of a three-dimensional constructional set and formed separate acting areas, including rare use of the projecting cubes at the sides of the stage to bring the actors out into the audience.
>
> (Chambers 1989, p. 143)

On this stage (a constructed rather than symbolist version of the platform) the story of the disaffected *Busmen* is played out. But these ideas began to appear in WTM productions a decade earlier. *The Judge of All the Earth* by Stephen Schofield, for example, created a simple, platform set and presented it as an afterlife, where a Guardsman, a Woman and a Bishop meet. All three characters approach God (who we never see) with different backgrounds and troubles. The aim is to break through religious pretension and create a sense of community based on innate human ethics. At the end when it seems they might finally see God, they actually see each other. The set was described as follows:

> The Judgement Throne is easily made of sugar boxes and wall paper (provided there is nothing against this in the new Act of Blasphemy and Sedition).
>
> (Schofield 1927, p. viii)

Like the later *Busmen,* this throne was placed on a devised set of blocks and steps. On this stage were placed just three characters and a disembodied Voice, directly engaging the audience with the message.

Comparable is one of Theatre of Action's productions, *John Bullion,* performed in 1934 when the company was still called Theatre of Action. The play, adapted from an earlier agit-prop piece, is a satirical presentation of typical characters of the capitalist society, from Deafen'em the press man to Fortune the financier, and the way that these characters are overcome by the workers.[8] The set, once again, is based on a multi-layered platform stage:

> The stage is divided into three levels or planes ... the height of the planes at this point is 2 feet. From here they slope down to stage level ... The ordinary stage level completes the list.
>
> (Goorney and MacColl 1986, p. 2)

The bare platform retains its prominence, but upon this unadorned stage emerges the concept of 'construction'.

Whereas in, say, *The Dreaming of the Bones* it is the ideas of Gordon Craig and the symbolists that so influenced Yeats, in *Busmen, The Judge of all the Earth* and *John Bullion* there is the notion of structured space. Through this concept, all progress beyond the simple platform to include multiple rostra or large suggestive props. Rather than a symbolist-inflected aesthetic like Craig, the WTM, Unity Theatre and

Theatre of Action were consciously tapping into a European avant-garde concept to be found in the work of figures such as Meyerhold and Piscator. Olga Taxidou provides one of the most telling comparisons of Meyerhold and Craig: the 'two men represent two very different, almost conflicting schools of Modernism – Meyerhold and Dialectical Materialism, Craig and Idealist Romanticism' (1998, p. 69). That said, Theatre of Action certainly claimed to be influenced by Craig as well as Meyerhold. There is a suggestion that in 1935 MacColl gave lectures to a training class, 'long, incoherent, disquisitions larded with quotations from Aristotle, Diderot, Goethe, Gordon Craig,[9] Richter, Appia and Stanislavski' (Goorney and MacColl 1986, p. xxxvii). Craig retained a minor influence even in the political tradition and marks yet another connecting node.

Meyerholdian techniques certainly had some effect in a British context, coming to the fore particularly in the work of Huntly Carter, who described the Russian as 'the greatest living creative and interpretative producer' (1929, p. 47). Although it did not always successfully implement the revolutionary platform stage, the WTM was certainly influenced by Meyerhold as it 'proposed to dispense with traditional staging techniques and, like the revolutionary theatre in Russia, to abolish the curtain' (Samuel, MacColl and Cosgrove 1985, p. 42). The earliest incarnations of Theatre Workshop, too, seemed to acknowledge the influence of Meyerhold with MacColl, suggesting that 'it was through Moussinac's book that we had our first real introduction to Myerhold's [sic] theatre and to some extent, at any rate, his ideas were to dominate much of our next production, *John Bullion*' (Goorney and MacColl 1986, p. xxxiv). Published in the same year as Tom Thomas and his WTM colleagues travelled to Germany to see the political platform stage in action, Moussinac's groundbreaking work *New Movement in Theatre* (1931) was vital to the staging decisions of Theatre Workshop. Its photographs largely illustrate a new preoccupation with the stage as a platform, a blank space on which a dramatic piece can be displayed. Of particular note in this book are the pictures of the Russian stage. In the development of his aesthetic, Meyerhold created stage sets that were substantially influenced by the utilitarian Constructivist visual art movement of the period and Moussinac's pictures provided the British reader with a perfect image of this Russian Constructivist platform.

In a violent rupture from naturalism, Meyerhold transformed the theatre back into a bare performance space, actively ridding the acting area of painted backdrops and revealing instead the natural walls of the theatre building (Leach 1994, p. 110; Schmidt, Levin and McGee 1996, p. 31). Significantly, some of his productions and techniques seemed to have had a particular impact in a British context. In a 1926 address to the English Playgoers Club, British director Basil Dean, who devised many of his own uniquely experimental performances, reflected that while the avant-garde across Continental Europe did have some influence over the British scene, 'none of these movements threaten radical influence over the English stage as does the modern Russian revolutionary theatre' (Dean c.1926). While it may well have 'threatened' the established conservatism of the British stage, it never held great sway. And yet, in keeping with Dean's hopeful premonition, as the 1920s and 1930s progressed the techniques of the Russian stage did have some influence.

Again, challenging the notion that the British avant-garde was anti-theatrical (either too polemic or too poetic), these local practitioners must have been attracted by the relationship between the stage and visual arts. The connections between theatre and sculpture or painting became important in Meyerhold's project, and collaborative productions were common. For one of his most celebrated productions, Crommelynck's *The Magnanimous Cuckold* (1922), Meyerhold joined forces with Constructivist artist, Popova to create a remarkable kinetic stage. Carter, discussing Meyerhold's innovative sets, pointed to the direct connection between theatre and the mood of the modern world, reflecting that 'he rightly saw that erections of wood, and iron, and steel express the spirit of the mechanical age upon which the world has definitely entered' (Carter 1929, p. 52). Once again the theatre and the outside world, art and life, reflected each other. Like the equipment in a factory, the stage became a machine for the actors who were themselves 'biomachines'. The set of *The Magnanimous Cuckold* was designed as a collection of moveable parts, wheels and windmills creating a kinetic space with which the actors could interact (Baer 1991). Carter was struck by the visual vibrancy of the set, celebrating the 'skeleton structure consisting of gangways, ladders, bars, swinging doors, gates, revolving wheels and other practical and symbolical parts' (1929, p. 77). Erast Garin, who joined Meyerhold's workshops in 1921 provided an in depth description of the staging for this production:

> The Constructivist set recalled the outlines of a windmill, but left the actor free to move about on the entire downstage area, which was completely bare of set and props. Stage right was a semicircular bench. The upstage area contained the construction, which consisted of two platforms at different levels connected by stairways, a bridge, and a slippery chute that might have been used for bags of flour. The platforms enabled the actor to move up and downstairs and to make use of doors and windows, but removed the narrative security of concrete naturalistic detail.
>
> (Schmidt, Levin and McGee 1996, p. 35)

This lengthy account is useful as it points to the centrality of a bare platform, but also details the innovations of the Meyerholdian stage – the steps, bridges and chutes. The construction provided a certain freedom for actors and signified a final division from the illusions of naturalism. Given their interest in non-naturalistic play structure, it is unsurprising that the overtly politically engaged practitioners in Britain followed Meyerhold (either directly or in parallel) towards a set design method that enabled such productions to be successfully and coherently realised. Upon this innovative, visually arresting stage, Meyerhold (and, following his lead, the artists of the British avant-garde) could create new methods of movement, based on acrobatics, and the physical actions of everyday work.

There are a number of notable connections between British workers' theatres and the innovations in Russia, but techniques from Germany too were instrumental for a number of companies. Piscator in particular is a name that reappears in writings and recollections from Unity Theatre (Chambers 1989, p. 143; Unity 1984, Introduction) and Theatre Workshop (MacColl 1973, p. 63), and his designs (including for his version of *The Good Soldier Schweik*[10] and Toller's *Hoppla, We're Alive!*) are again present in Moussinac's book. Undoubtedly his commitment to political engagement was key to his popularity with these two companies. He declared that 'we banned the word *art* radically from our program, our "plays" were appeals and were intended to have an effect on current events, to be a form of political activity' (Piscator 1980, p. 45). Again Piscator began with a platform-style stage and for his 1925 production, *In Spite of Everything*, he 'had a so-called "Praktibel" built, a terraced structure of irregular shape with a raked platform on one side and steps and levels on the other' (ibid., p. 94).

Through experiment, Piscator's stage became a space of innovation. His description of the 1927 production of Toller's *Hoppla, We're Alive!* reveals his creative approach:

> We had come up with a stage set that would display this cross section [of society] and lend it precision: a multistoried structure with many different acting areas above and beside one another, which would symbolize the social order.
>
> (Piscator 1980, p. 210)

Construction was a key element in Piscator's work, but so was technology, and many of his productions relied on back projection and film, including *The Drunken Ship* (1926) which used sketches by George Grosz: 'the action took place in a space bounded by three huge screens on which the appropriate pictures were projected at suitable moments' (ibid., p. 120). Although back projection was not used comprehensively in the British context, there is a particular example in Unity Theatre, with the company's 1937 production of *Aristocrats* by Nicholas Pogodin. Director Bert Marshall had trained at the Higher Film Institute in Moscow and employed his knowledge to create a cinematic impression of water flowing over the audience (Chambers 1989, p. 136).

Both Meyerhold's and Piscator's productions revealed a sense of experimentation and innovation, a search for a method that could take the platform-style stage and develop it in new, exciting ways. The political platform stage was a starting point, a placeless place on which to build, construct and create scene. In Britain, agitational theatre took a similar though not identical approach, gradually developing a sense of construction and scenic innovation on the 'rough-hewn boards'.

New lighting innovations

As Piscator's stage illustrates, the modern platform-style stage (in both its political and symbolist manifestations) provided new opportunities for technological advancement. The growth of technology on the stage in the local context had begun a number of years earlier. Indeed, the Victorians had experimented widely with the latest in stage technology, and it was perhaps the introduction of gas and then electricity into the theatre buildings that proved to be the defining moments of nineteenth-century theatre. The exploration of light as an artistic method to create mood, atmosphere and accentuate theme remained central as the twentieth century progressed. Craig's commitment to a mobile, flexible theatrical space where 'the earth is made to dance' led him to particular experiments in lighting effects. Indeed, his scene is largely created by light and colour. This provided an innate sense of movement rather than stasis as 'light *travels* over the scene – it does not ever stay in one fixed place' (Craig 1983, p. 126). Just as light was vital for Craig, it became pivotal for all practitioners and companies searching for a flexible method of creating atmosphere and scene. Many of the origins of these later experiments in lighting effects lay in the work of Adolphe Appia, a man Craig considered to be 'the only theater artist with whom he could have collaborated' (Innes 1998, p. 193), an admiration which marked another early connection between experiments in Britain and on the Continent.

Appia's problem, solved by his experiments in light and shadow, was how to create a *living* scene. He asserted, 'the dramatist-stage-director is a painter whose palette should be *living*; his hand should be guided in the choice of living colors, their mixture, their arrangement by the actor' (Appia 1975, p. 37). Appia devised definitions of 'diffused light' which allows for visibility and 'living light' which creates specific scene and atmosphere (Appia 1962, p. 76). Shadow, rather than being regarded as the antithesis to light and best avoided on the stage, was celebrated as a stage effect in its own right (ibid., p. 74). Like Craig, Appia marked a change in modern European theatre, Copeau referring to them both as 'precursors of great promise' without always agreeing with them (1990, p. 79). Appia's lighting effects were highly influential even over a politically engaged group such as Theatre Workshop. MacColl suggested that the company's use of Appia's theories began as early as 1933, when a member of the group, Alf Armitt, apparently conducted research into the Swiss technician and, as a practical outworking of his ideas created 'ten-pound barrel-type biscuit-tins fitted with 500-watt lamps "borrowed" from the floodlighting equipment used to illuminate the Salford greyhound-racing track' (Goorney and MacColl 1986, p. xxxi). How many companies and practitioners were directly influenced by Appia's ideas remains difficult to quantify. Yet it remains true that, whether consciously or not, the productions of the British avant-garde often turned to light as a method to create an Appia-esque living stage.

Such lighting innovations also had a developing local method in the work of Harold Ridge, who Ashley Dukes referred to as 'lighting expert and co-director' of Cambridge Festival Theatre (1942, p. 121). Basil Dean wrote the preface for the first edition of his book *Stage Lighting for Little Theatres*, which he described as a 'text-book containing a quantity of useful information of which many professional producers are profoundly ignorant' (Dean 1925).[11] Medley also referred to Ridge, 'whose theory of stage lighting, later elaborated in his book on the subject, was to teach me so much about light and colour' (1983, p. 117). Once again there is a perceptible genealogy between the innovations of the Cambridge stage and the later Group Theatre. Like Appia, Ridge was convinced of the lighting technician's status as an artist and saw the potential for new lighting effects to develop on a platform stage (Ridge and Aldred 1935, p. 119). He was particularly interested, not only in the way light can present scene, but also in the psychological effects of 'satisfying and harmonious' lighting (ibid., p. 104). He suggested that it was possible for the 'lighting to be subtly altered to assist what is felt rather than seen by the onlooker' (ibid., p. 105).

Like Appia and Ridge, Reinhardt too saw lighting effects as crucial to his aesthetic and his influential ideas certainly made some impact in the British context; Terence Gray claimed to be influenced by Reinhardt's work (Cornwall 2004, p. 76), as did Group Theatre (Medley 1983, p. 159) and Ashley Dukes met the German in 1926 (Dukes 1942, p. 106). Huntly Carter described Reinhardt's lighting techniques as follows:

> The new system of stage lighting is also bound up with intimacy. As the latter is largely based on emotional effects, so the main aim of stage lighting is to contribute as far as possible to the emotions of the drama.
>
> (1914, p. 12)

So, light was vital to the creation of atmosphere but more than this, it was central to the audience response, to the way spectators understood and reacted to the theme. It was now a symbol, a narrative device, a creator of scene, a commentator on the action, a reflection of individual consciousness.

In fact lighting effects in the British avant-garde resembled those advocated by Appia and Reinhardt, using light to both develop the scene and to suggest a particular atmosphere, even in plays that initially seem to be naturalistic. Benedick Scott's *The Lambs of God* (first performed in 1948 by Unity at the Theatre Royal, Glasgow) is a prime example of this. As well as, surely, being the first Scottish play to explicitly examine homosexuality, there is also, as Adrienne Scullion puts it, an 'expressionistic depiction of the industrial cityscape' (2002, p. 245). I quote here the opening stage direction:

> *The action passes in a sequence of daylight and moonlight scenes and covers a period of several weeks in the summer of a year in the 1930s. As regards the flight of time, the audience should use its own imagination. Time sequences will be suggested by lighting and music.*
>
> (Findley 2008, p. 206)

Again there is the empowerment of the audience here, using its imagination to create scene and, in an interesting connection with discussions in the previous chapter, time is, again, a concept in flux. Though 'suggested', the movement of time remained an illusive, subjectively constructed idea.

Yet light not merely contributed to the creation of scene, but actually acted as a commentator, particularly in the Expressionist movement, which, as mentioned, was vitally important for the British avant-garde. Take, for example, Stephen Spender's *Trial of a Judge* (performed in collaboration with Unity Theatre in 1938),[12] which opens with 'lights and colours suggesting illusion and uncertainty' (Spender 1938, p. 13). This play describes the growing anti-Semitism and increasing power of fascism in Europe. The 'illusion and uncertainty' of the opening light sequence reflects the complexities of an ever-changing socio-political scene. Indeed, it demonstrates the gradual breakdown in the very concept of truth that occurs during this play. The Judge later contemplates, 'that I am mad is perhaps true/ For the truth I see is truth, or was: and

perhaps truth/ As it exists in me, is mad' (ibid., p. 100). The lighting effects directly indicate the disintegration of truth. Yet, light
was not only employed as a method of illustrating danger but also
as emblematic of revolutionary change. MacColl's chorus of the
dead in *The Other Animals* declare that, 'the shadows fly before the
rush of light' (Goorney and MacColl 1986, p. 176) while, back in
Germany, Reinhard Sorge's Poet in *The Beggar* cries, 'one day I shall
stretch up defiantly toward the blue sun/ An eagle/ I shall spread my
wings/ Toward the fire of the sky' (Sokel 1963, p. 46). The association of light and hope is a common image but seemingly took on a
new political or social function here.

The new stage: cages and prisons

These new lighting methods and construction techniques upon
a platform stage could be used to create striking effects. As with
Meyerhold, the platform retained its pre-eminence, while upon this
empty stage, new scenic motifs appeared. In fact a number of recurring stage emblems can be discerned, often revealing an active move
away from naturalistic illusion and a shift towards imaginative space
that represented particular moods or themes. One such image is
the prison or cage.[13] It can be seen in both Continental Europe and
America, as well as Britain, and supplies us with a concrete example
of the avant-garde transformation of the theatrical through both
construction and light on the platform. As a useful starting point, in
The Future of English Poetic Drama (1938) Auden described the theatre
as a concept in terms of a prison:

> The novel is a park, the film is a window looking out on the world,
> but the stage is a box, it is a prison. We are in this prison with the
> audience, and the actors are in it too, and the important thing is
> that the actors can't get out and we share their imprisonment.
>
> (1988b, p. 517)

Perhaps it is this feeling of incarceration, uniting the audience and
actors, that led several playwrights to incorporate the cage image
into their work.

There are two main functions of the cage in the avant-garde: as
a symbol of the captivity of the human mind or the imprisonment

of the human body, or indeed a conglomeration of the two. The former is particularly noticeable in the Expressionist tradition with plays such as arguably the first Expressionist drama, Oskar Kokoschka's *Murderer Hope of Womankind* (1907) with its ever-present cage motif. The cage seems to signify separation, mental incarceration and oppression. Problematically it is also a comment on gender, playing an important role in the creation of a sense of the wild, savage female against the oppressed man. Indeed, the Woman tells the Man that 'here in this cage I tame a wild beast' (Ritchie and Garten 1968, p. 30). Conversely, and somewhat uniquely, in America Sophie Treadwell presented a similar cage image. In Kokoschka's play the cage is a symbol of mental anguish and isolation in an increasingly complex and unfathomable world. In *Machinal* (1928)[14] Treadwell's central character, Helen, finds herself imprisoned by circumstance. Married to a man she does not love, she is explored in similar terms as one of the central male figures in a German Expressionist play. By Episode Nine, however, she is imprisoned for murder in '*a prison room. The front bars face the audience*' (Treadwell 2003, p. 77). Treadwell's play is really unique here: to all intents and purposes this is a political comment on 1920's gender relations.

Coming out of an Expressionist tradition, Toller's *Hoppla, We're Alive!* (1927) also examines the concept of the cage as an identifiable prison. It seems to be a theatrical attempt to present his own experiences in prison, as, after his participation in the founding of a Socialist Republic in Bavaria, Toller was sentenced to five years (Dove 1993, pp. 71–93). In a letter of 1920 from his prison cell, Toller wrote, 'don't be afraid! I won't be beaten, I will not break down. Of that I am certain; prison walls shall not break my spirit' (1936, p. 54) and, later, in a correspondence of 1922, 'barbarism, moral and spiritual rottenness, lies, hypocrisy and profiteering are triumphant. But socialism is not beaten. One can throw revolutionaries into prison. But the idea for which they fight – is that slain by such methods?' (ibid., p. 179). So Toller experienced the prison at first hand, and this period of incarceration (and the intention and commitment revealed in these letters) proved essential to his plays. *Hoppla, We're Alive!*, originally designed by Piscator[15] starts thus: '*centre compartment where prisoners will be begins to light up. Façade of prison windows projected on to gauze and remains to end of scene*' (Toller 2000, p. 203). These projected images of the prison built on the idea of incarceration already explored in his 1921 *Masses Man*, where the Sixth Picture is presented as '*Boundless space. In its core, a cage, lit by a flickering shaft of light. Inside crouching down, THE SHACKLED PRISONER (face of THE WOMAN)* (ibid., p. 172). Toller's play marks a distinct move away from Kokoschka's vision to a more politically engaged perspective. While Treadwell's central character is confined after the murder of her husband, Toller's Woman is imprisoned for her political convictions. Accusing the Husband, she reflects:

> who robbed our brothers of a human face,
> Who forced them to be mechanisms,
> Degraded them to cogs in your machines?
> The State! ... You! ...

> (ibid., p. 180)

Using innovative *mise-en-scène* methods (projected sequences for *Hoppla, We're Alive!* and a constructed motif in *Masses Man*), Toller's plays began to utilise staging experiments for a political end. British companies attempting to stage Toller's plays often used similar avant-garde staging methods, retaining the visually experimental nature of the originals. Of note is a version of *Masses Man* presented by the People's Theatre, Newcastle-Upon-Tyne in the 1925–6 season. Norman Veitch recollected that the company 'used a permanent setting, changing its appearance for the different scenes by coloured lighting' (1950, p. 74). Rather than returning to a naturalistic set, British companies producing Toller's plays, of which, as mentioned, there were several, seemingly attempted to retain the German's innovative stage ideas.

This type of cage image can also be seen in the American canon with plays such as Upton Sinclair's *The Singing Jailbirds* (1924). Rather like in Treadwell's *Machinal*, the prison set means that the audience have to observe the action through prison bars. The opening song from the prisoners directly addresses the audience, 'Remember you're outside for us/ While we're in here for you', and illustrates both the sense of detachment and the idea of unity that permeate this play (ibid., p. 16).[16] Eugene O'Neill's *The Hairy Ape* (1921), too, contains the prison as a political statement, with Yank imprisoned on Blackwells Island where '*the cells extend back diagonally from right front to left rear. They do not stop but disappear in the dark background as if they ran on, numberless, into infinity'* (O'Neill 1971, p. 172). In a continuation of his imprisonment, Yank finally ends up in the gorilla's cage, reflecting society's association of the worker with the beast, the 'hairy ape'.[17] In many ways this is a class-based version of the cage for taming the man first seen in Kokoschka's *Murderer Hope of Womankind*. In both there is the sense of the man as animal, restricted behind bars. It is a symbol that appears again in Elmer Rice's *The Adding Machine* (1923), a play presented by the Stage Society in London in 1924 (Agate 1944, pp. 344–6):

> *In the middle of the stage is a large cage with bars on all four sides. The bars are very far apart and the interior of the cage is clearly visible.*
>
> (Rice 1997, p. 25)

Within this cage is the character of Mr Zero, according to the Guide, 'a very in-ter-est-in specimen; the North American murderer, Genus homo sapiens, Habitat North America' (ibid., p. 26). He goes on, 'he has opposable thumbs, the large cranial capacity, and the highly developed prefrontal areas which distinguish him from all other species' (ibid.). Again, the human is presented as the animal. This type of scientific voyeurism appeared as early as 1836 in that vital antecedent of both naturalism and Expressionism, Georg Büchner's *Woyzeck*. The Doctor presents Woyzeck before his audience as a specimen and the language used is remarkably similar to that of *The Adding Machine*:

> Just wiggle your ears for the young gentlemen while we're at it, Woyzeck. I meant to show you this before. He uses the two muscles quite independently.
>
> (Büchner 1979, p. 17)

Returning to *The Adding Machine*, Mr Zero is interpolated directly into a powerful economic system as a commercial object. The Guide even attempts to sell souvenir brochures to the visiting crowd.

There are similarities here with another play of the Continental avant-garde, Vladimir Mayakovsky's *The Bedbug* (1928). Yet, rather than a critique of the class system or the commercialisation of the body per se, Mayakovsky's play is a satirical take on Communist bureaucracy. After 50 years frozen in ice, party member Prisypkin is resurrected into a new world. It is a joyless society of regulations and protocol, a place where all the pleasures of former years have been reduced to historical analyses. The reincarnated Prisypkin is a rebel here, holding on to his flawed humanity. Placed in a cage (with the eponymous bedbug), Prisypkin, like Mr Zero and Woyzeck, becomes a specimen for study and entertainment. His final words transform this largely humorous piece into a profoundly tragic take on the perils of the Communist system which, though able to produce the passion and creativity of the October Revolution, could also lead to the unimaginative repression of Stalinism:

> Why am I alone in the cage? Dear ones, my people! Come in with me! Why am I suffering?
>
> (Mayakovsky 1995, p. 195)

It is this cage, the political emblem of Toller, Sinclair, O'Neill, Rice and Mayakovsky that is most reflected in the British context. The cage became one of the central scenic emblems in British avant-garde theatre, utilising both architectural construction techniques and innovative lighting methods. Perhaps one of the earliest uses of the cage in the British avant-garde is in the London Hammer and Sickle Group's *Meerut* (1931). In this agit-prop piece, each of the 'actors' had a pole that was used to create a prison effect. In *How to Produce Meerut*, Charlie Mann advised, 'wobbling bars look like a prison that is as farcical as the trial. It doesn't matter about the space between the bars being large, as long as the effect is symmetrical. You are not portraying a jail, but symbolizing imprisonment' (Samuel, MacColl and Cosgrove 1985, p. 106). At the final line of the piece, 'SMASH THE BARS', the 'actors' '*fling the bars down*' (ibid., p. 117). The intention was to make connections across the then British Empire, to create a sense of solidarity with the political prisoners in Indian jails:

> Workers of Britain, unite *your* power with the Indian toilers. This is your fight. Those who have jailed the workers in India are the men who cut wages and enforce the Means Test in Britain.
>
> (ibid., p. 117)

The prison construction meant that audience and 'actors' alike were, as in *The Singing Jailbirds,* viewing the action and each other through bars, thereby creating a sense of class-based cohesion and yet, concurrently, an appreciation of the isolation of the incarcerated prisoner. This simple use of props on a platform stage produced a highly effective piece. According to Tom Thomas, the production of *Meerut* encouraged other groups to start writing their own material in an 'amazing outburst of creativity' (ibid., p. 92). Its vibrant style and powerful theme of class unity appealed to many in the WTM and it was performed by a number of groups other than the London Hammer and Sickle, including the Red Megaphones in 1931–2 (Leach 2006, p. 20).

Meerut presents the working class as incarcerated in systems and MacColl's *The Other Animals* depicts a similar image. Whereas *Meerut's* cage was created through props employed by the actors, the cage in *The Other Animals* was a freestanding construction, similar in many ways to one of Piscator's scaffolds or Meyerhold's structures (Leach 2006, p. 191: Melvin 2006, p. 67):

> *In the centre stands a circular steel cage, broad at the base, narrowing as it reaches up into the darkness. Left and right of the cage and as far back as possible are two platforms raised above stage level.*
>
> (Goorney and MacColl 1986, p. 133)

Like *The Hairy Ape,* the central figure is presented as animalistic (or at least regarded as such by the hegemony) and the cage is a means of incarceration and control. Yet Theatre Workshop, employing Appia-esque light and shadow effects, transformed the static cage into a moving structure: '*an hour has elapsed. The cage appears to have increased its floor area and the shadows cast by the bars radiate over the stage like a great spider's web*' (Goorney and MacColl 1986, p. 176). This added to the sense that the prison is inescapable and all consuming; as the prisoner Hanau says 'only bars and silence' (ibid.).

But the cage emblem was not only used by those companies coming out of an agit-prop tradition. In fact two plays by associates of Group Theatre used a similar structure: Stephen Spender's *Trial of a Judge* and Auden and Isherwood's *On the Frontier.* As mentioned, Spender's intention was not naturalistic, but rather symbolic and suggestive. The physical stage was constructed by compartments throughout, visually representing political differences and oppositional forces. Act 5 presents an image of the prison where the Judge, Third Red and Fiancée are incarcerated:

> *The stage is separated into three cells. One, to the left is a yard, containing a tree. The second, the middle, is a prison cell, bare, white and simply furnished. The third, to the right, is a Guard Room.*
>
> (Spender 1938, p. 99)

The three constructed cells are the setting for the prisoners' final hours, and the concluding verses from the Red prisoners – 'O break of day/ The signal be/ Of man's release/ We shall be free/ We shall find peace' (ibid., p. 112) – again connect the visual, architectural stage image of the prison with larger political issues. The set for *Trial of a Judge* was designed by the artist John Piper and, in Sidnell's description seems to again resemble the sets of Piscator and Meyerhold:

> In practice, John Piper's abstract Expressionist setting – his first design for the theatre – was anything but dreamlike. The brightly coloured, severely geometrical screens and simple, stylized balcony helped to create a powerful – even terrifying – image of cruel and implacable force bearing down upon vulnerable individuals.
>
> (1984, p. 231)

Certainly, this is the impression given in Piper's edited works, which contain a watercolour study for *Trial of a Judge* with its platforms and bold geometry (Piper 1955, plate 218: Spalding 2009, pp. 103–4). Rather than the dreamlike symbolism seen previously in, say, Yeats's productions, Piper's set was utilitarian, somewhat brutal. The set paralleled the theme as the Black Troops began to exert authority: 'we are in no sense ideas:/ We do not discuss and cannot be discussed/ Indivisibly we ARE, and by our greater strength of being/ Defeat all words' (Spender 1938, p. 109). The Black Troops are dictatorial, immoveable and this was reflected in the set design.

The prison appears once again in Auden and Isherwood's *On the Frontier*. It is contained in one of the interruption scenes, forming

a self-enclosed episode within the linear narrative. The stage directions suggest the use of light to create the cage image: '*a ray of light,
barred with shadow, as if through a prison window, illuminates four
prisoners*' (Auden and Isherwood 1966, p. 128). Like MacColl, Auden
and Isherwood pointed to light and shadow as methods of scene
construction. In a similar manner to all the plays discussed here,
there is the sense that incarceration may last a time, but liberty will
be won:

> The night may seem lonely, the night may seem long,
> But Time is patient and that's where they're wrong!
> For Truth shall flower and Error explode
> And the people be free then to choose their own road!

(1966, p. 42)

These examples illustrate the profound importance of the cage/
prison for avant-garde expression, but also reveal the sheer range
of staging experiments. The platform retained its position, but, in
order to present an idea of place (and the political challenge that is
inextricably connected with it), the designers and playwrights used
radical construction and lighting effects that paralleled those used in
Continental Europe and America.

Limited experiment?

Although British theatre's experimentation with certain scenic
emblems and with light can be clearly discerned, there is seemingly little evidence for grand sets like the ones devised for *The
Magnanimous Cuckold* or *Hoppla, We're Alive!* Avant-garde British theatre largely seemed to develop a platform stage, often with multiple
rostra, without necessarily creating the complex constructions of its
German or Russian neighbours. I suggest that there are a number of
reasons for this perceived lack of revolutionary innovation.

For the workers in the WTM, it was largely a case of resources and
circumstances. One of the advantages of the agit-prop style was its
flexibility so that 'the preparation of special items dealing with events
as they arise, should be a matter of days only' (Samuel, MacColl and
Cosgrove 1985, p. 103). Performing in clubs and on the streets necessitated an extremely adaptable theatrical space. Yet, even away from

pure agit-prop, British practitioners retained a certain ambivalence towards such ambitious construction, with many concluding that the innovations, especially Piscator's ideas, were unworkable on the stage. For his 1928 production, *The Good Soldier Schweik*, Piscator developed a conveyor belt system that seemed to come directly from his readings of the play:

> Faced with the problem of putting this novel on the stage, this impression in my mind assumed the concrete form of a conveyor belt.
>
> (Piscator 1980, p. 257)

However, in reality, by his own admission, 'the belts rattled and snorted and pounded so that the whole house quaked. Even at the top of your voice you could hardly make yourself heard' (ibid., p. 260). Brecht also referred to the shortcomings of Piscator's staging, reflecting that 'the flies collapsed when heavy objects were hung from them, the stage broke through when we put weights on it, the motors driving the various essential machinery made too much noise' (2001, p. 66). Piscator's British contemporaries understood the disadvantages of such a stage while often retaining an admiration for his political and aesthetic commitment. In a meeting with German refugee actors from Piscator's company, MacColl said they 'spoke disparagingly of equipment which kept breaking down and which, when it did work, made so much noise that the actors couldn't be heard' (Goorney and MacColl 1986, p. xlii). Ashley Dukes, too, after watching Piscator's version of Toller's *Hoppla, We're Alive!* suggested that the innovations, though creative, meant that the 'gap between drama and treatment was altogether too wide' (1942, p. 129).

These quotations reveal an interesting pattern: the problem with Piscator's stage was that the dialogue, the message, the play text (the 'drama' in Dukes's case) could not be heard or clearly discerned – that the set, either visually or audibly, obscured the message. MacColl and Dukes's respective assessments of Piscator's stage point to the centrality of the written text (or in a broader sense the play's message) in the British avant-garde. This is unsurprising given the nature of the local scriptwriters, many of whom were poets first and foremost, and placed great emphasis on the word *a priori*. Even MacColl, a figure more readily associated with *performance* in drama and, more so, in music, said he aimed to create a 'new theory of dramatic poetry' (Orr and O'Rourke 1985, part 4). If the written word, the linguistic, *spoken* message of the play, in all its various guises, was at the centre of the British avant-garde, then the plain platform with rostra unsurprisingly remained the most popular method.

3
Language: Disturbing Words

Figure 4 Trap me in my words (© the artist Beth Fletcher)

Previous chapters have sought to create new dialogues between disparate companies and figures. However, in the area of language innovation there initially may seem to be more disagreement than accord with two clear sides forming: the poetic and the political. On the one hand, there were the Group Theatre dramatists; poets or prose writers first and foremost, playwrights like Auden, Isherwood, MacNeice, Eliot and Spender brought a keen sense of syntactical originality and creativity. On the other were the WTM, Unity and Theatre Workshop writers, with their roots firmly in political rallies. Such divisions have so far been seen to be arbitrary at best, but one might expect total opposition where language is concerned, with the poetic dramatists revelling in innovative experiments in verse while the political playwrights explored declamation and everyday speech patterns. Actually, such assumptions are again proved to be wholly inaccurate. Though, as revealed below, there were perceptible differences, the two groups had a great deal more in common in this area than one might initially expect. This chapter seeks to explore new linguistic methods across the British theatrical avant-garde as playwrights sought to create modern performances.

Poetry in theatre: a British tradition

Alongside an interest in contemporary innovations, there was also a commitment to revisiting the canon. In fact, this was not a new venture and, in many ways, when British avant-garde theatre focused on classic texts (particularly Shakespeare) it just continued the innovations of certain late Victorian/early Edwardian directors. Director, Tyrone Guthrie[1] assessed these new methods thus:

> Then came William Poel and after him Granville-Barker, who between them revolutionized British, and thence American, ideas of Shakespeare production. The text must be inviolate. If realistic scenery cannot – and it cannot – be suitably adapted to the constant changes of environment and atmosphere indicated in the text, then the realistic scenery must go.
>
> (1961, p. 183)

For Barker and Poel, the focus was on the language of the text. This is not to say that they were uninterested in the theatricality of the performance. In fact the opposite is true; both Barker and Poel were very concerned with bringing the text to the stage, with visually exploring the written word. But neither the extravagant spectaculars nor the mimetic drawing rooms of Victorian theatre could adequately place the Shakespearian text/language at the centre of the performance.

The companies associated with the British theatrical avant-garde adopted a similar, yet slightly less purist, attitude to the text. While Shakespeare and his contemporaries were revered as champions of a local, historical poetic drama, the plays were not seen as, in Guthrie's terms, 'inviolate'. In fact, the early decades of the twentieth century witnessed a number of innovative versions of classics which showed the potential of these old texts for a new theatre. Importantly, the understanding of the concept 'text' is not as a fixed entity. As Brecht suggested, the canon is no longer an esoteric body of work, stable and prescribed, but a tradition in flux, available to engage fully with new repertoires, theatrical conventions and, indeed, the contemporary world at large. Brecht's helpful conclusions can be seen practically in his description of his version of *Coriolanus*:[2] In the dialogue 'Study of the First Scene of Shakespeare's *Coriolanus*' he dramatises the key ideas. Here is the notion of 'amending' Shakespeare, of transforming the plays into contemporary comments (Brecht 2001, p. 259). The written text became 'raw material'; Brecht referred to the process of producing the canon is this way as textual 'vandalism' (2003, p. 79). A similar attitude prevailed in the Russian avant-garde theatre in the techniques of Meyerhold. He maintained that 'Shakespearization is not at all the restoration of the theatrical techniques of the Shakespearean age; it is mastery in the new material of his use of multiple levels, broad scope and monumentality' (Gladkov 1997, p. 120). Again, rather than fostering an uncritical reverence, Meyerhold focused on the contemporary. 'Shakespeare' actually became a method ('Shakespearization'), a way of presenting timely issues. The plays became malleable models for contemporary performance.

This attitude can be seen throughout the British avant-garde. Take the Russian Theodore Komisarjevsky's[3] version of *Macbeth* for Stratford-Upon-Avon (1933). With its innovative set and its innate timeliness (it became a direct comment on war) this production resembled 'a Vorticist nightmare' (Barker and Gale 2000, p. 152).

In 1940 a company led by Sybil Thorndike and her husband Lewis Casson took a version of *Macbeth* on tour around the Welsh Valleys. Thorndike enjoyed the experience, recollecting that 'this is the theatre we like best – getting right in amongst the people' (Morley 1977, p. 112). So the classic Shakespeare text became part of an inclusive social project, a means of reaching out to largely 'untheatred' communities. *Macbeth* was also the text of choice for the chief figure of the Scottish Renaissance, Hugh MacDiarmid, who apparently wanted to write a version in Scots in collaboration with MacColl (MacColl 1990, p. 257). Later *Macbeth* became part of Theatre Workshop's repertoire (1957). Littlewood's version, while using Shakespeare's words, set the play in the 1930s and presented Macbeth as 'Franco, an army general who became a dictator' (Leach 2006, p. 113). In these four instances *Macbeth* became a point of departure for productions that confronted the contemporary through the canon. Shakespeare's play became a comment on the modern world, with the fractures and fissures of the twentieth century invading this most canonical of texts.

I suggest that there are a number of reasons why the Elizabethans and Jacobeans[4] were such important figures for the development of theatre in this period. Shakespeare certainly continued to cast a large shadow over the local dramatic tradition; as Auden said in a 1947 lecture, 'how completely Shakespeare dominates!' (2000, p. 308) Perhaps partly it was the enduring vibrancy of the stories which could be adapted for a modern audience. For some it was the audience that Shakespeare's plays attracted and the perceived marginal position of his company within society. Certainly this was the case for Littlewood:

> Shakespeare's company was made up of leary misfits, anarchists, out of work soldiers and wits who worked their ideas in pubs and performed them as throwaways to an uninhibited pre-Puritan audience.
>
> (Goorney 1981, p. 130)

But, I suggest, the language of Shakespeare's plays was a real attraction. Terry Eagleton maintains that Shakespeare's plays reflect language's 'power to bend the world to its own will' (1986, p. 8); in MacColl's terms, 'hadn't Shakespeare teased and manipulated language till it fitted the hands like magic gloves?' (Goorney and MacColl 1986, p. xlvii) and, as Wyndham Lewis said in his manifesto in *BLAST*, bless 'SHAKESPEARE for his bitter Northern Rhetoric of humour' (1914, p. 26). Auden's final address in his *Lectures on Shakespeare* (2000) also concludes with a long section discussing language use. In all these descriptions, it is the inherent, compelling power of Shakespeare's language to create and shape experience that really stands out. So, it was the poetry and poetic prose that proved attractive.

And this attraction crossed all preconceived boundaries, with a number of playwrights even emulating Shakespearian syntax. In *The Dance of Death,* for example, Auden wrote, 'Thou hast thyself too well amused, not true?' (1933, p. 33) imitating the archaic pronouns of Shakespeare while also retaining his iambic pentameter. MacColl in his Expressionistic *The Other Animals* also seemed to adopt stereotypical Shakespearian speech patterns. As he speaks to the inmates, it is the doctor, Graubard, who litters his dialogue with these pronouns. While there are, as in *The Dance of Death,* moments of clear iambic pentameter – 'Fetch thou some warmer raiment for our friend' (Goorney and MacColl 1986, p. 175) – it is Graubard's physical response to his inmates that really stands out here. After speaking to the Architect and the Old Man, Graubard grasps his stomach and says, 'A stool! A stool! My kingdom for a stool!' (ibid., p. 174). MacColl turned King Richard's most famous exclamation into an ambiguous and far less tragic statement. Whether Graubard is calling for a place to sit down or (and given the pains in his abdomen this is perhaps more likely) pointing to an increasingly urgent stomach problem is unclear. Perhaps the pun, and the uncertainty that it leads to, is the point of the statement. What is plain, however, is MacColl's direct nod to Shakespeare's play. This peculiar interjection seems to encourage the audience to connect these poetic sections directly with Shakespearian verse and, of course, associate Graubard with King Richard, who in Shakespeare's play is a villain with a deformity. There is a discernible similarity in character here and the assumption (correct as it proves) is that, like Richard, Graubard will be defeated. A similar motif appears in Unity Theatre's music hall-style *Get Cracking*. The sketch in question is entitled *Hamlet Without the Prints,* and takes some of the most famous dialogue from this play and contemporises it through pun and word play. Making a direct comment on the economic tensions in society, the sketch begins

'2d or not 2d, that is question' (Unity 1942, p. 14). The final lines are shared between Hamlet and the First Citizen:

> The time is out of joint; oh cursed spite
> That you should deviate thus far to the right

(Unity 1942, p. 14)

The political implications are witty and clear. *Hamlet* became a comment on mid-war society, using linguistic travesty to satirically respond to hegemonic assumptions.

If tradition played a major role in the development of local dramatic language, then modern advancements were arguably just as vital. This meant looking not only to the Continental avant-garde but also to the growing power of technology in the modern age. The radio as a conveyor of the word is a recurring image in many of the plays of the British avant-garde.

Radio was a cultural phenomenon, a vital moment in the growth of twentieth-century technology, providing accessible entertainment for the majority. Indeed, many leading dramatists also worked in radio and this 1920s' innovation provided an important alternative career path for the British avant-garde playwrights. Auden, MacColl and MacNeice all contributed extensively to the programmes of this growing cultural medium.[5] In fact, some of the most innovative and influential plays were written for radio; both MacNeice and Dylan Thomas majored in this genre.

It is unsurprising, therefore, that this vital mode of communication reappears frequently in 1930s British avant-garde plays. MacNeice's *Out of the Picture* (1937), for example, is fragmented by radio episodes. It is a comic play with a linear storyline focusing on the artist Portright. But the oncoming war remains constantly in the background, affecting Portright's ability to make art. While the central plot continues apace, the short interruptions from the radio make comments or, indeed, just as importantly, do not make comments. The Radio Announcer provides both entertainment and information; able to shift between different characters, the Radio Announcer adopts first the academic tones of the Professor and, later, the Scottish accent of a veteran hurdler. He also brings updates on the Peace Conference from Geneva (1932–3) which provide a constant threatening backdrop to the farcical central story. The central notion that 'slapstick may turn to swordplay' (MacNeice 1937, p. 46) seems to sum up both the narrative of this play and the nature of radio. Moving between genres, the radio can be a devastating political commentator at one turn and a source of vaudevillian entertainment the next.

Like MacNeice, MacColl too theatricalised the radio. In fact his interest went right back to his 1934 play *John Bullion*, in which the Radio Announcer, fascinatingly just like the equivalent character in *Out of the Picture*, also documents the Geneva Peace Conference (Goorney and MacColl 1986, p. 8). There is no suggestion of any direct connection between these two plays, so we have an interesting and significant coincidence. There is, as might be expected, a discernible satirical approach, with a clear narrative of reportage and journalistic methods: 'Princess Marina today opened the extensive new Convalescent Home for Disabled Ex-Serviceman' (ibid.). But the servicemen are not the focus here, rather, in accordance with typical models of radio journalism, there is more concern with the Princess's outfit: 'the Princess was wearing one of the new ostrich-feathered muffs' (ibid.). The real nature of war is disguised beneath images of celebrity. War and its effect is further concealed by the financial gains war provides, with the news of famine in the Balkans and the rise of Hitler interrupted by updates on the bidding for engineering company, Vickers. The increasing price, directly connected to the rumours of war, fragments the news reports. This speech plays with the tones and structures of the radio to create an episode that critiques the capitalist response to war and the journalistic methods of chronicling it.

Auden and Isherwood too used the emblem of the radio in both *On the Frontier* and *The Ascent of F6*. In the former, the radio announcements respond to the bombing, whereas in the latter, Mr and Mrs A listen to a programme about travel, even though neither of them will ever get the opportunity to go abroad. This is one uniting feature of all of these representations of radio: like the newspaper, it is a linguistic medium that can both inform accurately and deceive. It taps into that important tension between objectivity and subjectivity, between fact and fiction, between impartiality and bias.

Poetry, drama and linguistic style

The so-called poetic dramatists (playwrights like Yeats, Eliot, Auden, Isherwood, Spender, MacNeice and, arguably, one could say MacColl) have often been read in contrast to the innovations of the Dadaists, the Expressionists or the Futurists overseas. This has been one of the primary reasons why British theatre has been under-researched as an 'avant-garde'. Whereas Continental experiments have been viewed as exciting examples of cross-generic, vibrant dramatic innovation, British theatre has been read through the lens of High Modernism. This has meant that the two have been understood as embodying profoundly contradictory positions (Puchner 2002, p. 7). In order to attempt to redeem these British plays in light of performativity, it seems pertinent to extricate them from this sort of dialogism. While there is, at times, an undoubtedly 'anti-theatrical' method (in fact, with a play like Wyndham Lewis's *Enemy of Stars* (1914), the very genre of drama is called into question by its poetic prose style), to present these plays as poetic artefacts as opposed to texts realised fully only in performance seems a little reductive. The search for a performative understanding of these texts is another reason why the term 'avant-garde' needs to be redeemed in a British context. Indeed, it is a project key to Olga Taxidou's 2007 book, *Modernism and Performance: Jarry to Brecht*. One of her aims is to deconstruct the divisions between the British theatre of Auden and Isherwood, and the innovations in the rest of Europe:

> Rather than read the Anglophone tradition in poetic drama as opposed to the theatrical experimentation on the Continent, the study underlines the parallels and intersections between the two.
>
> (Taxidou 2007, p. 70)

Taxidou's project can be taken further by bringing other plays into the dialogue as I seek to challenge the artificial boundaries between the poetic and the political traditions and between vibrant overseas performances and the innovations of the British scene.

This is not to say, of course, that verbal text became less important as practitioners and companies sought to create plays in performance rather than on the page. Rather, the two complemented each other. Given the prominence of the playwright in the British theatrical avant-garde, it is unsurprising that language remained a central focus of innovation. One might begin with a play that questions the very essence of theatre: *Enemy of the Stars*. Read alongside the other plays mentioned in this book, Wyndham Lewis's peculiar work (first written in 1914)[6] is virtually unique, termed a 'play' but resembling a complex melange of writing styles and images. Puchner points to the idiosyncrasies of this play, concluding, 'what is striking from the very outset about *Enemy* is that this dramatic text does not seem to be conceived for the theater at all; it is characterized by a total lack of theatrical – objective – correlatives' (2006, p. 118). Just as Lewis's play stands alone, so Lewis himself was somewhat disconnected from the other playwrights and companies mentioned in this book. It is a position he revelled in:

> There is no 'movement' gathered here (thank heaven!), merely a person; a solitary outlaw and not a gang.
>
> (Lewis 1975, p. 23)

The British avant-garde is in many ways defined by its lack of move-ments. But such an active repudiation of artistic groupings is unique. All the other playwrights and practitioners seem to have been com-mitted to some sort of creative relationship. But Lewis's proclamation does not mean that he was wholly isolated from the other figures of the British avant-garde. In fact, there are some obvious and fascinat-ing connections to be made. Group Theatre were certainly aware of *Enemy of the Stars*, and indeed connected it directly to its own inno-vations. Robert Medley pointed to Lewis's critique of 'the English francophilia as exemplified by Bloomsbury and Roger Fry' (1983, p. 90) and identified it with Group Theatre's approach. While Group Theatre did not entirely reject Bloomsbury and Fry (indeed, Doone and Medley knew and respected Fry), they recognised that, as they sought new methods and intentions, they were 'moving away in our own direction' (ibid., p. 90). This conscious decision to reject Fry's aesthetics created a fragile connection between Lewis and Group Theatre. Further, Stephen Spender was also extremely interested in Lewis's work and referred to him as 'a striking example of the clash in the mind of an artist between the wish to be modern and *avant garde*, and hatred of modern life' (1963, p. 217). What seems to unite the opinions of Medley and Spender is a fascination with Lewis's antagonism towards the established tropes. Neither would have claimed an uncritical affiliation with Lewis's ideas – quite the oppo-site. But both retain a certain level of admiration for his hostility to accepted methods. Perhaps, in typical avant-garde fashion, a tense unanimity arose because of what they were *against* rather than what they propounded.

The difficulty with *Enemy of the Stars* is one of genre and is inextricably connected with language use: is this piece a short story (written in prose) or a play (constructed through visual effects and speech – dialogue or monologue)? Such differentiation is intensely problematic, as Lewis experiments with an antagonistic, dialogue-based prose style, what William Wees usefully terms 'an exchange of blows' (1972, p. 183). It is, interestingly, reminiscent of Marinetti's ideas of poetry where he suggested, 'our poetry is essentially and unreservedly a poetry in revolt against established forms' (2008, p. 161). Again, antagonistic language use and the breakdown in conventional syntactical systems, led to a profound change in the nature of genre and literary/theatrical classification.

Lewis used language self-consciously; it not only transports meaning but is also its own site of contestation. Perhaps the tension is best summed up by what Arghol says to Hanp, 'again let me do a lot of extraordinary talking. Let me do a lot. Watch me most closely. Trap me in my words' (Lewis 2003, p. 172). Language seems to be an 'extraordinary' method, while retaining the ability to incarcerate its user. Strangely, Arghol tells Hanp to 'watch' him rather than listen to him. Hence spoken language is connected with the body and its movements. Nowhere is this clearer than in the sense of violence that pervades this complex text. Arghol's vicious dismissal of Hanp is described in extraordinary syntax:

> *Arghol's voice rings coldly in the hut, a bell beaten by dull words, in a series of calm strokes. The words only – not the tune of the bell at all – have grown harsher. But at last the words beat virulently – Hanp throws up his head, his eyes carbonic and his complexion lead.*
>
> (ibid., p. 177)

The 'battle' continues and the language becomes ever more confrontational as the physical violence increases. In the final scene Hanp attempts to sever Arghol's head and the final dialogue takes place as blood gushes from the latter's mouth:

HANP:　　It was you! I have done nothing.
ARGHOL:　Because I could not speak your tongue – in your barbarity!

HANP: You forced me, liar! All along, what were you doing?
ARGHOL: A question of words.
HANP: Words? Deeds! These are not words!

(ibid., p. 190)

It is a complex ending, providing very few answers. But at the centre of it lies an inability to communicate. Hanp's final sentence seems to make explicit a connection that permeates the whole piece: words are not abstract entities, but are active sources of meaning, affecting the material everyday. Communication therefore takes a different form and, alongside the abusive words comes a savage physical performance. With Hanp's final suggestion that 'words' are actually 'deeds', the distinction between action and verbal communication implodes entirely. Language as a physicalised mode, violent as (and, indeed, inextricably connected with) blood-letting, is further complicated by Lewis's preoccupation with visual art; in many ways his 'theatre' was a 'textual' version of his paintings, retaining the visuality of the latter (Puchner 2002, p. 119). Bringing these ideas together, the *Enemy of the Stars* is a striking example of an unusual form: a visual language game.

Lewis's linguistic intentions can be seen most clearly in his 1933 long poem *One Way Song*, in which he pointed to his plan to overhaul the English language entirely:

> Watch me push into my witch's vortex all the
> Englishman's got.
> To cackle and rattle with.

(2003, p. 29)

Stephen Spender admired this poem as 'finely planned. It contains five separate poems, but they are so ordered that the book has not only immense variety, but also the strength of unity' (1978, p. 37). This intention to 'Break out word-storms! – a proper tongue-burst' (Lewis 2003, p. 31) remained prominent in Lewis's dramatic texts and, indeed, could be used as a description for the projects of a great many of the playwrights mentioned in this chapter.

Enemy of the Stars is, in many ways, emblematic of a troublesome sub-genre: a sort of unperformable performance piece. However, it clearly reveals a contemporary preoccupation with language and genre. Though different in intention and realisation, Auden and

Isherwood's *The Dog Beneath the Skin* also experiments with language. While recognising the limitations of this play (Spender 1978, p. 57), Spender asserted, 'I like *The Dog Beneath the Skin* very much. In fact it deserves superlative praise ... also the poetry is beautiful: it is really final & brilliant' (1980, pp. 75–6). For all its peculiar characterisation and satirical critique of bourgeois mores, for Spender, it is the linguistic experiment that seems to excite him the most. It is unsurprising that with two of the foremost literary writers of the 1930s behind it, *The Dog Beneath the Skin* would be recognised for its particular innovations in language.

And the syntax is 'beautiful' and 'brilliant', as Spender had it. Its brilliance comes in part from the dynamic movement between tones. As mentioned previously, Auden admired Shakespeare for his juxtaposition of poetry and prose, the two linguistic modes developing analogously. Such a dialogue between poetry and prose is equally noticeable in *The Dog Beneath the Skin*. On the one hand there are, as might be expected, a number of poetic sections, including the vivid chorus speeches, particularly in the opening sequence and the epilogue. Actually, sections from this play either became or started out as stand-alone poems; for example, part of the opening chorus was originally published as 'The Witnesses' with just an added reference to 'Pressan' in the play version (Auden and Isherwood 1968, pp. 13–14; Auden 2007, p. 71) while Act II's opening First Mad Lady's speech is also published as part of the 'Five Songs' (Auden and Isherwood 1968, p. 65; Auden 2007, p. 60).

But, standing in comparison, there is some striking prose. When the First Lunatic points to the individuals that have published books that have, in his view, provided 'new classifications and forms of lunacy', he concludes, 'but we are not deceived. No foreign brand of madness, however spectacular, however noisy or pleasant, will ever seduce us from the grand old Westland Mania' (Auden and Isherwood 1968, p. 74). Both poetry and prose, then, are employed for political means. In a highly metatheatrical moment, the Financier attests, 'I've nothing against poets, provided they make good ... but the fact remains that most of them are moral degenerates or Bolsheviks, or both. The scum of the earth' (Auden and Isherwood 1968, p. 87). Poetry and the use of language became a site of political contestation. Attacked by the image of capitalism (the Financier) as 'degenerates', poets seem to have little commercial use. Perhaps this is what the

Financier means by 'provided they make good'. This is emblematic of a renewed interest in the place, intention and role of language in contemporary society. Words are not empty conveyors of meaning but are imbued with constantly shifting political intention. The Financier's comments question the independence and responsibility of the artist, and the worth of his/her output. It is a theme that can be seen time and time again in the plays of the British avant-garde.

Towards a political poetic

It could be easy to see the poetic dramatists in direct conflict with those from an agit-prop background, that the poets wrote their plays correspondingly, while those from a working-class political tradition simply used polemic in order to persuade the audience. There is some truth in this of course. Take an agit-prop sketch like *Four Proletarian Dialogues* by John Davidson, in which a Boy and Girl discuss the theoretical foundations of Communism:

GIRL: What do you mean by the class war?
BOY: The class war is the struggle between the working class and the capitalist class, and it arises out of the economic conditions of society.

(Davidson n.d.)

Although presented as dramatic dialogue such writing is far removed from the elegant poetry of Eliot or MacNeice. Often such polemic even found its way into the plays of Unity Theatre or early incarnations of Theatre Workshop. But as Theatre of Action (precursor to MacColl and Littlewood's later company) developed a street aesthetic fit for purpose, effective language became a central concern. As MacColl recollected, 'they [the agit-prop pieces] were built around a series of slogans – good slogans, but … well, we had begun to doubt the efficacy of slogans shouted at the top of the human voice at a small audience of shoppers or mill girls' (1990, pp. 207–8). His analysis here illustrated the company's commitment to the message; the slogans remained 'good slogans'. Yet, there was the gradual realisation that theatre required something more: sophisticated tone, clear intention and mature verbal style.

MacColl's memories illustrate a larger issue: the relationship between syntactical innovation and politics, art and polemics. With

Stalin's rise to power in Communist Russia there arose a number of tense discussions over the nature, importance and identity of art in Communist communities the world over. While the Communist Party of Great Britain (CPGB) was a comparatively small organisation, artistic culture in its myriad forms was vital to its identity. But the Party never really made definite, enduring decisions about art (Andrews, Fishman and Morgan 1995, p. 83). There is no doubt that the CPGB attempted to align itself with a Russian avant-garde in the 1920s, but this Russian influence continued as Stalin took control and a commitment to experimenting was sidelined to make way for Socialist Realism. This caused a problem for the practitioners affiliated to the CPGB who were engaged in inventive work (ibid., p. 91). While many artists had a tense relationship with the official Party, the CPGB's changing attitude towards art is emblematic of larger issues which remained unsolved. Should politically engaged theatre be written in the clearest prose style or should it be marked by artistic excellence, innovation and poetry? What if the poetic style becomes difficult to follow or makes complicated political ideas even harder to grasp? What if it is rejected by audiences who view it as pretentious or impenetrable? The CPGB tensions were, therefore, part of larger, far-reaching debates.

To provide some sort of answer to this conundrum, it seems particularly useful to return to a number of representative plays. And on the whole, it would be incorrect to suggest that, while those from a poetic tradition sought vibrant forms of linguistic discourse, those from an overtly political background shunned artistic expression in favour of diatribe. A number of these latter writers, indeed, were fascinated by language and by its poetic uses. It should also be remembered, of course, that those claimed as poetic dramatists were often just as committed to producing political plays as those working with the WTM or Unity Theatre. As MacColl's above memories illustrate, even the groups with the closest ties to the labour movements and the political rally started to look to new ways of using language.

In fact, language became such an important aspect of Theatre Workshop's aesthetic that they employed Australian language coach Nelson Illingworth to help the company with pronunciation and diction. Littlewood recollected, 'there we were every morning, singing, chanting, producing pure vowels and throwing consonants into them like straws into a stream' (2003, p. 203). Interestingly,

Illingworth marks another clear connecting point for the British avant-garde. As well as working with Theatre Workshop, he also had some association with Unity and got into some heated debates with Bert Marshall during the production of Pogodin's *Aristocrats* (Chambers 1989, p. 134). He was also on the 1935 membership list for Group Theatre (Sidnell 1984, p. 272). The presence of Illingworth across the spectrum of the British avant-garde again points to the importance of language. But his work also challenged that perceived tension between the poetic and the performative. Illingworth's system relied on the relationship between the actor's physicality and speech: the 'sound was produced by the whole body, not simply the larynx' (Leach 2006, p. 90). Just as Yeats's poetry relied on the symbiotic relationship between speech patterns and dance, and Lewis claimed that 'words' are 'deeds', so Illingworth's system attempted to assess language as inextricably connected with the body. Again, speaking became, in and of itself, a physical performative act.

Returning to MacColl's *The Other Animals*, one can clearly see the importance of linguistic experiment. Littlewood remembered, 'the writing was often dazzling, so dazzling that it tended to obscure the meaning' (2003, p. 311). Again adapting a clear Expressionist style, MacColl created a syntactically vibrant piece combining prose, verse and arresting imagery. In general, Expressionist plays challenged the very notion of language – 'grammar and syntax were ruthlessly overthrown, articles eliminated, sentences clipped, new words created' (Garten 1959, p. 105) – and this is certainly true of *The Other Animals*, which uses syntactical experiment as a political mode. The opening voices are clear examples of this as they discuss the hegemonic repression of a revolution-focused minority. These monologues are written in free verse, a form that MacColl came back to throughout the play. Interestingly, he rarely used strict meter, but largely created a more fluid poetic voice:

> Shags opened the breast of the wheeling gull
> As he rode the shifting current of the air.
> His perfect flight
> Was a reminder,
> Constantly before their eyes,
> Of the gulf
> Which lies between

> Their world, half-fish, half-bird,
> And his,
> All bird,
> Perfect.

> (Goorney and MacColl 1986, p. 134)

The political intention of this speech, given by the Second Voice, is clear; the bird's sense of freedom and physical wholeness is presented in sharp contrast to the deformity of the hegemony. The stylised fragmentation is a vital device, providing, at first, a sense of unimpeded flight. But it goes on to fracture still further, with interruptive commas and unusually short lines. This stylistic splintering reflects the 'half-fish, half-bird' of the repressors.

The poetic form of the opening voices is further stressed by the subsequent dialogue between the guards in Robert Hanau's cell. Their distinctly unpoetic language – 'Home again, brother! There's no place like home./ Christ, how this place stinks!' (Goorney and MacColl 1986, p. 135) – creates a sort of Brechtian *Verfremdungs-Effekt,* an interruption to the initial dreamlike syntax by the brutal blasphemy of the guards. This jarring juxtaposition is not unique to MacColl's work but can also be seen in the plays of Auden and Isherwood, MacNeice and even Eliot. Retelling the story of Archbishop Thomas Becket's death in 1170, Eliot's *Murder in the Cathedral* (1935) is a play of contrasting voices. Nowhere is this more clearly seen than in the post-murder scenes. The Knights who have just killed the Archbishop move downstage and address the audience directly. The speeches are written in an everyday prose style and provide some sense of justification for the Knights' actions. In many ways, as the First Knight's speech suggests, the presentations resemble those in a court of law (Eliot 1969, p. 276). The Priests' response to this event uses a poetic voice with an irregular metre. It leads into the final Chorus prayer with its King James pronouns and a sung *Te Deum* in the background. The differing voices of this final section audibly reflect a tension throughout: the peace of the cathedral is brutally interrupted by a violent act, the poetry is interrupted by the prose. In many ways, the Knights' speeches also resemble those of the Living Newspaper as political dialogues. There are appeals, presentations of a case and justifications of action with the intention of persuading the audience of their position. Given the Medieval subject matter and the archaic poetic voices, the Knights' speeches give the impression that the modern has suddenly burst through.

Founder of Mercury Theatre Ashley Dukes concluded that 'Expressionism is, or should be, one form of the poetry of the stage ... the aim of expressionist drama is clearly allied to that of imagist verse and impressionist painting' (1942, p. 52). So, while the form is defined by syntactical innovation, it is also defined by the image. Dukes clearly connected this to the act of painting and, as we have seen, this connection made a substantial difference to the very structure of these plays. Yet Dukes was conscious of another influence, that of Imagism.

Spender described the Imagists' project in his 1963 text, *The Struggle of the Modern*. He suggested that they, 'stripped poetry back to the primitive situation in which the outer experience produced a poetic reaction on the sensibility. This is when it strikes off an image, like a spark. The image is the basic unit of poetry' (Spender 1963, p. 110). Understanding the Imagists' project as committed to a 'hardness of outline, clarity of image, brevity, suggestiveness, freedom from metrical laws' (Hughes 1972, p. 4), a similar attitude can be seen in a broad range of examples from the British theatrical avant-garde. Given the well-documented connections between the originator of the movement, Ezra Pound, and Eliot and Lewis, one might expect such influences in their work. However, the parallels (if not direct connections) can be seen in a number of performance pieces. The image as an incisive, condensed trope is a recurring motif.

The images created in the British avant-garde were, in keeping with the Imagist movement, often vibrant. But they were also infused with intention: poetic pictures with political design. Take, for example, the dialogue between light and darkness. This is a well-established trope, as in *Macbeth's*, 'Stars, hide your fires,/ Let not light see my black and deep desires' (Shakespeare 1967, p. 64). While this dualist image remained in the British avant-garde, it was now imbued with political fervour and a growing complexity.

'Light' and 'dark' as political motifs unexpectedly recurred time and again. The device is evident in Auden and Isherwood's *The Ascent of F6* in which the Chorus affirm, 'the future, hard to mark/ Of a world turning in the dark' (1966, p. 118) and MacColl's *The Other Animals* where Hanau maintains, 'we have lived through a long night/ But now the sun stands poised and ready/ On the furthest ridge of Capricorn' (Goorney and MacColl 1986, p. 188). In both, darkness is associated with repression and ignorance whereas light is a moment of revelation. But there are also moments where this hierarchical opposition (darkness as evil, light as revolutionary freedom) is disturbed. The analogy becomes particularly troubling in Spender's *Trial of a Judge*. At first it seems a straightforward dialogism; the Black Chorus are representative of fascist violence. However, the image becomes increasingly complex:

> But now all crumbles away
> In coals of darkness, and the existence
> Of what was black, white, evil, right
> Becomes invisible, founders against us
> Like lumber in a lightless garret.
>
> (Spender 1938, p. 46)

The darkness acts as a covering, concealing the contrasts between formerly diametrically opposed terms and ideas. The well-established oppositional pairings start to collapse. Further, the Mother presents the now complex understanding of light thus:

> Beloved sons,
> You start on that difficult journey
> Away from the light and towards the light.
>
> (ibid., p. 68)

The 'light' is both the easy route, the conventional path *and* aim of the rebel. Those wishing to challenge political subjugation must leave the light of mainstream society and enter the light of subversion.

There are some interesting connections to be made here. Though a traditional image, the light/dark dialogue is suddenly a political comment. Often, as with the Mother's description in *Trial of a Judge*, these images are not wholly straightforward. Furthermore, and in conjunction with this, there is also a fascination with astronomy; the light/dark image, with its strong political overtones, connects the struggle for social change in its very broadest sense with the enduring patterns of the universe. The images in our extracts from *The Ascent of F6* and *The Other Animals* bear this out. As *Macbeth* reveals, this was not a twentieth-century innovation. However, the relationship between the astronomical and the light/dark image was dramatically modernised in the historical avant-garde. In *The Star Turns Red* (1940), for example, Sean O'Casey pointed to the star that 'shone when it led the kings; so shall it not shine when it leads the people. It leads no more, and never shall till its silver turns to red' (1950, p. 256). This quasi-Messianic image will only lead the people again when it is imbued with Socialistic potential. This connection between the universe, political change and people (as individuals and in communities) brings new purpose and potency to the traditional light/dark image. It is a clear example of the dialogue between the British poetic tradition and new Expressionistic innovations.

However, it also marks a challenge to the accusation that the British poetic dramatists were anti-theatrical, as using this light/dark dialogue was not only a poetic decision but was worked out in performance. This is perhaps best illustrated by Eric and Anna's meeting in Auden and Isherwood's *On the Frontier*. The stage directions describe the encounter as follows:

> *The spotlight illuminates a small area in the middle of the stage. The various chairs and table should have been pushed back, so that they are visible only as indistinct shapes in the surrounding darkness. Enter ERIC and ANNA L and R respectively. They advance slowly, like sleepwalkers, until they stand just outside the circle of light, facing each other.*
>
> (Auden and Isherwood 1966, p. 67)

The shadowy furniture almost represents a threat in the dark with Eric and Anna, slightly illuminated by the 'circle of light', emblematic of an attempt to bridge the 'frontier'. At the end, they step into the light and, though through death and destruction it appears that the repressive governments have succeeded, Eric and Anna defy them by finding 'peace/ Only in dreams' (ibid., p. 121), emerging into the light that had been kept from them. The light/dark image that has been so linguistically prevalent in the other plays mentioned here is also revealed through innovative lighting effects.

Poetry is often regarded as distinct from everyday methods of speech and, further, entirely irrelevant to the contemporary experience of the majority. But I would suggest that it has a place in all manifestations of the avant-garde since it is an intrinsic human experience. To substantiate this claim it is useful to turn to MacNeice's introduction to his 1942 radio play, *Christopher Columbus*:

> For man, we should always remember, is born poetic. Hence the dominance of nursery rhymes in the nursery and of poetry in all early literatures. Poetry, in this one sense at least, is more primitive than prose; it was easier on the ear and less strain upon the mind [...] but the modern public, we shall be told, is not at home to poetry. This I do not believe ... He may dislike *the idea of poetry* but that is because he has been conditioned to think of poetry as something too sissy, infantile, difficult or irrelevant.
>
> (1944, p. 11)

Eliot agreed:

> Verse becomes the most effective medium for these multiple levels because it intensifies the emotional content of the plays and allows the actors to achieve a connection with the audience that prose cannot, thus reversing the standard argument that prose drama was more accessible.
>
> (Badenhausen 2004, p. 127)

So, as well as reflecting modern life, poetry could actually be a more effective means of voicing contemporary concerns. For the playwrights of the British avant-garde, poetry became a multi-faceted entity and, rather than present declamation and dialect in contrast to the poetic voice, I prefer to see all these innovations as part of a similar project: an attempt to fashion a workable linguistic method to explore the contemporary.

The poetics of declamation

Responding to the 1936 events in Spain, Jack Lindsay wrote *On Guard for Spain* (presented by Unity Theatre in Trafalgar Square in 1937), a declamatory poem that acts as a useful transition point for the current argument. The poem was written for performance, to be split amongst a number of different voices, and narrated some of the key moments in Spanish Civil War history, uniting them with more personal reflections and challenges to the audience. Thus, Lindsay juxtaposed a melodramatic, Hollywood-style train departure, where the central character remembers his lover's 'tearwet lashes', with 'Workers of the World we cry/ We that have forged our unity on the anvil of battle' (Lindsay 1937, pp. 3, 1). Lindsay, comparing his piece to the theatre of Brecht in Germany and the New Deal in the United States, referred to it as 'a distinctive type of mass-declamation' (ibid.) which differed from innovations overseas. For Spender, however, this combination of poetry and declamation made for an unsatisfactory performance. He called it 'effective recruiting propaganda' but 'supremely untruthful as poetry' (Chambers 1989, p. 85). And it is certainly true that Lindsay did not really seem to reconcile the two modes in this piece. However, *On Guard for Spain* is a vital model: an attempt to ally the powerful challenge of declamatory propaganda with the nuances of a poetic form. While it is not unequivocally successful in this endeavour, it does provide an introductory template. As many of the theatre companies and practitioners of the political tradition turned to declamation as a persuasive theatrical form, they also retained a particular interest in the vibrancy of a poetic voice. Indeed, the declamation itself is often infused with a particular poetic spirit that means that any clear distinction between the two becomes impossible.

Given that the political rally was such a vital model for WTM, Unity and Theatre Workshop, it is perhaps to be anticipated that the language patterns of these events should find a way into their theatrical projects. The striking rhetoric of the rally with its passionate oration can be seen throughout the British theatrical avant-garde. With the performative nature of modern politics, such a connection between the on-street rally and on-stage theatre is hardly surprising. Indeed, Raphael Samuel pointed to the strong connection between theatre and political protest, reflecting that 'a political demonstration is necessarily an act of street theatre, albeit one with a multitudinous cast, and a rhythm and tempo of its own' (Samuel, MacColl and Cosgrove 1985, p. xv).

MacColl spent a great deal of his youth attending political rallies and, predictably, declamation was crucial to Theatre Workshop's performances. Even in his later works agit-prop declamation remained prominent. He explored the progression of the Theatre Workshop aesthetic thus:

> The Agit-Prop basis of our work was still very obvious, particularly as acting was concerned, but now it had style, nuance. We were no

longer deafening the audience with slogans, we were developing arguments in what we considered to be a new, exciting theatrical language.

(Samuel, MacColl and Cosgrove 1985, p. 248)

This is an accurate summary of the syntactical changes in the company; the powerful oration of the Red Megaphones' agit-prop formed a foundation point for a more refined language. Theatre Workshop's 1945 ballad play, *Johnny Noble* is a prime example of this grounding in agit-prop declamation. Its clear emotive story of Johnny and Mary, lovers who seem to be irreparably separated by the dangers of work, unemployment and war, is supplemented by conspicuous moments of declamation. This convention can be seen in the Newsboy's (a character coming out of the company's experiments with the Living Newspaper form) proclamations and in the songs. But there is also a disembodied narrative from the Mic. Voice. With statements like 'the unemployment figures can now be said to be stabilised at two and a half million. No immediate deterioration is expected' (Goorney and MacColl 1986, p. 45), the Mic. Voice is, like the Newsboy, a Living Newspaper character. However, the declarative voice does not only speak in slogans or headlines but also in a poetic form:

If only one could choose one's moments of eternity – but inexorable time divides and sub-divides again until nothing is left of a moment but an insubstantial memory.

(ibid., p. 59)

This is 'theatrical language' at work; the declarative remains, but it is now tempered with the poetic. And the audience seemed taken with this exciting and varied story: 'we played *Johnnie Noble* [sic], our story of a Hull fisherman, his life in unemployment, and war. The audience lapped it up, they loved the songs. We had a wildly enthusiastic reception' (Littlewood 2003, p. 346).

Dialect, accent and vernacular speech

If polemic declamation came from the political rally, from the street protest, then inevitably, the spoken rhythms of the industrialised urban space followed suit. This was, quite clearly, predominantly an attempt to make a particular political point, to ally the theatre with the working class, and to speak for and to an alternative audience to that which frequented the established theatre. Although both working primarily in a linear naturalistic style, this new interest in regional accents was obvious in plays like Walter Greenwood's *Love on the Dole*, which discusses the effects of unemployment on a Salford street, and D. H. Lawrence's Nottinghamshire-based miner plays. Judging the proliferation of regional accents is one of the harder tasks of the archivist, as photographs are no help and the plays are often written without any obvious dialect, presumably because there was the expectation that most actors would use their own regional accent without the need for direction. One might suppose, however, that lines like 'and that's how they do it to you. There's always a good time coming – but the workers never get it' in WTM's *The Theatre and Ours* (1932) would only be effective if spoken in the everyday vernacular of the actors/audience (Samuel, MacColl and Cosgrove 1985, p. 140).

There are, however, clear examples of regional accents in a few of the play texts which provide workable models for understanding regularly used speech patterns. A helpful example is Vance Marshall's naturalistic *A.R.P.* (Unity 1938). Granddad's distinctly cockney, 'I see Earthquake won the free firty an' they're agoin' to hang that Hoxton chap wot killed his missus' (Marshall 1938, p. 1) illustrates Unity's commitment to placing regional, identifiable accents on the stage. Later that year, this play was rewritten as a Living Newspaper and performed across Britain, altering the script to make it relevant to local communities (Chambers 1989, p. 149).

Presumably, regional accents would have been an important part of connecting with specific local audiences. It was, to borrow a phrase from Theatre Workshop's Howard Goorney, an attempt to challenge the speech patterns of the established theatre, which was dominated by 'the language of the cocktail bar rather than the workshop' (1981, p. 2). In fact, from the early experiments of Theatre Workshop, the company was committed to finding, in MacColl's terms, 'a dramatic utterance which would crystallise, or at least reflect a kind of working-class speech' (1990, p. 269). This decision was clearly reflected in *Johnny Noble*, which contained a wide range of local accents belonging to the fishermen of Hull, a miner in Durham and a Bolton-born soldier.

All this is not to say that the political groups were unconcerned with actor training. Rather, as mentioned, with the cross-group work of Nelson Illingworth, it is very clear that developing vocal skills was absolutely vital. Even in the earliest WTM productions, such a commitment to engaging with useful acting techniques was evident. Indeed, in *How to Produce Meerut* (1933), the author suggested, 'inflection of the voice is most important ... the sketch offers most unusual opportunities for voice-acting' (Samuel, MacColl and Cosgrove 1985, p. 107). Further, it must be recognised that there is no inherent conflict between good projection and the use of regional accents, and there are notable examples of the two coexisting, particularly in the speeches of some of the most prominent politicians of the period: figures such as Aneurin Bevin or Ramsay MacDonald.

Local accent and dialect also appeared in a range of plays that would more readily be associated with the poetic tradition. Such syntactical experiments became a vital part of the poetic drama movement. Eliot's voices in the second section of *The Waste Land* concluding with the line 'Goonight Bill. Goonight Lou. Goonight May. Goonight/ Ta ta. Goonight. Goonight' (1969, p. 66) persisted in the theatre works of the so-called poetic dramatists; these playwrights continued to experiment with accent and dialect. Eliot's own *Sweeney Agonistes* contains Londoners, Americans and a Canadian. Indeed, the whole basis for *Sweeney Agonistes* lay in the search for a new rhythm, one created out of 'colloquial speech' (ctd. in Rainey 2005, p. 143). International language patterns, therefore, were at the heart of Eliot's project here. From the Manager in Auden's *The Dance of Death* with his peculiar, suggestively foreign vowels to the Cockney Left Foot in his collaboration with Isherwood, *The Dog Beneath the Skin,* accent and dialect are frequently explored.

However, there was a difference in intention here. For Auden and Isherwood, using accent in their plays was, predominantly, an aesthetic decision. It created a multi-vocal, experimental linguistic method, just as it had done in Eliot's *The Waste Land*. Further, and the Left Foot is a case in point here, accents were used for comic effect. This stands in sharp contrast to the objectives marked out by Theatre Workshop and Unity, to create a real working-class speech for the stage. Yet, it would be easy to set the two in opposition. Actually, despite the contrast in purpose here, working with local dialect was, again, part of a distinct commitment to experimentalism. For all these playwrights, linguistic innovation was extremely important; exploring regional speech patterns was a crucial aspect of this.

Non-communicative language

In the presentation of political ideas, the battle between communication and non-communication became paramount, and it was further complicated by the British avant-garde's use of noises and impenetrable language systems. This was certainly not unique to Britain. Rather, across the Continent, such non-communicative methods had dominated the avant-garde scene. Marinetti advocated Words-in-Freedom, where the poet would 'begin by brutally destroying syntax as he talks ... Handfuls of essential words in no conventional acceptable order' (2008, p. 123). The *Verse ohne Worte* of Hugo Ball and the Dadaists explored the very character of language itself. Tzara's description of poetry as 'vigour and thirst, emotion faced with a form that can neither be seen nor explained' suggests a move away from formal language systems and towards a dynamic series of expressions, intrinsically connected to the psyche (1977, p. 75). Furthermore, 'psychic automatism' as André Breton termed it, attempted to crystallise the intricate workings of the subconscious in a textual form: 'dictated by thought, in the absence of any control exercised by reason, exempt from aesthetic or moral concern' (1972, p. 26). This was not a destructive Dadaist breakdown of language; rather, in many ways, such language actually expressed the subconscious more effectively. Perhaps, as Breton seems to claim, it is a purer, more 'authentic' syntax, a way of articulating the workings of the modern mind (Melzer 1994, p. 182). So a questioning of the reliability and objectivity of language was imbued into the very fabric of the historical avant-garde.

Furthermore, there are a number of moments where language breaks down entirely, when it seems, somehow, unable to cope with the strains of modern society. It is a theme exemplified by a range of theoreticians throughout the twentieth century. While Ferdinand de Saussure presented structures for understanding language and its relationship to the world in his collected lectures, *Course in General Linguistics* (1916), he also pointed to the arbitrary nature of the sign itself. This, coupled with the potentially paradoxical notions of chronological, historical stability and changing societal construction of the language system, means, 'the linguistic sign eludes the control of our will' (Saussure 1983, p. 71). Of course, in later decades this theme was taken up and explored to the point of combustion by

Jacques Derrida, amongst others. While there seems to be no direct connection between Saussure and the practitioners of the British avant-garde, the questioning of preconceived assumptions about language systems remained an ever-present theme. For all, language was not merely an empty receptacle for theme, but rather a legitimate focus of study in and of itself.

The solidity of language was questioned in a number of different ways, not least through the widespread use of rhythm: taps, knocks and drumming. These all became methods of communicative discourse as traditional linguistic systems seemed to collapse. But there were also examples of language itself becoming more (or less) than a method of disclosure. One of the key precursors for this theatrical questioning of language's reliability can be found in the work of the Belgian writer Maurice Maeterlinck[7] for his plays are full of syntactical uncertainty, reiterating phrases like 'Who was it made that noise?' and 'I hear again a sound I do not understand' (Maeterlinck 1912, pp. 48, 109). There is the constant, overwhelming sense that there is no real way of comprehending the terrors and confusions of the modern world. When Basil Dean tried to convince Maeterlinck to give permission for a British performance of *The Bluebird,* he focused on the language of the play:

> In permitting it to be done you would be doing a great service to young theatregoers in this country who so badly need just that inspiration of poetry and light and optimism that the play will bring to them.
>
> (1948, 2/7/12–2/7/27)

So, for Dean, Maeterlinck's poetry illustrated the complexity of modern methods of expression but also provided an inspirational poetic elegance.

Pushing this further, Antonin Artaud directly challenged the supremacy of recognisable language, advocating a complete break with a strict alphabet:

> We must first break theatre's subjugation to the text and rediscover the idea of a kind of unique language somewhere in between gesture and thought.
>
> (2010, p. 63)

Artaud's solution for Western theatre's obsession with language, of course, was the Theatre of Cruelty, a theory that has had a tremendous influence over contemporary dramatic form. While Artaud first published his *Theatre and its Double* in 1938 it did not make a real impact in Britain until many years later. Yet, while there was no British equivalent for Artaud's visceral, expressive, dynamic ideas, it is interesting to note that the solidity of language was being questioned across the modernist avant-garde.

Again, the techniques of Expressionism are vital to this discussion, revealing moments when language seemed an unsatisfactory mode to truly express the concerns of the modern world. The *Schrei,* for example, is that ecstatic moment of heightened emotion, used when language is unable to cope with the pain or despair or confusion of the modern world; it is the dramatic equivalent of Edvard Munch's *The Scream* (1893), the lone figure crying out while the world around him seems to disintegrate and fragment. In the British avant-garde it is most clearly seen in MacColl's *The Other Animals* when Hanau shrieks, 'Hanau is dead!/ They murdered him with voices!' (Goorney and MacColl 1986, p. 158). Obviously language does not break down entirely here; the character is able to enunciate his feelings clearly. In fact, it directly resembles Toller's use of the Expressionistic *Schrei* in *Transformation* when Friedrich smashes the sculpture and cries, *'I'll smash you up. Victory of the Fatherland'* (2000, p. 91). The *Schrei* leads to action rather than speech; after Hanau is killed, Robert dances away with Morning and Friedrich 'smashes' the statue. In the face of language that has started to disintegrate, action and movement seem to adopt new power. What is particularly interesting about *The Other Animals* example is that it is language ('voices') that has killed Hanau. With language as such a formidable opponent at the beck and call of the hegemony, Hanau finds that a scream is his clearest method of expression.

Language becomes even more complex at the end of *The Dog Beneath the Skin* when the masked characters become animals:[8]

> *The* General *as a Bull, the* Vicar *as a Goat,* Iris *as a Cat and* Mrs Hotham *as a Turkey…The* General *is addressing them, but only a bellowing is audible. His hearers respond with various animal noises, barking, mewing, quacking, grunting, or squeaking, according to their characters.*
>
> (Auden and Isherwood 1968, p. 178)

The characters are unable to communicate, condemned to respond to each other in animalistic noises. It is a striking modern day Tower of Babel, the confusion of language in response to the arrogance of the Pressan Ambo inhabitants. Unlike Hanau and Friedrich whose ability to speak coherently and calmly begins to dissolve in the face of outside hegemonic pressures, the characters in *The Dog Beneath the Skin* can no longer speak properly because they have simply lost their intrinsic humanity. Whereas Hanau and Friedrich ironically find clarity in their moments of linguistic breakdown, the community of Pressan Ambo find only chaos and a disintegration of human individuality.

But largely, British dramatists were far more interested in recognisable discourse than revelling in non-communicative confusion. As a general rule, playwrights from across the British theatrical avant-garde sought a language system that spoke directly, whether through the declamation of agitprop, the free verse of the poetic dramatists or the local dialects of the expected working-class audience. The examples above reveal the British theatrical avant-garde's commitment to exploring language in the modern world as a complex, shifting system. But, in order to really explore contemporary society, language was a means of expression and explication, not an impenetrable network of signifiers.

Speaking to an audience

Language innovation was evident throughout the British theatrical avant-garde from the poetry of Auden and Isherwood to the declamation of the Unity Theatre Living Newspapers. However, the key to understanding these innovations is to explore the intended audiences for these plays. If language is, at its heart, about communication and dialogue, then surely it is vital to ask who the actors were hoping to communicate with. In many ways, it is here that the differences between the practitioners can be most clearly seen.

In Group Theatre's *First Manifesto* (1934) there is a list of company participants and, while the usual suspects are mentioned (actors, producers, writers, etc.), the audience is also seen as a vital contributor to the creative process (Medley 1983, p. 146). After the performance of *Sweeney Agonistes* in the same year, Medley described this audience as 'lively and informed' (ibid., p. 152). Such close communication between stage and audience is summed up in Auden's 1935 *Manifesto on the Theatre*, in which he wrote 'in practice every member of the audience should feel like an understudy' (1986, p. 273). And, while such an objective is a formidable challenge, Spender concluded that 'the most important of these problems – that of finding an audience – they have solved better than anyone for a generation' (1978, p. 60). Eliot, too, was preoccupied with finding an audience and addressing it directly. Connecting the power of linguistic innovation with actor–audience communication, Eliot reflected, 'what we have to do is to bring poetry into the world in which the audience lives and to which it returns when it leaves the theatre' (1951, p. 27). For Group Theatre and its affiliates, direct communication with a supportive audience was imperative to the success of performances.

Group Theatre's audience was, of course, largely middle class, a collection of artist friends and left-leaning supporters. There were also those searching for a working-class audience; WTM, Theatre Workshop and Unity all sought a new audience, distinctly proletarian. So, consequentially, what defined Glasgow Unity's *The Gorbals Story* (Robert McLeish, 1946) was that it 'attracted that truly popular audience the company had never quite succeeded in bringing into the theatre before' (Hill n.d.). *Uranium 235* (1946), Theatre Workshop's challenging play about nuclear physics, was enjoyed by the holidaymakers of Butlins where 'every scene, including the Atom Ballet was applauded, sometimes cheered, as though it was indeed a Variety Show' (Goorney 1981, p. 52). Indeed, it mirrored a similar contemporaneous production in America, *E=mc2* (Haillie Flanagan, 1948), a Living Newspaper that also looked at the history of nuclear physics (Billington 2007, p. 25). Against all the odds, *Uranium 235*, a scientifically complex play, seemed to entertain and reach out to a new audience. While there is no doubt that this noble objective was not always realised, it remained a decisive intention (and a troublesome challenge) for these politically engaged groups.

Verbal expression became a focus for some of the most striking experiments in the British theatrical avant-garde. However, as the playwrights and companies explored new methods, textual language became just one of the performance signifiers. Terence Gray analysed this transformation:

Words, then, once supreme in the theatre, once the solitary vehicle of drama, are now but one of several factors, and must decrease in importance as the developing forces prove more efficient for the work.

(1926, p. 25)

Gray's conclusion is not entirely accurate, of course; whether there has ever been any real theatre in which the word has been the 'solitary vehicle' is debatable. Yet his animated evaluation does point to the growing importance of the performative, the visual and the fruitful relationships between theatre and other art forms.

4

Character: The Screaming Man and the Talking Feet

Figure 5   Marionette (© the artist Beth Fletcher)

The plays of the British avant-garde attempted to make sense of a world in which the individual subject had been fractured by war, unfulfilling work, unemployment, transformations in class and gender relations, and an overwhelming sense that the overarching narratives of former times had broken down. The characters of these plays embodied those contemporaneous challenges. In general, there was very little attempt to create illusion and characters remained theatrical (often metatheatrical) figures. Of course, the most well-known example of this sort of consciously theatrical characterisation can be found in Luigi Pirandello's *Six Characters in Search of an Author* (1921), described by Tyrone Guthrie as 'one of my favourite plays' (1961, p. 212). While there was an eclectic range of figures presented in the British avant-garde, they were almost unanimously united by a similar commitment to representational as opposed to individualised or psychonaturalistic characters, thereby reflecting Auden's manifesto proposition, 'the drama is not suited to the analysis of character, which is the province of the novel. Dramatic characters are simplified, easily recognisable and over life-size' (1986, p. 273). Now, as with many other facets of the theatrical experience, characters had to serve a greater purpose, become emblematic of specific political and/or artistic projects. Prefiguring Auden, Yeats suggested that a theatrical focus on character was actually a modern invention as 'when we go back a few centuries and enter the great periods of drama, character grows less and sometimes disappears' (1961, p. 240). Yeats was not, of course, suggesting that theatre history is characterless, but rather that psychological analyses of character in any naturalistic sense are not to be found. It is to this vibrant theatrical past that Yeats wished to turn.

Ancient modes reinterpreted

Once again, there are connections to be made here with a British folk play tradition and with Continental *commedia dell'arte*: the former with the Mummers' play characters like the doctor, the hero and the villain, and the latter with Harlequin, Pulcinella, Pantalone, and the other 'masks' that made a real impression on the theatre of the early decades of the twentieth century. In Russia, for example, Meyerhold's *commedia dell'arte* characters (and particularly the clowns) were 'though profoundly unrealistic ... theatrically expressive, full of potential, and even subversive' (Clayton 1993, p. 75). So these ancient characterisations provided artistic freedom and a *potential* challenge to hegemonic structures. The attraction for a practitioner such as Meyerhold is clear and the merits were as welcome in the British scene as in the theatre of post-Revolutionary Russia.

There are a number of examples of these stock characters, but perhaps the most potent is the symbol of unchecked capitalism which seemed once again to cross that boundary between the poetic and the political. The Financier in Auden and Isherwood's *The Dog Beneath the Skin*, Fortune in MacColl's *John Bullion* and the Capitalist in WTM's 1931 *Art is a Weapon* (a sketch originally from New York), Crabbe in Herbert Hodge's *Cannibal Carnival* and Slusher, 'the great Lord High Extortioner' (Unity 1936/7, p. 2) in *The Fall of the House of Slusher* are all confident expounders of the economic status quo. They all understand art in purely commercial terms or, as in *Art is a Weapon*, as a detached metaphysical concept soaring 'miles above the common place of daily routine, above politics, above party strife' (Samuel, MacColl and Cosgrove 1985, p. 146). These can be read in parallel to figures like Domin in Karel Čapek's *R.U.R.* or Fayette, the Industrialist in Clifford Odets's *Waiting for Lefty*, two plays we will return to later in this chapter. Capitalism and all its perceived defects are encapsulated in one figure. The similarities between, say, the war-mongering businessman/financier, emblematic of a brutal capitalism in the plays of the British avant-garde and the greedy, avaricious Pantalone are obvious, though there is not necessarily any polemical, agitational impulse in the presentation of the traditional Pantalone. Similarly, while there was no real political intention in a genre like melodrama, a form that dominated the British theatrical scene in the nineteenth century, the heroes and villains continued to populate the stage. Placed in this British avant-garde, the villain became the political dictator or the mercenary businessman while the hero was imagined as a freedom fighter, a political martyr or an engaged member of the working class.

This search for simplified, representational character found new impetus in the work of Edward Gordon Craig. His concept of the *Übermarionette* advocated a profound change in the nature of the on-stage protagonists that chimes with and pre-empts the British avant-garde's commitment to depictive, theme-centred characterisation. He suggested, 'the actor must go, and in his place comes the inanimate figure – the Übermarionette we may call him' (Craig 1983, p. 95). Craig insisted on stylised, puppet-like gesture, and particularly facial gesture, so that the individual, distracting idiosyncrasies or adopted 'actorly' mannerisms disappeared. For Craig, the *Übermarionette* provided an escape from the irritating on-stage individuality of the human.

A number of other older traditions influenced the British avant-garde endorsement of the representational character. For Group Theatre, for example, the mask became an important motif. Productions of Eliot's *Sweeney Agonistes,* Auden's *The Dance of Death* and *The Dog Beneath the Skin* used masks as a means to construct character, creating striking visual effects. After watching a production of the first two in 1935 Benjamin Britten commented on the 'décor & very lovely masks by Robert Medly [sic]' (Evans 2009, p. 281). In the later *The Dog Beneath the Skin*, the masks of the Lunatics added to the unreal grotesqueness of the Red Light District Scene and stood in sharp contrast to Alan's normal face (Sidnell 1984, p. 163). For all three, the masks were central to the non-naturalistic intentions and, while the mask is, of course, present in the established aesthetics of both the ancient Greek and Roman stage and *commedia dell'arte*, there was a renewed interest in it on the cusp of the new century. Consider the intentional contrast between the artist's own face and the red-lipped masks that surround it in James Ensor's *Self-Portrait with Masks* (1899) or one of the masked ladies of Picasso's *Les Demoiselles D'Avignon* (1907). Again, use of the mask marked a pertinent connection between the theatre and the visual art of the historical avant-garde, though it first re-emerged in this modern theatrical setting in the work of Yeats and Craig. The innovations of the latter were connected with his ongoing commitment to reassessing the acting figure for a modern theatre. And this sense of modernity and contemporaneous exposition was vital to Craig's appropriation of a mask tradition. This was not, as he made clear, a nostalgic or scholarly exercise, a sham-Greek motif (Craig 1983, p. 23). It was a particularly modern theatrical concept and, just as with the *Übermarionette*, employed to overcome the inherent and inescapable problem of the actor:

> The face of the actor carries no such conviction; it is over-full of
> fleeting expression – frail, restless, disturbed and disturbing ... the

mask will return to the theatre; of that I grow ever more and more assured.

(ibid., p. 21)

And it became a central avant-garde motif in a Continental European context. Alfred Jarry's *Ubu Roi*, for example, also used masks to present the actors as marionettes, ridding the stage of unintentional human characteristics. In the program notes for the 1896 premier at the Théâtre de l'Oeuvre, Jarry mentioned the 'cardboard masks of actors talented enough to depersonalize themselves voluntarily' (1965, p. 81). Jarry's description points to both the objective here (an intentional 'depersonalization') and the importance of employing accomplished actors who were able to deal with this process successfully. It is interesting that while the mask hides the actor in one way, this device actually requires a high level of skill to be used successfully.

So why was such an ancient and historically loaded feature as the mask to enjoy a resurgence in this British avant-garde context? I suggest a number of reasons, all of which relate directly back to its historical uses. The mask 'makes strange', transforming the face into a peculiar parody. In this modern context, therefore, the mask acted as a direct challenge to naturalistic methods of characterisation; empathetic association with a character in a mask is almost impossible. The mask also makes the character visible. Again, the aim is not subtlety but obvious, intentionally artificial construction. This means that in a play such as *The Dog Beneath the Skin*, masks are extremely effective grotesque motifs. Auden suggested that the masks of this play, 'exaggerate the obvious' (1988, p. 501), taking images of the modern world and creating something larger and distorted. The characters Alan meets as he wanders through the cityscape are terrifying simulations of humanity; the Chorus describes the local inhabitants of the street with their 'faces grey in the glimmering gaslight: their eyeballs drugged like a dead rabbit' (Auden and Isherwood 1968, p. 55). While the vibrant Red Light district stands in sharp contrast to the colourless street, the occupants seem to be subverted examples of humanity. The masks are vital to the prevailing mood of desperation, exploitation and the strangely dynamic, exciting grotesque. Further, and connecting the argument back to earlier conclusions, the mask acts as a cage, incarcerating the wearer and enabling him/her to only see the world as brief glimpses through the apertures. Certainly, this is true for the women of the Red Light District in *The Dog Beneath the Skin*. The descriptions of the 'pleasures' to be found here explicitly point to S&M, drug taking and paedophilia, thereby trapping the women in the desires of the customers.

While there was a proliferation of grotesque masks, the noble mask of the Japanese tradition also made an appearance. Dispensing with the individual expression of the human face, these masks provided a playwright like Yeats with a way of dealing effectively with the mythological subject matter in plays like *The Only Jealousy of Emer* (1919) (Kermode 1957, pp. 79–80). Negating any sense of naturalist illusion, the Japanese Noh mask meant that theatre moved from the plane of character analysis to symbolist storytelling. For Yeats, this led to different ways of understanding story and character and, in many ways, a device akin to Craig's *Übermarionette*:[1]

> A mask will enable me to substitute for the face of some common-place player, or for the face repainted to suit his own vulgar fancy, the fine invention of a sculptor, and to bring the audience close enough to the play to hear every inflection of the voice.
>
> (Yeats 1961, p. 226)

Again, it is an act of 'making strange', but in *The Only Jealousy of Emer* it is not the grotesque, comic mask of the *commedia dell'arte* that is needed but the tragic, noble mask of the Noh.

Isolation: psychoanalytical science and the fragmented mind

Yet, as always, this appropriation of theatre history was coupled with a notable commitment to original, contemporaneous experiment. This was particularly evident in the British avant-garde's continual presentation of the isolated figure and the individual psyche. In many ways this was a cognitive quest taking on the mantle of Sigmund Freud and others in an artistic context. With the advent of such psychological theories, the way a human being could understand him/herself was transformed. Descartes's *cogito ergo sum* appeared to be unravelling. This was directly reflected in the presentation of character on the stage. Given that the 'modernist character comes to the stage partly de-substantiated' (Fuchs 1996, p. 35), it is unsurprising that avant-garde theatre began to interact, consciously or otherwise, with modern scientific methods in an attempt to study the fragmented psyche on stage. In fact, Freud confronted the presentation of theatrical character through his own psychological interpretations. The basic premise of his 1905–6 paper, 'Psychopathic Characters on the Stage', is that the illusory suffering of the central character is the source of enjoyment and interest for an audience. This suffering is mental, 'within the soul of the hero himself' (Freud 1960, p. 146). Freud returns to Hamlet as a prime example of this type of character but this tortured figure became ever-more prevalent in the modernist avant-garde, responding to a combination of new theoretical and scientific understandings of selfhood and the tensions in contemporary society.

This scientific, psychoanalytical representation of the human appeared on stage in plays like Nikolai Evreinov's *The Theatre of the Soul*. In 1915, Edith Craig and the Pioneer Players produced the English version (translated by Marie Potapenko and Christopher St John) with a set dominated by a red pulsating light, visually representing the central figure's heart (Cockin 2001, p. 180). It confirmed this company's commitment to artistic innovation and to engaging with plays from the Continental avant-garde. In the opening speech the Professor alludes to some of the foremost psychoanalytical thinkers (including Freud) and introduces the play as a 'genuinely scientific work' (Evreinov 1915, p. 14). Following Freud's concept of the triune self, Evreinov presents three characters, the Rational Entity of the Soul, the Emotional Entity and the Subliminal Entity. The play examines the conflict between these facets of the self, particularly between the Rational and Emotional as they fight for pre-eminence and decide whether the Man should stay with his Wife or choose to run away with the alluring Dancer. The Subliminal Entity sleeps throughout the play until the end when the Emotional Entity appears to commit suicide. In many ways it is an overly simplistic rendering of modern psychoanalytical methods. In her introduction, St John recognised its crudeness but suggested that this was a 'virtue rather than a defect' given the 'astonishingly simple' nature of the psyche (ibid., p. 8). Despite its limitations this play illustrates a broader point: the British avant-garde's fascination with the individual on a psychological level. The theatre had become a vibrant medium for the examination of modern methods of understanding the self and, further, this theatrical self was subject to fissures and ruptures.

The disconnected protagonist of Evreinov's play was a persistent image in British avant-garde theatre; though surrounded by other characters, this figure is detached from them, occupying a central position in the play while remaining isolated. Though presented and realised in differing ways, this is true of such characters as Robert Hanau (*The Other Animals*), Michael Ransom (*The Ascent of F6*) and the Judge (*Trial of a Judge*). Not resolutely alone, nor indivisibly connected to those around them, these characters stand apart and the narrative follows them as a central motif through the play.

There is a distinct Expressionistic parallel here, as the plays associated with this movement often focus on a central man (and it generally is a man)[2] and his circumstances. An example can be found in a play that made a great impact on Ashley Dukes: Reinhard Sorge's *The Beggar* (1912).[3] Dukes travelled to Germany in 1919 and attended the theatre in Cologne. The theatre was producing this play, which he regarded as 'the first expressionist drama, and perhaps the best because it never left the plain of poetry' (Dukes 1942, p. 51). Here the Poet is the central character and the entire play is focused on his experiences, which drive him 'into much loneliness and tortured grief' (Sokel 1963, p. 40). He is a struggling artist committed to producing his plays on the stage but, leaving his Patron and returning to his family, he finds an insane Father and conventionally bourgeois Mother and Sister. While he does communicate with others the dialogue is full of gaps and a lack of understanding. There is affection but there is also pain, separation and death. His response to his Mother's death is typical of an increasingly isolated figure: 'the abyss gaped and darkness shrouded us/ You failed to see me' (ibid., p. 88).

For Expressionists like Sorge, this central man is a culmination of various social and philosophical ideas. In some ways he is a religious figure, a Messianic saviour. In others he is the modern man, struggling to cope with the isolating nature of contemporary, industrialised society. At times he is an emblem of a Nietzschean new man, an *Übermensch* instilled with the potential for individual inner regeneration rather than a societal revolution. Yet in all cases he is resolutely alone, either as an ardent individualist standing firmly against the assumptions and values of modern society, or as an outcast (voluntary or otherwise), crumbling beneath the horrors of a modern world.

In plays like *The Beggar* the world is wholly mediated through the mind of the central character and the narrative storyline is structured accordingly. If perceived entirely through the individual, subjective consciousness, society becomes an infinitely complex place; it is impossible to make generalised presuppositions or to fully grasp any sense of objectivity. It therefore, by definition, breaks through so-called bourgeois assumptions and the previously concretised postulations of governments and leaders. As a result, reading the world through the subjective is an inherently revolutionary process. It does remain crucial, however, to remember that this focus on the individual psyche was present in the naturalist tradition and not to presume that the British avant-garde stood in irreconcilable contrast to nineteenth-century innovations. But whereas naturalism dealt with the interaction between subjectivities, the avant-garde (and particularly Expressionism) examined single subjectivities existing in predominantly non-communicative relationships with others.

This highly subjectivised, modern, Expressionistic world is discernible in a play like MacColl's *The Other Animals* with the appearance of dead revolutionaries, Piera, Gaudry and Guthrie, who seem to be based only in Robert's psyche; they disappear as quickly as they arrive and are introduced at the start as dead already. This subjective conjuring of characters was a recurring emblem across the British theatrical avant-garde. Take Eliot's *Sweeney Agonistes* in which the characters do not seem real but rather images lodged in the imagination of Sweeney or, to take the play's own description, 'meat to be made into a stew' (Eliot 1969, p. 121).[4] Both these plays are grounded firmly in the contemporary, but this modern world is understood through the mind of the protagonist. This leads us to a particular accusation levelled at much of the British theatrical avant-garde, particularly the poetic tradition: there is a distinct absence of incident. This would obviously be a profound difficulty in the dramatic genre, a mode that relies on action and the audience reaction to it. But it is this 'interior action' that becomes a source of drama. While naturalism largely prided itself on objective analysis of contemporary society, plays like *The Other Animals* or *Sweeney Agonistes* rejected such a detached empirical approach, preferring instead to read contemporary circumstances (the dull everyday, the urban landscape, revolution, class relations, war) through the collective or individual psyche. This does not lead to a lack of action as much as an intensification of action.

Focusing on the psyche of the central figure enabled practitioners across the historical avant-garde to explore different facets of the human mind. Unsurprisingly in light of this, dreams were a recurring motif. Once again this was building on movements in medicine and psychoanalytic thought. Not only did the narratives investigate the complex modern mind but, as we have seen, this preoccupation with the dreaming subconscious affected the actual narrative system, with the juxtaposition of naturalistic scenes and dream sequences. This meant that performances could explore extremely complex, at times incoherent, ideas and images. While, according to Freud, dreams could be intelligible, hallucinatory desires, they could also defy logic and reasoned argument. This 'dream-distortion ... [which] makes a dream seem strange and unintelligible to us' (Freud 1991, p. 168) was used to great effect across the modernist avant-garde, creating narratives and characters that at times seem to respond in a fairly naturalistic manner, and at others seem to utterly violate rational rules.

Both *The Other Animals* and *Sweeney Agonistes* are constructed in a highly fragmented style that resembles (or indeed embodies) the human experience of dreaming and waking. The former certainly retains some sense of linearity, but moves between scenes enabling the central character to be on a train one minute and battling with Graubard in the prison the next. The fragments of *Sweeney Agonistes* are constructed a little differently and presented explicitly as fragments – the Fragment of a Prologue and the Fragment of Agon. The structure of this piece points back to Eliot's interest in the work of the Cambridge Ritualists and connects this play, despite its ultra-modern focus, with ancient Greek traditions. Despite the differences, one of the by-products of this sort of structure is that it becomes a far more suitable medium for the discussion of the psyche and the subjectivised world which is intrinsically fragmented and non-linear.

The 'subjective structure' is equally evident in a play like Toller's *Masses Man* which is written in self-titled 'pictures'. Some of these resemble the scenarios of the poetic drama tradition so, while they are not naturalistic in any conventional sense, they are constructed through recognisable dialogue. Juxtaposed with these are the 'dream pictures'. But *Masses Man* has a uniquely autobiographical element which marks it as a particularly fascinating example of this dream/ 'reality' mode. As mentioned with reference to the cage as a scenic motif, the first draft was written as Toller languished in a prison after his participation in an attempted revolution in Bavaria (1919). Perhaps MacColl and Eliot associated or empathised with their respective isolated characters,[5] but Toller actually *was* this figure, the drama acting as a sort of imagining of his own psychological/personal-political anguish. He addressed this in his 1921 introduction to the play:

> The drama *Masses Man* in its totality is a vision, which literally 'burst' out of me in two and a half days ... the atrocities of the days of revolution had not yet become a psychic image of the days of revolution; they were somehow still painful, agonizing, psychic *fragments*, psychic *chaos*.
>
> (Toller 2000, p. 128)

While the poetic, nightmarish visions of Robert Hanau and Sweeney's 'bogeys' are imaginative interpretations of the modern world, *Masses Man* seems to have directly emanated from the isolation of the playwright. In many ways Toller became a Hanau or a Sweeney, graphically implicated in his own creative construction.

With this focus on the human mind, it is unsurprising that a number of plays (including *The Other Animals* and *Sweeney Agonistes*) examine the spiritual, which continued to impinge despite the British avant-garde's commitment to exploring the material contemporary world. Of course, again, this examination of the spiritual can be seen throughout the European avant-garde, from Strindberg's 1898 *To Damascus* and onwards. In order to understand the intention behind this focus on the divine, I want to discuss three plays which, like *To Damascus*, have at their heart a quest narrative: Vladimir Mayakovsky's *Mystery-Bouffe* (1918), André Obey's *Noah* (1931) and, from a British context, MacColl's reworking of Ben Jonson's *The Devil is an Ass, Hell is What You Make It* (produced by Unity Theatre in 1950). In all these examples, the playwrights took key motifs from a broad Judeo-Christian tradition and reconsidered them in a contemporary, theatrical context. For Obey, it was the Old Testament story of the Flood that formed the basis for his play. *Mystery-Bouffe* and *Hell is What You Make It* both take audiences on a journey through the afterlife. So, in many ways these plays consciously represent a clear genealogical progression from the medieval mystery plays, placing Biblical and traditional Christian stories on the stage. Yet it is in their contemporaneousness that parallels begin to form between them.

Michel Saint-Denis, who first produced *Noah* in Britain, at the New Theatre London in 1935, reflected that, 'nobody reading the play to-day can fail to be struck by its topicality' (Obey 1965, p. vii). And there are a number of moments when this can be clearly seen. As Noah watches the last people on Earth die, he cries, 'but men keep on swimming – men are still swimming over this dreadful waste of water. Oh! I hope, I only hope. He saw it from up there [sic]. I hope He saw it too, that was something for Him to see! – And now they're dead' (ibid., p. 20). In this post-First World War (with a looming Second World War) context, the idea of seemingly chaotic, over-whelming suffering must have been particularly poignant.

While *Noah* focuses on a specific Old Testament incident, *Mystery-Bouffe* and *Hell is What You Make It* describe the spaces associated with Christian ideas of eternity: Heaven, Hell and, the specifically Catholic, Purgatory. Both plays, interestingly, are based in theatrical traditions, the former in the medieval mystery play mode and the latter in Ben Jonson's satirical critique of seventeenth-century society, which is itself framed by a semi-parodic modification of the tradition of the morality play. Yet the audience is struck not by their connection with established tradition, but with their modern outlook. Subtitled 'A Heroic, Epic and Satiric Representation of Our Era', *Mystery-Bouffe* is a passionate interpretation of the class struggle. Like *Noah,* a flood is at the centre of this narrative. After the flood, we are left with the Clean (representatives of capitalism) and the Unclean (the workers). Such a 'them and us' attitude is just as evident in *Hell is What You Make It,* with Adamson as the worker compared to the petty, amoral symbols of the aristocracy, the government and big business. While Jonson's play situates the action in London, MacColl transported the narrative to Hell, basing the adaptation very loosely on the original. The selfish, mercenary characters are updated and placed in Hell, but we see the scene not through the eyes of a young inexperienced devil but through Adamson. The group are disgusted that they should find themselves in Hell but it is Adamson who is eventually offered the chance to escape the work of Hell for the restful idleness of Heaven. As might be expected, Adamson refuses, concluding (with an obvious Communist idealism) that it was his responsibility to build Hell and create a better society.

While both *Mystery-Bouffe* and *Hell is What You Make It* focus on a spiritual afterlife, what is striking is their commitment to contemporary material analysis. Heaven is transformed from a grace-bestowed reward to a society the workers can create. The Man (an apparition played by Mayakovsky himself) gives an invitation:

> come all
> who are not pack mules,
> and all
> for whom life is cruel
> and unbearable!
> My kingdom – earthly, not heavenly, –
> is for you

> (Mayakovsky 1995, p. 89)

The Soldier's later proclamation, 'it is near –/ that joy-filled home of the future,/ earned by labor' confirms that the Promised Land is not a spiritual benefaction but an earthly, political objective (ibid., p. 124). And a similar image appears in *Hell is What You Make It* where Adamson reflects, 'Paradise belongs to the people of Paradise. They made it, fought for it' (MacColl 1950, p. 86). In the spirit of Michel Saint-Denis's introduction to *Noah* above, established theatrical narratives infused with recognisable spiritual imagery were transformed into topical analyses of contemporary society.

Modern humanity: the nameless, the dead and the non-human

While the individual psyche retained a pre-eminent position in the plays of the British avant-garde, many were also populated by numerous characters who seem to have little sense of individuality. This can be clearly seen in the naming devices employed. A number of the characters are not given real names; rather they are denoted in descriptive terms. At times characters are referred to as 'Man' or 'Woman', providing them with no real subjectivity. In Spender's *Trial of a Judge,* for example, there is the 'Judge', the 'Fiancé' and the 'Mother'. It is a convention seen readily throughout the Expressionist plays of the Continent and America in works such as Treadwell's *Machinal*, which contains characters like 'Mother' and 'Doctor', and Toller's *Masses Man* with its 'Companion' and 'Husband'. In this example there is even a group called 'the Nameless', explicitly obliterating any sense of individual subjectivity at all. The 'Lunatics' in Auden and Isherwood's *The Ascent of F6* use a numbered system to suggest a lack of individual character and, again, this same device is utilised across the avant-garde; returning to Toller's *Masses Man*, there are the numbered guards and bankers. These characters do not require any specific characterisation as they are fulfilling clear narrative roles.

Nowhere is this clearer than in *The Ascent of F6*, which contains the characters of Mr and Mrs A. Detached from the actual journey up the mountain, these figures are vital, providing a commentary on the events. They represent a majority who work in dull jobs and seek their 'moments of happiness' (Auden and Isherwood 1966, p. 43) by living vicariously through celebrities, in this case, Michael Ransom. Their response to Ransom's climb – 'England's honour is covered with rust/ Ransom must beat them! He must! He must!' (ibid., p. 64) – illustrates the patriotic fervour that is invested in Ransom's attempt. The Abbot, in conversation with Ransom, perhaps puts it most succinctly when he says, 'you could ask the world to follow you and it would serve you with blind obedience; for most men long to be delivered from the terror of thinking and feeling for themselves' (ibid., p. 58). Rather than reason independently, Mr and Mrs A remain overawed by the messages transmitted from those in power. The play concludes[6] with their imagined ownership of a statue in Ransom's honour. Whereas in Toller's *Transformation* Friedrich smashes his monument that represented 'victory of the Fatherland!' (2000, p. 91), Mr and Mrs A valorise the statue, saying 'he belongs to us now' (Auden and Isherwood 1966, p. 123). Indeed, they resemble another denoted character: Mr Zero in Elmer Rice's *The Adding Machine*. He too does not seem to see through the deceits of the hegemony. In using the denotation terms, 'Zero' and 'A', the playwrights were directly commenting on the position of these character types in modern society; insignificant and unnoticed by the hegemony, real names are conspicuous by their absence. Yet the names also represent the position these characters have adopted for themselves, active participators in their own subjugation. Lieutenant Charles's final comment to Mr Zero, 'if there ever was a soul in the world that was labelled slave it's yours' (Rice 1997, p. 58) could just as easily be applied to Mr and Mrs A.

The lack of individualised naming devices points to a breakdown in our understanding of the unique human. This theme is examined still further in the frequent images of death. In all three of the 'Biblical' plays above, for example, death becomes an extremely complex image, with the recently deceased descending to Hell in *Hell in What You Make It*, the travels through eternity in *Mystery-Bouffe* and the annihilation of the world in *Noah*. In fact, death and various images or motifs connected with death appear across the local, historical avant-garde. And by escaping the chronological restrictions of pure naturalism, death need not be quite as final as one might expect. The British theatrical avant-garde is full of characters who are already dead; as Clive Barker has it, 'ghosts walk the stage throughout the 1920s and 1930s' (Barker and Gale 2000, p. 215). Barker's comment is substantiated by Harry's accusation in Eliot's *The Family Reunion* that 'one is still alone/ In an over-crowded desert, jostled by ghosts' (1969, p. 294). Even the isolated figure we have been looking at, disconnected in some way from the world, was still 'jostled by ghosts'. Whether tangible figures or metaphorical emblems, the dead took a prominent position in these plays.

This appearance of the dead can lead to profound incredulity, as in MacColl's *Uranium 235* in which Giordano Bruno, speaking to a reincarnated Paracelsus, accuses him of being 'dead a hundred years' (Goorney and MacColl 1986, p. 91). Paracelsus's response, 'I speak across a grave with a voice full of earth and stars' (ibid., p. 91), reveals the theatrical ability to move beyond even this most powerful and unalterable of barriers. Yeats's ghostly spectral images in his Noh-influenced analysis of the Easter Rising, *The Dreaming of the Bones*, create similar bewilderment as the 'dizzy dreams can spring/ From the dry bones of the dead' (Yeats 1979, p. 125). The dead return, demolishing any sense of naturalistic realism and bringing with them challenges, advice and 'dizzy dreams'.

However, and vitally, death was also presented in its traditional manner, as an irrevocable event. Given we are here concerned with the individual, it is interesting to note that death was often negotiated specifically through one figure rather than generally through statistics. Even when statistics are used, as in MacColl and Littlewood's dramatisation of the Gresford Pit Disaster in *Last Edition*, this is backed up by specific human examples. Yes, there was 'a total loss of life ... [of] 265' but, specifically, this was 'Joseph Andrews, of Wrexham, dead/ Thomas Anders, of Wrexham, dead' (Goorney and MacColl 1986, pp. 25–6). The finality of death, as exemplified in the very syntax of *Last Edition*'s Gresford Pit episode, is especially important in discussions of war. Mr A in *The Ascent of F6* sums up the ethical importance of presenting death in this manner:

> If you had seen a dead man, you would not
> Think it so beautiful to lie and rot;
> I've watched men writhing on the dug-out floor
> Cursing the land for which they went to war.

> (Auden and Isherwood 1966, p. 72)

Again, though not specifically named, there is a sense of *specific* death here. Mr A is a key witness, presumably imagining his own friends and comrades in the First World War. This type of personal detail breaks through statistical circumlocution. Death is personal, violent, gruesome and, importantly, final. Obviously, it is crucial to stress this, especially in theatrical presentations of war and its consequences.

One of the most striking theatrical examples of this dialogue between death and, for want of a better term, 'beyond death' – or the 'reanimated body' (Perdigao and Pizzato 2010, p. 3) – can be found in Irwin Shaw's *Bury the Dead* (1936). Again this was a play that entered the British repertoire in 1938 with Andre van Gyseghem's version for Unity Theatre. It captured a sense of the Zeitgeist; left-leaning practitioners in Britain were trying to balance the horrific recollections of the First World War with the need to fight against the growth of fascism in Spain (Chambers 1989, p. 150). While focusing clearly on the barbarity of war it also provided the dead with voices in order to provide a direct comment on the experiences of the common soldier. The play is highly sensory; the causes of death are described in extremely visual terms by the Doctor, but the soldiers who are digging the graves focus on the smell, with the reiteration of 'they stink! Bury them!' (Shaw 1936, p. 7). Unlike Mr A's described soldier, these infantrymen do not 'lie and rot', but rather rise and challenge. Such a defiance of natural and biological order leads to panic for the Generals, the Voices and the Women. As the First General says, 'those foundations will crumble utterly if these men of yours come back from the dead. I shudder to think of the consequences of such an act. Our entire system will be mortally struck' (ibid., p. 27). Indeed, with the change in the First Soldier's attitude, from a complaining, subordinate soldier to a challenging voice to the army hierarchy telling his Sergeant to 'shut up', the First General's worst fears are realised (ibid., p. 25). Like the 'beyond death' soldier in MacColl's *Johnny Noble* who encourages Johnny to 'take the world in your hands ... and wipe it clean' (Goorney and MacColl 1986, p. 66), the servicemen return from the dead to directly protest against the socio-political status quo.

Dead soldiers with a grudge reappear again in Hans Chlumberg's *Miracle at Verdun.* In Britain it was first produced in 1932 at the Embassy Theatre again under the direction of van Gyseghem, and Theatre Workshop (as Theatre of Action) attempted it in 1936. In a poignantly prophetic manner, the play recounts a 1939 visit to three First World War battlefields. The tourists are implicated in a commercial project, complaining about the price of the trip and its value for money. When the play moves to local communities, the inhabitants largely seem equally self-interested, while the short scenes that focus on the prime ministers of Germany, England and France are satirical studies of governmental leadership. It is against this backdrop of self-promotion that the soldiers of the Verdun graveyard are resurrected. The caretaker Vernier explains why the French and German soldiers died together:

> They were being shot at from both sides. They had to crowd together for cover. They were killed or wounded by the same shells. They had to bind each other's wounds – share each other's cigarettes – iron rations – gas masks.
>
> (Chlumberg 1932, p. 20)

The soldiers represent a sense of friendly solidarity that cuts across falsely constructed antagonism. Their response to the audience before returning to their graves provides a clear challenge. Soldier Weber asserts, 'the same state of rottenness, the same blind quarrelling ... Hatred as bitter and strong as before ... Goodness further from us than ever ... What did we die for?' (ibid., p. 93). Once again, the dead return to confront the living.

Here it is the broken post-war body that returns. But in Thornton Wilder's *Our Town* (1938), an analysis of a small community through the first decades of the twentieth century, there is a 'reanimated body' that was not involved in conflict. Although direct links are quite difficult to substantiate,[7] there are remarkable parallels between this American play and MacColl's *Landscape with Chimneys*. Both plays look closely at a small community. Both situate their communities on a platform stage rather than propose a naturalistic sense of scene construction. The action for both is mediated by the Stage Manager, who becomes a character in his/her own right. He/she is able to communicate with the audience and with the actors; the Stage Manager acts as an active narrator, not merely telling the story but also interacting with it. Both plays conclude with an element of tragedy and a challenge to the audience. It is fascinating that two playwrights working in different nations (and, notably, a few years apart) constructed their studies of local communities in strikingly similar ways.

At the end of *Our Town*, the dead are able to speak to one another and make comment on the world beyond their graves. The central character in this section is Emily who has recently died. She decides that she wants to return to the past as an act of remembrance. Yet the process of returning is a painful one. Emily is struck by the way humans take their lives for granted: 'oh, earth, you're too wonderful for anybody to realize you' (Wilder 1938, p. 124). There is a strong connection to be made here; Wilder's, Chlumberg's and Shaw's returning dead all comment on the living and all are, in some sense, dissatisfied by what they find.

Death is also anthropomorphised, making an appearance as a central character. Although the plays of the British theatrical avant-garde are negotiating particular contemporary issues, there is a long-standing tradition of the figure, Death. Most abiding is the character of Death in the medieval mystery play, *Everyman*, who appears as a moral challenger to the title character. Death confirms that, 'every man will I beset that liveth beastly,/ Out of God's laws, and dreadeth not folly' (Anon 2002, p. 66). Interestingly, despite the differences, Death acts as a similar moral gauge in two twentieth-century examples: MacColl's *The Other Animals* and Auden's *The Dance of Death*. In both, Death dances on to make comment and points to an ineludible conclusion. In the former she appears as an old woman in the final scene. In contrast with the character of Morning who dances away with Hanau, reflecting an abiding sense of hope, Death is connected solely with Graubard. Death is presented as Graubard's mother; he is owned by her, unable to escape and follow Hanau (Goorney and MacColl 1986, p. 197). She represents the decay of the Doctor's ideas and, in a typical socialist approach, the inevitable victory of the proletariat over the bourgeoisie. Death embodies something equally broad and far-reaching in *The Dance of Death*. In his synopsis, which appeared in the 1934/5 programme, Auden suggested that, 'Death symbolises the decay which exists within a class of society' (Auden 1988, p. 542). So the figure of Death became a metaphorical model. It was a vital recurring motif in the British theatrical avant-garde; not only is it an inevitable experience of a number of (we might say all) characters, but also an emblem of a larger issue: the breakdown of formerly more stable concepts.

All these interpretations (the finality of death, the return of the dead and Death as a character) can be found in J. B. Priestley's play *Johnson Over Jordan*, produced by Basil Dean in 1939. In a fascinating connection, Britten wrote the music for this piece, just as he did for a number of other plays mentioned in this book. Auden and Isherwood's *On the Frontier* acts as a sort of bridging device. Dean mentioned this in a letter to Britten dated 21 December 1938:

> You may recall that I met you at Professor Dent's party after the last night of the production of 'On the Frontier' ... I am very anxious to talk with you about a new play by Mr J. B. Priestley which I am going to produce early in the New year [*sic*]. The play is a symbolical work and calls for a certain amount of incidental music in the first act.
>
> (Dean 1938)

Britten duly wrote the 'incidental music', which surely was partly modelled on the music he had written (and Dean had obviously admired) for *On the Frontier*. This marks a useful connection between the Group Theatre project and a more mainstream theatrical producer and director like Basil Dean.

Johnson Over Jordan begins with the death of Robert Johnson and then returns to moments of his life, once more breaking through the barrier between life and death. Here again there is a Masked Figure of Death who guides Johnson through the various sections of his life. Death's advice to Johnson is reminiscent of the warning Emily receives in *Our Town*. Death confirms, 'You can't go back. In that world you <u>are</u> really dead. To try and force your way back there would be to bring evil into your house. You must take your road' (Priestley

1939, act ll). To cross that impermeable border between life and death here is extremely dangerous and potentially destabilising.

Priestley's play concludes with the suggestion of a final death, a moving from a temporary death to a more permanent state. The stage direction reads:

> *He walks slowly towards the starry opening, and is seen silhouetted against it. A trumpet swells, then the music swells triumphantly, and the curtain slowly falls.*

(ibid., act lll)

This play combines the key devices examined in this section: the humanoid figure of Death, the pervious space between life and death and the eventual permanency of death as the characters finally find (or are forced to accept) a final peace. In a modern world dominated by two large-scale wars, state-sanctioned killings and the growing threat of fascism, it is unsurprising that the dead seem to populate the plays of the modernist avant-garde.

Animals, mannequins and robots: new characters for the modern stage

So character became a profoundly complex on-stage presence, battling with mental fragmentation, the inevitability of death and an overwhelming sense of powerlessness. In response, new methods of character construction appeared. Strindberg summed up the beginnings of this transformation in character presentation in his introduction to *A Dream Play* (1901): 'Time and space do not exist ... The characters split, double, multiply, evaporate, densify, disperse, assemble' (1982, p. 175). As the early decades of the twentieth century progressed such fragmentation was augmented. In this flexible theatre unencumbered by the typical rules of space, time or logic, the actor did not need to inhabit the same character throughout the performance. Rather than attempting to disguise transitions between characters, playwrights would often draw attention to them. It is most acutely revealed through the conversation between the Manchester businessmen in MacColl's *Uranium 235*:

> This jumping about from one character to another is bloody confusing. One of these performances I'm going to come on in

the Greek scene dressed as a Manchester businessman. That'd
shake 'em!

(Goorney and MacColl 1986, p. 94)

The audience is immediately aware of the theatrical construction
here, the characters becoming representatives of a central theme: in
this case, the history of nuclear fission. But the speech also forces the
audience to consider their expectations of character and context. The
Businessman's proclamation, 'that'd shake 'em', explicitly points to
the discomfort caused by a tension between character and context.
Rather than hide this concern under illusory pretence of narrative
linearity, MacColl compelled the audience to attend to it.

For MacColl, this ability to move from character to character without necessarily concealing this shift partly came from his company's
grounding in agit-prop and, later, the Living Newspaper. Indeed,
describing the performance intentions of *Newsboy,* the Federal
Theatre Project's Alfred Saxe pointed to the flexibility of character;
he wrote, 'push a lever and a character springs up like magic – press
a button, he disappears, changes quickly to another character'
(Samuel, MacColl and Cosgrove 1985, p. 290). Saxe's description is
infused with the imagery of the factory and/or modern technology.
It again reveals an ambivalence in the modernist avant-garde; while
the modern industrial world is a place of subjugation and exploitation, it is also charged with experimentation and the 'magic' of innovation. It is also, of course, a recognisable *Verfremdungs-Effekt,* a nod
to the conscious theatricality of the play.

But this metatheatrical moving between characters is made
even more explicit in MacNeice's *Out of the Picture.* Here the Radio
Announcer acts as a central narrative device, taking on a number
of roles as the play progresses. These changes in character are
signified visually and audibly. Becoming Professor Joseph Vint in
order to give a talk about Chekhov and Aristotle (creating a further layer of metatheatricality, of course), the Radio Announcer
'steps back and forward again, puts on a false moustache and pince-nez'
(MacNeice 1937, p. 28). Later, becoming the 'veteran low hurdler'
Mr MacDonald, he *'takes three steps back and forward again and
speaks in a Scottish accent'* (ibid., p. 79). There is no sense of full and
consistent characterisation here and, interestingly, it is in keeping
with Alfred Saxe's advice above. The small movements (walking
forward and back) and the costumes or accents used here could

provide clues for the audience, maintaining some sense of logical progression.

This commitment to non-illusory, non-linear character led to a number of fascinating and unusual experiments. In *The Dog Beneath the Skin*, for example, the very composition of the human body is brought into question. This can, of course, be most noticeably seen in Francis's disguise. Becoming a dog enables Francis to see the world from a different perspective:

> As a dog, I learnt with what a mixture of fear, bullying, and condescending kindness you treat those whom you consider your inferiors, but on whom you are dependent for your pleasures.
>
> (Auden and Isherwood 1968, p. 173)

The title brings a slightly different perspective to bear here. Francis is a dog *beneath* the skin. Certainly the disguise allows him to be a dog, but the title suggests that Francis actually *is* the dog. Perhaps Auden and Isherwood were pointing to these profound transformations in Francis's attitudes. In pretending to be a dog Francis's perspectives change utterly; rather than return to his human identity when he removes his disguise, actually Francis retains his new way of looking at the world. He will always see society from a dog's perspective, littered with hierarchical injustice.

One of the play's potential endings sees the animal theme continuing with the occupants of Pressan Ambo transforming into various creatures. Unlike Francis, whose experience as a dog allows him to empathise more keenly with others, the metamorphosis of the Pressan Ambo community suggests an overwhelming lack of humanity. In many ways, their fate resembles the final transformation of the characters in Eugène Ionesco's *Rhinoceros*. In both plays, the characters choose the bestial as opposed to the human and, consequentially, lose their innate human characteristics. Yet, in both there is the rebel; Francis is followed by Alan and a selection of others who decide to oppose the prevailing views of the village and, despite his loneliness and almost certain destruction, Ionesco's Bérenger resolves to remain human and 'put up a fight against the whole lot of them!' (Ionesco 1978, p. 124).

Even when the human body remains fairly stable, as in the character of Alan, it is still presented as fractured and subject to peculiar transformations. As he sleeps, Alan's feet come alive with the stage directions suggesting, '*The* Right Foot *speaks in a cultured voice, the* Left Foot *has a cockney accent*' (Auden and Isherwood 1968, p. 112). It is a bizarre moment, faintly reminiscent of Tristan Tzara's characterisation in his 1921 *The Gas Heart* in which the Nose, Eye, Mouth, Ear, Neck and Eyebrow all become individual characters. By June of 1936 Auden, certainly, had allied himself with Tzara, at least politically, when he 'allowed his name to be used as one of the twelve signatories to a questionnaire which asked writers to declare themselves either for or against Franco and fascism. The other signatories included Louis Aragon, Heinrich Mann, Pablo Neruda, Stephen Spender and Tristan Tzara' (Osbourne 1980, p. 141).[8] But this example also tapped into the popular cartoon form. Oversized shoes had become a defining motif in the comic strip by the thirties (Varnedoe and Gopnik 1991, p. 410). Feet had become funny. Perhaps Auden and Isherwood were also tapping into this burgeoning popular form here.

This example from *The Dog Beneath the Skin* presents the very notion of the human as subject to rupture. It is made all the more clear in the play's presentation of the non-human anthropoid. Alan's downfall is centred on his devotion to Miss Lou Vipond. Presented as a famous beauty, Miss Vipond is actually a shop mannequin:

> *Alan stands embracing* Miss Vipond *who is a shopwindow dummy, very beautifully dressed. When the dummy is to speak,* Alan *runs behind it and speaks in falsetto.*
>
> (Auden and Isherwood 1968, p. 141)

Here there seems to be a direct comment on the human perception of beauty and the commercialisation of the body. The dummy represents the constant lure of attractive simulacra.[9]

The dummy reappears in MacColl's *Landscape with Chimneys* in which the young worker Jessie dreams she is a film star:

> *She, free from the attentions of undesirable suitors moves slowly into the shadows and returns holding in her arms a tailor's dummy wearing evening dress with the price label still attached. She dances with her dream lover lost in an ecstatic region where she is Cleopatra and Juliet and the star of a thousand Hollywood epics.*
>
> (MacColl 1951, p. 29)

Though MacColl was certainly more patient with his character than Auden and Isherwood, the intention here is similar: the 'real' is rejected in favour of the conventionally appealing image. The explicit mention of the 'price label' also implicates this short scene in the capitalist system. The modern economic structure, like the dummy in evening dress, is empty, a poor commercialised masquerade hoodwinking the general populace. Rather than connecting with the human, both Alan and Jessie are content to occupy a dream world of simulations. This seems to be a coincidental parallel between two plays that, despite their differences, contain provocative and challenging images of the modern world. For Craig, the *Übermarionette* (the non-human anthropoid) provided an escape from the infuriating peculiarities of the human, but Auden, Isherwood and MacColl seemed to subvert this: it was not a positive method of overcoming the human, rather it was emblematic of the tensions in the modern world, which reduced the individual to a commercialised product or an unreal image of manufactured perfection.

In many ways, the presence of the mannequins in *The Dog Beneath the Skin* and *Landscape with Chimneys* pre-empted the 1975 conclusions of Polish theatre director Tadeusz Kantor. Kantor confronted Craig's idea of the non-human replacing the human and rejected it. However, he maintained that the non-human (the 'mannequin') could stand in contrast to the actor:

> The MANNEQUIN in my theatre must become a MODEL through which pass a strong sense of DEATH and the conditions of the DEAD. A model for the live ACTOR.
>
> (Kantor 1993, p. 112)

In MacColl's play and the Auden/Isherwood collaboration, it is the sharp contrast between the live actor (Alan and Jessie) and the mannequin that brings a sense of poignancy to the scenes. Interestingly, given the amount of dead characters in the modernist avant-garde, the mannequin became an image of the 'absence of life' (ibid., p. 112), not a figure to be emulated but a motif to suggest death.

Unusual non-human characters reappeared across the avant-garde (Segal 1995). The Italian Futurists created synthetic, robotic characters that challenged notions of humanity (Berghaus 2000, pp. 438–9). In Cocteau's *The Eiffel Tower Wedding Party*, two actors are dressed as Phonographs, 'their bodies are the cabinets, their mouths are the horns' (Cocteau 1963, p. 161). The body is transformed by the modern world around it. Of particular note for this discussion is Karel Čapek's *R.U.R.* (1923) with its juxtaposition of naturalistic dialogue, poetic monologue and fantastical subject matter. Čapek visited Britain in 1924 and wrote the illustrated *Letters from England* (1925) in response to his experiences there. *R.U.R.* is a play that enjoyed some interest in Britain; Basil Dean was granted the licence to perform it in 1923 (Dean 1923) and there is the suggestion that it was presented by the People's Theatre, Newcastle in its 1926–7 season (Veitch 1950). It was also regarded by Plebs League lecturer and Labour MP, Ness Edwards as one of the 'precursors of workers' drama' (Samuel, MacColl and Cosgrove 1985, p. 186). It focuses on a robot manufacturer, Rossum's Universal Robots and charts a robot revolt that ends with the virtual annihilation of the human race. But this is not a typical science fiction Armageddon story; rather it has some profound comments to make about human nature and the class struggle. These robots are programmed to imitate human actions, thereby producing accurate simulations. This is clear in Domin's new plan:

> I mean that each factory will produce Robots of a different colour, a different language. They'll be complete foreigners to each other. They'll never to able to understand each other. Then we'll egg them on a little in the same direction, do you see? The result will be that for ages to come one Robot will hate any other Robot of different factory mark.
>
> (Čapek Brothers 1966, p. 57)

Initially, this mimicry of human characteristics requires encouragement by the humans themselves. However, the robots evolve into independent simulacra, adopting typical, hegemonic human actions for their own end. When Alquist asks why the robots have murdered the humans, Radius replies, 'slaughter and domination are necessary if you want to be like men. Read history, read the human books. You must domineer and murder if you want to be like men' (ibid., p. 94). Ness Edwards described this play as a theatricalisation of the class struggle, where 'the robots are the world workers ... [as they] combine throughout the world. They are the producers of the world's goods, and the distributors' (Samuel, MacColl and Cosgrove 1985,

p. 186). The connection is obvious, though not without its problems, as Ness Edwards goes on to suggest[10] and as Radius's exclamation above indicates. Yet, *R.U.R.* does point to the mechanisation of the working-class body and the potential for revolution.[11]

Redeeming the human

So the modern consciousness was often presented as irreconcilably isolated, as painfully splintered or even as overwhelmed by the non-human. Yet the British avant-garde also provided some solutions to these issues. Indeed, there was a potent commitment to recon-nection, to creating community. Constructing these relationships was part of a conscious objective: to break through the ignorance of individuals like *The Ascent of F6*'s Mr and Mrs A, representative of a disenfranchised majority. Politics were at the centre of the British avant-garde and much of the theatre sought to inform the audience, to create engaged communities, to, in MacColl's words, 'awaken a population that was still drowsy from its 100-year old sleep of impe-rial greatness ... who were afraid to shout for what was theirs for fear it would disturb the neighbours' (1990, p. 183).

I have been careful to maintain a sense of diversity when discussing the politics of the British theatrical avant-garde, for despite obvious similarities, the political intentions of, say, Group Theatre and Theatre Workshop differed quite considerably. And it is important to note that the playwrights, directors and actors of the British avant-garde did not all come from the same socio-political background; some claimed a working-class origin, others were materially privileged. This, of course, made a great deal of difference in terms of natural class affiliations and, potentially, political perspectives. Yet, it would be true to say that a majority of the playwrights and companies mentioned here (with some well-publicised exceptions, namely Wyndham Lewis and, per-haps, Eliot) were committed to a broadly left-wing political position. These affiliations ranged from Auden and Isherwood's 'leftist ten-dency' (Williams 1989, p. 61) to Unity playwright Jack Lindsay who claimed with fervour that 'Communism is English' (1939, p. 64).

In fact there is a growing (though at times wavering) sense of political unanimity which counteracts the almost overwhelming feeling of isolationism and fragmentation of psyche. The reaction to the Spanish Civil War (1936–9), an event that created significant ripples in the British context, serves as a case in point. This event was the inspiration for a number of performances, including Jack Lindsay's mass declamation, *On Guard for Spain* (1937) which, according to Angela Tuckett of Bristol Unity, was 'in demand everywhere' (1980, p. 11), Unity's version of Brecht's *Señora Carrar's Rifles* (1938) and Theatre Union's production of Lope de Vega's *Fuente Ovejuna* (*The Sheep's Well*, 1937). In later years plays by Federico García Lorca, killed during the Spanish Civil War, were performed by both Theatre Workshop (*The Love of Don Perlimplin and Belisa in the Garden*, 1945) and Unity (*The Shoemaker's Wife*, 1947), reigniting an interest in this important event.[12] In fact many individuals associated with these groups actually went to Spain to fight against Franco (Chambers 1989, pp. 86–7; Leach 2006, p. 36).

With these volunteers went Auden and, though he was unable to do a great deal, his participation caused a lot of publicity (Osbourne 1980, p. 132). He was joined by a number of others, including Spender and MacNeice, 'as short-term visitors, or reporters, solid with the Republican cause, anxious to do something, but not actually fighting' (Cunningham 1989, p. 420). Their Group Theatre companions, while often concerned to maintain their commitment to aesthetics rather than to a particular political position, were also anxious about the situation in Spain:

It is true that many of us involved with the Group were concerned about the issues of the day – unemployment, the struggle for democracy in Spain, the rise of Fascism in Germany and Italy.

(Medley 1983, p. 159)

There is a remarkably similar proclamation in Merseyside Unity Theatre's contribution to the Liverpool Daily Post (18 June 1937):

Our material deals with the most urgent political issue of the day – the need to rouse support for the Spanish people in their fight against international fascism and to warn: Madrid Today – Merseyside Tomorrow.

(Dawson 1985, p. 1)

There is no doubting the differences between Group Theatre and MUT, yet the very expressions used here are strikingly alike: the importance of the modern, the concern with specific 'issues' and the fight against fascism. Here there is a sense of unity; as Auden wrote in his 1937 poem *Spain*, 'our hours of friendship [blossom] into a people's army' (1979, p. 54). Once again, and in keeping with the spirit of the avant-garde, unity appeared when practitioners fought *against* a formidable force.

And resisting that force required a group mentality, off stage and on. The productions these collaborations engendered not only addressed the situation in Spain but, in a broader sense, encouraged engagement and solidarity in response to a range of twentieth-century events. While the isolated man did reappear, there were perhaps more examples of individuals uniting, generally in the face of repressive forces; in many ways the theatre reflected a growing sense of solidarity that must have been central to the everyday experiences of the company members. One of the most striking examples, in fact, was not directly associated with any of the so-called political theatre groups. Rather, it came from a collaboration between Basil Dean and Louis MacNeice. Entitled *Salute to the Red Army* and performed by well-known actors like Sybil Thorndike, Laurence Olivier and John Gielgud at the Royal Albert Hall in February 1943, this was a highly ambitious piece, both in form and content. The aim of the pageant was to encourage the British audience to show their support for their war allies in Russia; as the final speech reflects, 'our eyes today look East/ To where our comrades fight/ Their Battle with the Beast/ That rages day and night' (Dean and MacNeice 1943, p. 39). In many ways this remarkable piece resembles a Theatre Workshop or Unity Theatre Living Newspaper. With its Newsboy, declamatory passages and persuasive argument directed towards the audience, the similarities are striking. And the sense of community is at the very heart of its success. The Spokesman and Spokeswoman call on the 'working people of Britain' to unite with the Russian people (ibid., p. 20). There is recognition that amidst that term 'working people', there are important distinctions, and the Speakers list a comprehensive range of occupations in order to bring some sense of solidarity to this broad epithet. There is also a very specific focus on women's experience with the Woman calling 'upon all the women of Britain to greet their sisters, the women of Russia, and to greet their brothers in the Red Army' (ibid., p. 23).

This pageant was not without its issues, of course. In many ways it was a nationalistic reading of war and did not address some of the problematic class issues. At times it resembled a piece of war-time propaganda. In fact the final speech was delivered by the then Foreign Secretary, Anthony Eden. Yet, its innovative style marks it as a fascinating example of theatre as a uniting force. In calling for complete working-class unity with a Communist state, it still remains one of the most engaging British examples of the political pageant genre.

MacColl's *Johnny Noble* also advocates this sense of community. With its fragmented structure, commitment to exploring real historical conditions and mixture of declarative statements, dialogue and poetic lexicon, it resembles the Living Newspapers of Theatre Workshop's earlier incarnations. Johnny's response to his experiences in Spain reveals the importance of creating unifying groups in the modern world:

> You know, Mary, I used to feel lost, as if there was no place in the world for me. There seemed to be no sense in being born. But I've learned something. There's a lot of people like me in the world. We're everywhere, and we're important.
>
> (Goorney and MacColl 1986, p. 56)

Unsurprisingly, this is a recurring theme in MacColl's plays. It is even present in his most Expressionistic play, *The Other Animals*, with its focus on the protagonist, Robert Hanau. In many ways the fragmented presentation of Robert Hanau represents Britain's clearest example of the Expressionistic isolated man. But, in the final scene this central figure becomes two distinct characters permanently as Graubard murders Hanau while Robert dances away with the symbolic character of Morning. Despite Graubard's suggestion that 'my world will survive you, Hanau', the prisoner recognises that he is part of a larger, persistent political group that will continue on after his death to challenge Graubard's destructive hegemony (ibid., p. 194). There is a notable parallel here with Upton Sinclair's *The Singing Jailbirds*, a play that enjoyed numerous British productions from groups affiliated to the ILP and WTM (Leach 2006, p. 14; Samuel, MacColl and Cosgrove 1985, p. 22). Red's final conversation with Nell illustrates this connection between the present and the future. He reflects, 'mankind is only at the beginnings of its life, Nell. You and I have suffered its birth-pangs, and those who come after us will have an easier time' (Sinclair 1924, p. 73). Unity works across generational divides here, just as it does in *The Other Animals*. Even in his delirium Hanau becomes aware of the present and future political collective, replying to Graubard's threats, 'you hate us because you envy us,/ You envy us because we walk upright/ And constantly remind you/ Of your own mis-shapenness' (Goorney and MacColl 1986, p. 192).

This political solidarity required an identifiable enemy, of course. Certainly, this is the case in the two MacColl plays mentioned and, indeed, in Dean and MacNeice's pageant. However, it is also clearly perceptible in a number of the plays found in the British avant-garde repertoire. *Waiting for Lefty* (1935) by American Clifford Odets was a highly influential piece for Unity Theatre, which really founded its reputation on it in 1936 (Chambers 1989, p. 41). Creating some contention for ignoring copyright protocol, it was also produced a year earlier by the Red Megaphones (Harker 2007, p. 46). This play is based on the events behind the New York taxi strike of 1934. Opening at a union meeting, the play presents a range of different views, bringing the political forum to the stage. During the piece, they are waiting for their chairman, Lefty. His off-stage murder is the spark that ignites the final cries of 'Strike!' Harold Clurman evoked the play in his analysis of American Group Theatre, *The Fervent Years*:

> Deep laughter, hot assent, a kind of joyous fervor seemed to sweep the audience toward the stage. The actors no longer performed; they were being carried along as if by an exultancy of communication such as I had never witnessed in the theatre before. Audience and actor had become one.
>
> (1957, p. 138)

In Clurman's description there is a clear nod to the importance of solidarity, not just on the stage but also between stage and auditorium. This sense of unity is there from the start as voices from the audience interrupt Harry Fatt (Odets 1979, p. 5). The audience are immediately implicated as part of a disillusioned, but potentially revolutionary striking force. The subsequent episodes are brought together by Agate who cries, 'it's war! Working class, unite and fight! Tear down the slaughter house of our old lives. Let freedom really ring' (ibid., p. 30). In its very syntax, Agate's cry resembles the final sentences of Marx and Engels's *The Communist Manifesto*. Again, solidarity and antagonism are presented as a vital dialogue.

So while the isolated man remained an important emblem, a growing sense of community (specifically a political community) was increasingly evident. In light of this, and harking back to previous traditions, particularly to the ancient Hellenic stage, playwrights saw the merit of employing a chorus. Again, these on-stage figures are not characters in any illusory pseudo-naturalistic sense. Often, they provide vital background information or comment on the action, as in Eliot's *Murder in the Cathedral* or Auden and Isherwood's *The Dog Beneath the Skin*. In Spender's *Trial of a Judge* we have a useful illustration of some of the ways the chorus model could be updated in the British avant-garde. The start of act III plays two choruses off against one another: the Red Chorus, the broadly left-wing political challengers, and the Black Chorus, representative of a Nazi-style faction who have been gradually infiltrating the government and other powerful institutions:

> *The two choruses remain at their respective sides of the stage, divided by the gap containing the speakers' rostrum and the balcony above; except when one or another speaker leaps forward excitedly onto the rostrum to make a longer speech.*
>
> (Spender 1938, p. 53)

So, the Red Chorus is an emblem of the protesting victims of the State, while the Black Chorus is a mob, intent on a fascist ruling government. Extending the narrative chorus mode, Spender imbued the tradition with a strong political message. Just as with the mask, a technique of antiquity was updated for a modern audience.

Here was a commitment to bringing solidarity to the stage, to overcoming the almost overwhelming feeling of mental and physical fragmentation so prevalent in early to mid-twentieth-century society. This sense of cooperation, like the use of stock characters or the challenge to the finality of death, broke through theatrical illusion. Inextricably linked with this non-naturalistic, representational characterisation was a renewed interest in the physicality of performance. The body became a site of political and artistic contestation. If read through the recent conclusions of Erika Fischer-Lichte, it is unsurprising that a theatrical movement so committed to enquiry and intellectual questioning should focus so heavily upon the corporeal. Fischer-Lichte suggests, 'Man is *embodied mind*. No human can be reduced just to body or mind, and even less to a battlefield where body and mind fight for supreme authority. The mind cannot exist without the body; it articulates itself through physicality' (2008, p. 99). Consequentially, an inquisitive, analytical theatre must centre its enquiry on the human body. The mind is not detached from the body, but rather is an integral part of it. In light of this it is perhaps inevitable that, like their compatriots overseas, the practitioners of the British avant-garde developed new methods of movement, often crossing those generic boundaries between dance, acrobatics and dramatic theatre. Beginning with dance in the very broadest sense, the next chapter aims to develop a cross-disciplinary dialogue.

5
Crossing Genres: Movement and Music

Figure 6 A lace of rigging (© the artist Beth Fletcher)

Manifestations of popular, contemporaneous culture appeared regularly on the British stage throughout the first half of the twentieth century. As we have seen, cinema, radio, print journalism and variety theatre forms impacted poetic and political groups alike, once again contradicting any artificial divisions. But this was, I suggest, a reflection of a larger growing preoccupation with cross-generic forms more generally; surely if the barrier between the concepts of so-called 'high' and 'low' art could be eroded and traversed, then the boundaries between other genres could display a similar element of flux. Although naturalistic theatre contained moments of music and dance (examples include Nora's rehearsed dance for the costume party in *A Doll's House* or the dance at the start of act three in Chekhov's *The Cherry Orchard*), these were intrinsically part of the linear narrative rather than acting as independent artistic modes. This was also true of melodrama where music was used to create atmosphere, captivating the audience rather than enabling them to critically assess the action.

The British theatrical avant-garde sought to reinstigate a fruitful dialogue between these three genres – drama, music and dance in its broadest sense. In rejecting illusionism, embracing new methods of characterisation and staging, and in the re-establishment of the communicative relationship between audience and actor, a way was opened to re-examine the complex dialogues between genres and to begin to break down, or at least reposition, generic borders. Rejecting the notion that the avant-garde was purely concerned with a destructive nihilism, Berghaus refers to a 'liberated art practice' engendered by experimentation (2005, p. 39). In this British context, nowhere was the 'liberated art practice' clearer than in the fruitful juxtapositions of music, movement and drama.

Crossing genres: music, dance and the dramatic form

Connecting this with an avant-garde sensibility is not to say that the Victorian and Edwardian performance spaces were entirely devoid of music and movement techniques, or indeed wholly lacking in cross-generic dialogues. The operetta, for example, enjoyed particular success with the collaborative works of Gilbert and Sullivan in particular, and the remarkable popularity of Oscar Asche's Arabian Nights-inspired *Chu Chin Chow* (1916) clearly revealed the demand for theatre that combined engaging storytelling with musical interludes. Melodrama too (literally 'music drama') used music to heighten the emotional tone of a piece, complementing the stock characters and the formulaic narratives. But perhaps the nineteenth-century music hall was the clearest example of a vibrant local dance and music culture and, furthermore, could provide an initial model for the British avant-garde. The variousness of its parts and its fragmented yet engaging non-Aristotelian form would prove to be an important precursive model.

Just as they were vital to successful music hall performances, 'circus numbers [movement], music and theatre' (Kift 1996, p. 53) were also the central inter-generic fundamentals of the British avant-garde. This is not, of course, to suggest that the music hall was an *active* antecedent of the avant-garde; in many ways, with its largely escapist intention (ibid., p. 42), it was an antithetical tradition. Yet, while the differences have to be noted, the inter-generic music hall variety structure remained a highly influential method. In his *Manifesto on the Theatre,* Auden asserted, 'the music hall, the Christmas pantomime, and the country house charade are the most living drama of to-day' (1986, p. 273). Eliot agreed in his 1923 discussion of music hall performer, Marie Lloyd, in which he said, 'I have called her the expressive figure of the lower classes. The middle classes have no such idol: the middle classes are morally corrupt' (1966, p. 458). For both Auden and Eliot, the music hall represented a vibrant tradition that could be adapted in the dramatic mode. They may well have concurred with Marinetti's understanding of variety theatre as 'melting pot of the many elements of a new sensibility in the making ... a bubbling fusion' (2008, pp. 186–7).

Unsurprisingly, given the connection between music hall and the working class, the other companies also saw the benefits of using it in their theatre. WTM's sketch and revue pieces apparently 'owed ... [their] popularity perhaps as much to the indigenous tradition of the music hall and the concert-party as to the more highly disciplined European examples' (Samuel, MacColl and Cosgrove 1985, p. 44), while Unity players had long been interested in music hall 'as the popular entertainment of their own class' (Chambers 1989, p. 242). MacColl and Littlewood's *Last Edition* Living Newspaper explicitly amalgamated 'fantasy, satire, agit-prop, music hall, folk song and dance' (Goorney 1981, p. 22).

This is certainly not to say that the British theatrical avant-garde accepted the music hall uncritically, either as a model of working-class entertainment, or as an example of a vibrant inter-generic method. MacColl's rejection of the music hall as emblematic of uncritical performance, containing only the 'rosy glow of nostalgia' (Goorney 1981, p. 128) caused him to dismiss Theatre Workshop's celebrated 1963 production *Oh What a Lovely War!* as, '"the nadir" of Theatre Workshop, its entertainment imperative warming the hearts of friends and foe alike' (Paget 1993, p. 258). This would, one might surmise, be a universal concern; certainly the music hall provided an exciting, dynamic archetype, but its connection with escapist nostalgia and sentimentality would always ensure it would be a problematic antecedent.

If music hall provided a certain local cross-generic model, then there are a number of other forms from across Europe that had some impact in a British context. Certainly, whatever the discernible links between the Continental European and British avant-gardes in this area, there were noticeable parallels. Generic boundaries can, of course, be traversed and negotiated in a number of different ways; a polyphonic, inter-generic theatre is the central aim, but the methods, techniques and philosophies pertaining to create this aesthetic are all markedly different. Of course, one of the major influences in this area has been Richard Wagner and his search for a synthesis of arts, presented in his *Opera and Drama* in 1851.[1] He concluded that dance, music and poetry had long fought against each other, and rather than perpetuate this inter-generic tension, his conclusions centred on the restoration of unity (Wagner 1970, p. 124). According to Appia, Wagner advocated an 'organically united' work of art capable of synthesising all aspects of performance into one integrated whole (Appia 1962, p. 132). No doubt his ideas were extremely significant, even to left-wing politically engaged theatre companies like Theatre Workshop who, in typically Wagnerian terms, tried to 'create a theatre of synthesis in which the actors will be able to sing, dance and act with equal facility' (Samuel, MacColl and Cosgrove 1985, p. 242). But Wagner's model privileged music and its seamless juxtaposition of the arts went against the fragmentation of the avant-garde. So, in spite of Wagner's undoubted influence, British avant-garde theatre often posed a challenge to his synthesised ideal.

When it came to a true synthesis of the arts, it was Copeau rather than Wagner that produced the most influential model, particularly for Terence Gray's Festival Theatre (Cornwall 2004, p. 138) and, influenced by the Cambridge experiment, Group Theatre (Medley 1983, p. 116). Copeau's commitment to the 'plain rough-hewn boards' marked an obvious connection with many of the British practitioners, and his highly trained actors, many of whom worked with him for a number of years, 'were mimes, acrobats; some could play musical instruments and sing; all could invent characters and improvise' (Roose-Evans 1989, p. 46). For Copeau, then, his artistic dialogues came together in the human figure on the stage. Diaghilev, too, another important figure for Group Theatre, constructed fruitful dialogue between the arts, what the Ballets Russes company member Léonide Massine termed as a 'complex spectacle' which contained and juxtaposed 'poetry, literature, painting, music and choreography' (Drummond 1998, p. 172). Both these cross-generic models came out of a particular ballet tradition that was to have a tremendous impact on the British avant-garde. In very different ways, Diaghilev and Copeau sought to create integrated works of art; for the Ballets Russes it was a 'total, aestheticized environment' (Garafola 1989, p. 96), for Copeau a 'sense of collective playfulness leading to a unity of dramatic purpose' (Hodge 1999, p. 56). With reference to Group Theatre's preoccupation with Copeau and Diaghilev, Sidnell perhaps provides the clearest explanation of the way the British company employed the two contrasting aesthetic perspectives:

> In the Group's early days, Diaghilev's extravagant theatrical collages and the zealous purification of the theatre undertaken by Copeau were the great, contrary inspirations.
>
> (1984, pp. 258–9)

Both aimed for a certain artistic synthesis, yet, from Group Theatre's perspective anyway, there was a particular perceived difference in style between the visually elaborate Diaghilev and the more intentionally simplistic stage of Copeau. Using dance as a catalyst, both sought a cross-generic theatre, and it was this aim that so influenced Group Theatre. Though markedly different in the actual realisation of these intentions, a united total theatre somewhat reminiscent of Wagner's ideas was the central objective.

However, in the establishment of new dialogues between the arts, there was an endemic, and in many ways, diametrically opposed perspective: that of Bertolt Brecht. The influence of Brecht over the British theatrical avant-garde has already been described in detail, but his inter-generic connections are extremely useful to the discussion. Whether the companies and playwrights were actively aware of Brecht's ideas remains difficult to fully assess; however, what is undeniable is that Brecht's ideas were certainly paralleled in the British context. Nowhere is this more evident that in his concept of Epic theatre. As is well documented, Brecht's primary argument against the Wagnerian-style synthesis rested on the use of emotion. Whereas Wagner sought a method that largely appealed to the audience's emotions, Brecht wanted to retain, and indeed actively exploit, the audience's powers of reason. Brecht suggested that if Wagnerian *Gesamtkunstwerk* was employed in the theatre, all the separate arts would be lost to a synthesised whole, which would merely immerse the audience in the play and produce an empathetic emotional response rather than a more detached inspection of the thematic concerns on the stage (Brecht 2001, p. 204). If, as Theodor Adorno put it, Wagner's concept 'combines the arts in order to produce an intoxicating brew' (Adorno 1981, p. 100), the artwork, rather than relying on the audience's imaginative reason, would produce instead a work that powerfully suppresses logic in favour of emotion. This was Brecht's primary concern with Wagner's method and, instead, he posited a model in which all the arts were utilised while retaining their autonomy: actors, stage-designers, playwrights etcetera 'unite their various arts for the joint operation, without of course sacrificing their independence in the process' (Brecht 2001, p. 202).

The British avant-garde plays can be read through both the united integrated model of Copeau and Diaghilev, *and* the more fragmented approach of Brecht. In fact, as the British avant-gardists sought new ways to juxtapose and reinstate dialogue between genres, these methods often coexisted within the same work to produce highly complex, cross-generic compositions.

Dance, movement and the modern world

While searching for a type of 'total theatre', the core of both Copeau and Diaghilev's aesthetic projects was dance, and movement techniques in all guises became vital to the projects of all the British avant-garde companies. Indeed, the analysis of modern methods of movement was a key factor across the historical avant-garde. As the industrialised world seemed to speed up and indeed create new movements, the arts, reflecting this, devised works that could attempt to make sense of it. Futurism, in particular, celebrated movement in this modern context, with Marinetti affirming that 'we say that the world's magnificence has been enriched by a new beauty: the beauty of speed' (1972, p. 41). Modern speed, both as beauty and as tyrant, became a concern for British artists.[2] Even static images of the new age seem to develop an innate sense of speed; Steven Spender's famous pylons carve their way through the landscape and 'there runs the quick perspective of the future' (1985, p. 39).

Of course, the Industrial Revolution led not only to a perceived speeding up of the world, but also to the mechanisation of the body. In a modern world, the body was employed in new ways, and machinery, in its various guises, was central to this change. In fact Auden addressed the relationship between man and machine in the capitalist world in his 1933 *How to be Masters of the Machine* in which he reflected that although the machine theoretically had enabled everybody to reach a better standard of living, in reality, 'they have so far made a majority of mankind wretched' (1986, p. 317). This 'wretchedness' is connected to the subordination of the body by the hegemonic owners of the machinery. The resultant poor wages and living conditions only served to augment this sense of 'wretchedness'. This is not to say that the practitioners of the British theatrical avant-garde were anti-machine per se; rather, as Auden recognised, the mechanisation of the modern world could potentially lead to the gradual improvement of the everyday lives of all. But British artists did largely understand the negative effects of the machine. Many of the movement techniques employed in some way attempted to resolve this problem. Furthermore, the sense that the body intrinsically represented freedom was also vital to the aesthetics of many practitioners and groups. While this does not necessarily point to an overt political comment, it does indicate the importance of the emancipatory body in the modern world. If, as Terence Gray suggested, 'the human body is man's natural means of self-expression' (1926, p. 27) the physical can act as a powerful challenge to hegemonic forces.

But the turn to new movement methodologies was not only a political commitment but also an aesthetic necessity. The innovations in the basic *mise-en-scène* of the British avant-garde resulted in movement coming to the fore. The platform stage meant that the actor suddenly seemed vulnerable, unable to hide behind the scenic apparatus of the 'well-made play' or costume spectacular. Peter Brook usefully refers to a search for a flexible stage of mobility, a moving towards a new 'nakedness of theatre' (1968, p. 87). His very imagery here denotes a sense of exposure and it is the actor (and indeed his/her relationship with the audience) that is at the centre of this 'naked' theatre. In this, the body becomes an important aspect of performance, a political site of meaning construction as well as the fundamental element on an uncluttered, presentational stage.[3] Perhaps MacColl put it most succinctly when he reflected that 'ever since *Newsboy* we had been conscious of a crippling need for movement training and we talked longingly of a theatre where the actors could handle their bodies like trained dancers or athletes' (1990, p. 254). His description is an interesting one; the notion of a 'crippling need' reveals the importance of developing a method of movement that could overcome the company's current 'disability'.

Dalcroze's eurhythmics to Meyerhold's biomechanics

This 'crippling need' seemed to be an almost universal concern in the British avant-garde and was solved by looking to a number of key figures across the European Continent as well as developing methods independently as the need arose. Theatre Workshop discovered a partial answer to their 'crippling need' in the Eurhythmics of Emile-Jacques Dalcroze. Dalcroze perceived a certain pleasure in effective movement:

> This condition of joy [which] is brought about in us by the feeling of freedom and responsibility, by the clear perception of the creative power in us, by the balance of our natural powers, by the harmonious rhythm between intention and deed.
>
> (1917, p. 33)

Using the body to its fullest potential, he felt, created a sense of both joy and freedom. Both these elements remained important to the Theatre Workshop aesthetic. Littlewood used Dalcroze's ideas to encourage actors to express themselves in the body, both individually and as part of a group (Holdsworth 2006, p. 56). She thereby, through sustained study of Dalcroze's work, created a method of movement that both assisted the performance of the actor and created an innate sense of community on the stage.

In fact, the influence of Dalcroze crossed that boundary between the marginal, regional political groups and what was perceived as more established theatre. Marie Rambert is arguably one of the greatest and enduringly influential figures in British dance, and her name lingers on through the Rambert Dance Company. After training with Dalcroze she accepted an invitation to join the Ballets Russes to assist with their production of Stravinsky's *The Rite of Spring* (1913) (Rambert 1972, p. 54). Her connection with the British theatrical avant-garde was through her work at the Mercury Theatre with her husband Ashley Dukes who, as well as translating Toller's *The Machine Wreckers* for the ILP, also worked with Group Theatre on *The Ascent of F6* (Auden 1988, p. 502).

But the British avant-garde looked to Russia too as it sought a remedy for the 'crippling need'. As we have seen, Meyerhold's Constructivist staging was comparatively influential in British theatre, and the biomechanical methods that complemented his *mise- en-scène* were also important as companies sought to present the body on the stage. In fact his techniques gained a British following in the 1920s and were explored in some detail by Huntly Carter in his 1925, *The New Spirit in the European Theatre* and his 1929 *A New Spirit in the Russian Theatre*. He writes, 'M Meierhold's [*sic*] busy brain has come to grips with a new system of acting called Bio-mechanics, which is all a part of a game of destroying illusion' (Carter 1925, p. 234). For movements like the WTM, the aim was 'to transcend the written word – as in Meyerhold's "bio-mechanics" and Eisenstein's circus acrobatics – by a theatre of swirling physical movement' (Samuel, MacColl and Cosgrove 1985, p. 42). In both of these descriptions, biomechanics, just like the turn towards non-linear structures or stock characters, acted as a challenge to conventional modes of theatre and as an interruption to any sense of illusion.

A brief description of Meyerhold's method will reveal its appeal to the British theatrical avant-garde. It taught the individual actors how to move in harmony with themselves, the theatrical space and their fellow performers. Meyerhold suggested that 'the basic law of Biomechanics is very simple: the whole body takes part in each of our movements' (Gladkov 1997, p. 96). It is a style of movement that markedly resembles physical exercise and establishes a sense of rhythm upon the stage, combining it with other methods of movement such as ballet, gymnastics and eurhythmics; Meyerhold created a theatre in which the whole body of the actor was pre-eminent (Gordon 1974, p. 78). The actor is not purely a voice or a face; the audience's attention is directed towards the whole body in flux. Through this method of movement, the audience could attend to the actor's skill and dexterity (Kleberg 1993, p. 75).

The movements themselves presented a vision of the Revolution, a means of recapturing 'man's primordial joie de vivre' (Symons 1971, p. 200) and were inherently political. Movement became a direct political challenge because it is liberating; it indicated an equality within humanity and provided an emancipatory vision of the future. It also connected art with the working process. Biomechanics upon a machine-like stage recognise 'the fact that the factory is the real creative force in the world' (Lodder 1990, p. 2) and many of the movements are similar to actions one would engage in within a factory setting. So, rather than reject the mechanisation of the body out of hand, Meyerhold's method allowed for its liberation, presenting it as revolutionary rather than as an image of the suppression of the masses by the owners of industry. As Carter went on to say, 'the actor must know himself and all his movements as though he were a machine or machines' (1925, p. 234). In many ways, biomechanics hovered between the two contrasting opinions of the machine; it was at once a force for exciting, democratising progress *and* an instrument of subjugation.

With its direct connection to the working class and to the very concept of a Communist revolution, it is unsurprising that these movements were explored specifically by the British agit-prop based companies. The theory originated in a variety of scientific (William James's idea of reflexology) and industrial (Frederick Taylor's studies of the movement of unskilled workers) concepts and, no doubt, it was this sense of the modern and the urban that attracted the city-based British companies like the Red Megaphones. Certainly, the WTM employed a number of these techniques, perhaps most noticeably in a piece like *Their Theatre and Ours* (1932), a direct discussion of the very notion of a workers' theatre and its importance to the class struggle. It is most discernible in this piece because it is a work of contrasts and comparisons, particularly focusing on the marked disparities between conventional, illusory drama and the workers' theatre. Whereas the music-hall star *'starts to dance [if possible] and sings in a sloppy style'* (Samuel, MacColl and Cosgrove 1985, p. 141), by comparison, the workers are highly disciplined in their actions, mirroring the self-control of the Meyerholdian actors: 'the troupe marches on well-disciplined, singing enthusiastically and in well-marked rhythm the following song, with each word well brought out and distinct' (ibid., p. 138). The unity of the rhythmic movement and song is vital to the success of this scene, markedly differing from the ill-disciplined sentimentality of the emblems of bourgeois and/or escapist entertainment. As the play says, *'it is vital that the strongest contrast in style be made between the burlesque inset scenes of the capitalist theatre and films and the serious passages'* (ibid., p. 138).

The disciplined biomechanical systems are also seen in Theatre Workshop's post-war *Landscape with Chimneys*. In *Their Theatre and Ours*, and indeed in *Landscape with Chimneys*, there is the continual sense that, like Meyerhold, the companies were developing specific working-class methods of movement based on particular working-class experience and inextricably connected to the industrial (Leach 2006, p. 82). Certainly this is true of *Landscape with Chimneys* with its inserted factory mime sequence; in this scene the Stage Manager draws attention to the exertion of the actors as factory workers by asking the audience to 'note the play of light on the muscles' (MacColl 1951, p. 28). Yet, rather like the portrayal of Yank and his comrades in O'Neill's *The Hairy Ape*, who are described as *'hairy-chested, with long arms of tremendous power'* (O'Neill 1971, p. 137), there is also a note of danger in the movements:

> There's something disturbing about so much strength. Who are they? Does it matter?
>
> (MacColl 1951, p. 28)

The play suggests that through the movement of the actors, the audience can perceive a revolutionary possibility. The biomechanical methods became a political challenge in and of themselves. Working at a machine, the working class are a subjugated minority. Yet, in their movements and the muscular bodies that have been formed by these movements over the years, there is an inherent possibility of revolution. It is a theatrical representation of that central premise of Communist ideology: 'what the bourgeoisie, therefore, produces, above all, is its own grave-diggers. Its fall and the victory of the proletariat are equally inevitable' (Marx and Engels 1987, p. 94).

Modern dance: Theatre Workshop's experiments with Laban

The arrival of a German refugee, Rudolf Laban, marked another crucial development in Theatre Workshop's aesthetic. Laban came into contact with the company during his exile from Nazi Germany, arriving in England in 1938. Although his work was never overtly political, Laban did gradually develop a specific interest in, what he termed, 'the ugliness of the class struggle' and certainly wanted to reveal the 'dollars, depravity and deceit' of modern life (Laban 1975, pp. 41, 45).[4] In 1943 the Manchester Dance Circle was established and members of the pre-war Theatre Union (the precursor to Theatre Workshop) joined the classes (Preston-Dunlop 1998, p. 229).

This was not the company's first exposure to Laban's theories; while at RADA Littlewood had received some formal training in Laban movement techniques (Goorney and MacColl 1986, p. xxxvii). However it was the addition to their number of Laban's apprentice and talented dance student Jean Newlove in this period that really cemented the relationship (Preston-Dunlop 1998, p. 223). The new Laban-based movement techniques were created by these three figures (Littlewood, MacColl and Newlove) working together. Often these innovations are attributed to Littlewood alone, but Newlove played a vital role in the realisation of Laban's ideas, even creating new methods of movement based on her mentor's systems; indeed she invented the dab-thrust which was, apparently, 'not as light as a dab nor as heavy as a thrust' (Leach 2006, p. 126).[5] Although Laban's major interest remained in movement techniques and dance as genre, he became increasingly concerned with the relationship between the human body and drama, particularly during this time in England. Indeed, in 1943 he was invited to assist in a production at Highbury Little Theatre (Preston-Dunlop 1998, p. 226). MacColl and Littlewood appreciated this obvious connection between dance and drama, and greatly admired Laban's work. The feeling seems to be mutual; in a letter to Littlewood he apparently declared, 'I consider your group to be the only one in England which is, in the true sense of the word, experimenting in the use of all these factors which go to the creation of real theatrical art' (Goorney 1981, p. 161).

MacColl reflected that Laban had 'blazed across the firmament of the dance world like a comet bringing light where there had been darkness' (MacColl 1990, p. 253) and the company was impressed with three specific aspects of his innovative aesthetic. Firstly, Laban's key interest was the human body. Unlike Meyerhold whose method was heavily influenced by James's ideas of reflex, it was the way the body revealed inner *emotions*, moved through space and interacted with others that really dominated Laban's work: 'the whole, living person' (Laban 1975, p. 3). He suggested that 'an observer of a moving person is at once aware, not only of the paths and the rhythms of movement, but also of the mood the paths themselves carry, because the shapes of movements through space are always more or less coloured by a feeling or an idea' (Laban 1966, p. 48). He posited here a connection between the gesture or movement and the thought processes in the mind of the individual. The human body, as a central concern of theatre, can therefore represent 'inner attitudes and conflicts' (Laban 1975, p. 177). With the Theatre Workshop's focus on political agitation and revolutionary change, this new function of the body could be extremely useful.

Secondly, this body became politicised, not (in contrast to Meyerhold's biomechanics) associated specifically with the company's Communist approach per se, but democratised, actively challenging the ownership of the physical by the hegemony. The human body could, through these methods, break through the 'whirring and clanking of [the] thousands of wheels and chains' (Laban 1975, p. 48) of the industrialised twentieth century. The wisdom ran that in capitalist society, the body had been shaped and moulded by factories, shipyards and mines, but Laban's theories suggested that the body could be redeemed and used in a different way. Although not everyone could be a dancer as such, Laban did suggest that everyone could learn how to use their body in an effective way, regardless of body shape, size or health; all individuals were potential dancers 'not potential performers of steps, but potentially in touch with their own souls through the experience of gesture and moving' (Preston-Dunlop 1998, p. 64). As such the body became a site of democratic intent, a method of challenging the political status quo and a source of individual (and indeed community) freedom.

In discussing the active potential of the body, Laban imagined it in space and connected this specifically with movement, suggesting that, 'movement is the life of space' (Laban 1966, p. 94). The question remained however: how could the body move effectively through this non-static space? Laban conceived of a 'kinesphere', split into zones, possible targets of movement (Laban 1966, p. 29). The dual instincts of stability (which is not lack of movement, rather the embedded weight of the body) and mobility work within this space to produce a feeling of harmony (Laban 1966, p. 152). Every movement made is distinct and yet connected with the previous and the future movements. In order to discern certain specific movement techniques, Laban created a list of named actions including dabbing, flicking, pressing, gliding and slashing and created a method of notation which works rather like a musical score.

These terms made an obvious impression on MacColl, Littlewood and Newlove. In 1945 Theatre Workshop toured with their folk music-infused *Johnny Noble* and their adaptation of Molière's *The Flying Doctor*. These plays were premièred in Kendal and were later taken as far afield as Sweden and what was then Czechoslovakia. *The Flying Doctor* required specific movement techniques, and the ideas of Laban could be clearly seen. The plot is orchestrated by Sganarelle, a witty servant in the tradition of *commedia dell'arte* and Beaumarchais's Figaro. In Theatre Workshop's production Sganarelle was played by Howard Goorney, and later, in correspondence with Goorney, Newlove recalled, 'I remember quite clearly getting you to leap up with a flick' (Goorney 1981, p. 160; Newlove 1993, p. 154). This is a term adapted directly from Laban's work. MacColl's adaptation play compels the actor playing Sganarelle to be tremendously dextrous, and the movements he integrates into his play, including jumping out of windows, are extremely demanding. These movements were, of course, integral to the original Molière script, but in Theatre Workshop's version, the nature of these movements was transformed by the addition of the Laban method. Newlove remembered, 'Howard was able to move flexibly and with ease, accompanying his speech with entrechats, spins' (ibid., p. 154). The agility of body directly reflects Sganarelle's nimble and astute mind, which frequently enables him to manipulate and deceive the other characters. In addition, the ability to move effectively also suggests the pre-eminence of the lower-class servant over the other, and predominantly upper class, characters, particularly the father (Gorgibus) and the lawyer. His notable superiority of movement, especially over the rich yet elderly and infirm Gorgibus, is a distinct part of this reversal of the typical social hierarchy, and the audience begins to question the accepted assumptions about class and position. The distinctive difference in movement styles visually signifies the reordering of class positions and the possibility of lower class pre-eminence; a political comment is made through movement.

Laban's methods were equally in evidence in *Uranium 235* (1946). Newlove recollected that 'we wanted to show the splitting of an atom, not simply describe it in words' (Goorney 1981, p.160), which reveals an important aspect of Theatre Workshop's work and of MacColl's plays: that is, the literary text was not a completed composition but was adapted and interpreted in performance. The nuclear fission process is initially presented in the form of a dance in which a dancer depicting a neutron eventually penetrates a group of other 'neutrons' and 'protons'. This singular action creates the destruction of the atom, and 'all [the other particles] leap away from her and land on their knees' (Goorney and MacColl 1986, p. 110). Although the term 'leap' could be a generic term of general movement, the influence of Laban's terminology is again surely in evidence here and Newlove mentioned this innovative dance sequence in her 1993 book, *Laban for Actors and Dancers*. She also saw a clear connection between the symbols connected with science and those used by dancers. Both are coded ways of understanding actual events and movements (Newlove 2003, p. 120). The final leap is the concluding act of a closely choreographed dance sequence before which the dancers are described as 'limbering up' in preparation. It is a self-conscious, stand-alone scene (in keeping with Brecht's notion that the arts should remain independent of one another), which effectively reflects a scientific problem in a visual manner.

Somewhat surprisingly, Theatre Workshop were not the only company to present atomic fission through dance. In 1939 Donald Hatch Andrews produced an atomic ballet for the national meeting of the American Chemical Society in Baltimore. As a Professor of Chemistry at Johns Hopkins University, he was approaching his subject from an entirely different perspective to MacColl. Furthermore, given that his ballet was performed six years before the annihilation of Hiroshima and Nagasaki, its symbolism and intention also differed from Theatre

Workshop's version. Yet, although there seem to be no connections between the two, the finished product was remarkably similar:

> Ballerinas costumed to represent carbon (in black), hydrogen (in red), oxygen (blue), etc. pirouetted around on stage.
>
> (Murchie 1981, p. 633)

For Guy Murchie, who cited this event in his book, *The Seven Mysteries of Life,* atomic fission, just like the movement of the planets, resembles a musical score; a scientific understanding of the world can be regarded as a 'melody', suggestive of organised notes and rhythms (ibid., p. 634). It is little wonder, then, that Andrews (from his scientific frame of reference) and MacColl (coming from a theatrical background) used dance to signify these scientific concepts.

These two influences – Meyerholdian biomechanics (or at least the emulation of a similar idea) and the Laban methods – were, of course, profoundly different in style and intention. While Meyerhold began with the movement itself in a similar manner to a reflex – in James's terms 'I saw a bear, I ran, I was scared' – Laban started with the emotion, 'dazzled by the vision of the inner life' (Laban 1975, p. 95). Yet, though contrasting, both were useful as Theatre Workshop continued to develop its aesthetic: methods of liberating the body from the constraints of capitalist society and presenting it as a site of revolutionary challenge.

The Dance of Death: the influence of ballet

While Rudolf Laban and, to some extent, Meyerhold played a key role in the development of Theatre Workshop's aesthetic, it was the ideas of Diaghilev, Copeau and Cocteau that proved instrumental in the evolution of Group Theatre. Although members of the WTM and Theatre Workshop were both influenced by ballet as dance genre, neither group really formed specifically balletic methods.[6] For Group Theatre, by contrast, the methods of these three Ballets Russes-connected figures, with their focus on creating a modern inter-generic ballet rather than centring on conventional ideas, were absolutely crucial to the company's aesthetic.

These balletic conceptions of dance began to come together in Auden's *The Dance of Death* (1933). Auden, as poet first and foremost,

largely regarded as a proponent of poetic drama, was actually fascinated by dance and movement. His *Manifesto on the Theatre* contends
that 'drama is essentially an art of the body. The basis of acting is
acrobatics, dancing, and all forms of physical skill' (Auden 1988,
p. 273). For a playwright so preoccupied with language and the written text, such a claim is remarkable, and illustrates the significance
of movement methods for Group Theatre, and indeed for his own
plays. Once again, Auden's pronouncements enable us to move away
from any assumption that the so-called poetic dramatists focused
almost exclusively on the written text.

Auden's approach had an obvious precursor in Yeats's plays.
Yeats, perhaps even more than Auden, had a great interest in dance.
Indeed, the dancer is not just an important figure in his plays but
remains a vital image throughout his work; as Frank Kermode suggests 'the Dancer is one of Yeats's great reconciling images, containing life in death, death in life, movement and stillness, action and
contemplation, body and soul' (1957, p. 48). Similarly, in light of
Kermode's conclusions, it reconciles the literary image with the performance-based one. It is not that poetry (the written image) and
performance stand in contrast, but rather that they complement
one another. Yeats's influences in this area were varied which meant
that his concept of dance was multi-faceted and, at times, difficult to
fully grasp (Flannery 1976, p. 208). Certainly there were ideas from
Japanese Noh theatre. And it is the way the body moves in Noh
theatre that excited Yeats. He wrote, 'the interest is not in the human
form but in the rhythm to which it moves, and the triumph of their
art is to express the rhythm in its intensity' (1961, p. 231). But there
were also connections to be made with modern free dancers, namely
Loie Fuller whose 'Chinese dancers' he praised in his poem *Nineteen
Hundred and Nineteen* (1991, p. 144).[7] Further, in Ninette de Valois,
dancer with Diaghilev's Ballets Russes, he found an artist who really
captured his imagination (Flannery 1976, p. 209). But, though all
these influences played their part, Yeats's search seemed to continue
on without ever really finding a solution:

Should I make a serious attempt, which I may not, being rather
tired of the theatre, to arrange and supervise performances, the
dancing will give me most trouble, for I know but vaguely what
I want. I do not want any existing form of stage dancing, but

something with a smaller gamut of expression, something more
reserved, more self-controlled, as befits performers within arm's
reach of their audience.

(Yeats 1921, p. v)

Perhaps, like many of the practitioners across the historical avant-
garde, Yeats was clearer about what he didn't want than what
he did.

The Dance of Death became one of the most important and experimental moments in the British avant-garde. Its success, as Ashley
Dukes suggested in 1935, was its 'correlation of acting, movement
and words' (Haffenden 1983, p. 157). The sheer diversity of Auden's
piece revealed his commitment to creating fruitful dialogue between
earlier traditions and the contemporary. It also showed a particular
interest in the juxtaposition of artistic genres. The play is politically
engaged, not as workers' theatre, but as an analysis of the demise of
the middle class for the middle class. It is what Sidnell describes as
'politically tendentious choreography' (1984, p. 71).

The piece begins in a similar manner to Yeats's *Four Plays for
Dancers*, on a platform where 'the stage is bare with a simple back-
cloth' (Auden 1933, p. 7). On this presentational stage, Auden
created an image of class tension and the disintegration of the bourgeoisie in a highly metatheatrical manner with, in a similar way to
MacColl's later *Landscape with Chimneys*, the Theatre Manager and
the Stage Hands as characters. At the centre of this play is Rupert
Doone's Dancer Death, a representative figure for the declining middle class. Gradually, as the play progresses, the Dancer finds himself
in a number of hazardous situations culminating in his portrayal of
the Pilot, whose 'ambition is no less than to reach the very heart
of Reality' (ibid., p. 28). He seemingly fails in his aim, eventually
dying amidst a sea of stereotypical bourgeois concerns, such as land
ownership, industrial growth and nationalism. There is the continual
sense that the middle class has brought the current situation entirely
upon itself, with Karl Marx finally insisting that 'the instruments of
production have been too much for him' (ibid., p. 38).

The dance sequences are of vital importance in this play to provide a visual image of this process of class fracture. One of the most
powerful episodes is 'The Ship of England' scene. The ship represents a particular national identity, one of unity, jingoistic pride

and the assumption that God is championing the Nation's cause. The Dancer's interlude visually contradicts this notion of English selfhood:

> *During the storm the formation gets more and more disintegrated.* Dancer *gradually works into a whirling movement which culminates in a falling fit.*
>
> (Auden 1933, p. 21)

In addition, playing the Pilot in the later scene, the 'Dancer *falls and staggers up being paralysed from the feet up*' (ibid., p. 31). Reminiscent of a Brechtian *Verfremdungs-Effekt*, it is the interruptions in the dance that mark the political comments, those moments when movement becomes impossible or limited. The middle class, caught in a position of its own making, finally becomes unable to move. There is a profound sense of inevitability about this conclusion, visually presented by the struggles of the Dancer; movement is suddenly a crucial method to comment on class politics.

In many ways Auden's play is markedly similar to Kurt Jooss's 1932 piece, *The Green Table*.[8] Performed in London just a year before Group Theatre's version of Auden's *The Dance of Death*, Jooss's choreographed work contains a scene entitled 'The Dance of Death', again with the lead character, Death. Jooss's version, however, connects Death specifically with war rather than the death of a class. But there is a similarity in political intention. Jooss seemingly wanted to point to society's class structure with the masked Ten Gentlemen, 'powerful manipulators of world affairs (as in politics, high finance or industry), who are in discussion. At the height of an argument they draw pistols and shoot. War breaks out' (Jooss 2003, p. 31). Auden's play, though not specifically about war as such, does look at nationalism (and the consequences of bourgeois nationalism which include xenophobia and the potential onset of war) and the structure of a society where those in power advocate, like the Doctor, that 'there's to be no excitement of any kind – no politics, for instance, something quite peaceful, something shall we say, about the country or home life' (Auden 1933, p. 23). Both pieces, then, though explicitly different in intention, seek to uncover through movement the underlying structures of society and render visible those issues that are largely suppressed by the hegemony.[9]

The Dance of Death was in many ways a theatrical starting point for Group Theatre and for Auden. With Doone's connections with the Ballets Russes it is unsurprising that Diaghilev and Copeau formed the basis for the company's ballet technique, and that their influence should be seen in plays from *The Dance of Death* onwards. Copeau was certainly an important founding figure for Group Theatre (Sidnell 1984, p. 57), not just in the creation of the platform stage, but also in the evolution of movement methods. Indeed, Copeau made the connection between the specifically revolutionary theatre of Meyerhold and his own less overtly political stage, reflecting that 'about the same time, Meyerhold in Russia and myself in France were expressing the same unlimited dramatic ambition by asking for a *bare stage*' (1990, p. 111). There is no doubt that these two aesthetic projects were very different in terms of intention and realisation, but Copeau posited an analogous parallel: an empty platform-style stage. On this 'bare stage', then, Copeau placed his highly trained actor. His commitment to training was absolute, choosing his students from a young age in order to educate them in his theatrical methods (ibid., p. 38). This sort of training advocated the 'actor as instrument' (Hodge 1999, p. 68). I suggest that it was this concern with this 'actor as instrument' that really interested Doone and Group Theatre. This was a figure who could dance not just for the entertainment of the audience, but could also play a particular role, who could portray theme and relate arguments.

Copeau, like Meyerhold, was interested in the human body on the bare stage, but rather than connecting movement with the industrial, Copeau's movements were largely a reassessment of more ancient forms, as he put it, 'of renewing one's good faith in ancient traditions and rhythms' (1990, p. 40). In fact, this was vital to his whole theatrical concept, and, with the Group Theatre's commitment to older established forms, was certainly one of the reasons for the company's interest in his ideas. The group's focus on 'folk and medieval sources' (Medley 1983, p. 133) would inevitably lead them to Copeau rather than Meyerhold.

The influence of figures associated with the Ballets Russes was instrumental in the creation of Group Theatre's aesthetic and, correspondingly, to the plays of Auden, Isherwood, Spender and MacNeice to a greater or lesser extent. Indeed, there was a direct connection between the Ballets Russes and Group Theatre in the person of Rupert Doone. Doone had worked briefly with the Ballets Russes before Diaghilev's untimely death in Venice in 1929. Robert Medley points to this defining relationship and the effect of his death: 'In 1929 Rupert finally joined the Diaghilev Ballet at Covent Garden as a "premier danseur" ... the dream was shattered only a few weeks later by a telegram from Venice announcing Diaghilev's death' (Medley 1966, p. 3). Though Doone's association with the Ballets Russes was a brief one, Diaghilev's influence remained central to Group Theatre's aesthetic. The Ballets Russes' *premier danseur* Léonide Massine revealed Diaghilev's idea of 'total theatre', asserting, 'I don't know whether one can call this a sort of artistic policy, but he [Diaghilev] certainly felt very strongly one thing, that ballet is not only what you see on the stage, dancers, but ballet is part of a very complex spectacle' (Drummond 1998, p. 172). Doone took this notion from the Ballets Russes and applied it to Group Theatre productions.[10] Diaghilev was specifically concerned with rejuvenating every aspect of the theatre and, although dance was the obvious foundation point, his contemporaries consistently alluded to his commitment to crossing genre divides. The underlying priority in reimagining this multi-generic theatrical space was the resolution to create a wholly anti-naturalistic aesthetic (Garafola 1989, p. 78). So dance was not a component in a dramatic illusion, but rather a contributor to a highly metatheatrical, self-conscious performance.

In another connection with the Ballets Russes, Jean Cocteau was also extremely influential for Doone's company. According to Medley, Doone spent time with Cocteau as a 19-year-old in Paris, assisting him in his production of *Romeo and Juliet* at the Theatre Pigalle (Medley 1966, p. 2). Auden, too, was greatly influenced by Cocteau from early in his playwriting career. Like Diaghilev and Copeau, Cocteau aimed for a Wagnerian-style *Gesamtkunstwerk*, using dance as a starting point and adding other elements to create a highly original, satirical system. This was particularly in evidence in his groundbreaking *Parade* (1917), a collaboration with Satie, Picasso, Massine and Diaghilev, which illustrated Cocteau's search for a multimedia theatrical space that challenged established theatrical modes (Williams 2006, p. 3). Cocteau's understanding of the inter-generic theatrical space was just as clear in the preface to *The Eiffel Tower Wedding Party* (1922):

The new generation will continue to experiment with forms in which the fairy, the dance, acrobatics, pantomime, drama, satire, music, and the spoken word all combine to produce a novel genre.

(1963, p. 158)

From these experiments, then, a totally new genre of performance was emerging. It could no longer be termed 'drama' or 'dance'; rather it was an imaginative amalgam, an original formal challenge to drama as simply the realisation of the spoken word.

So, the ideas associated with the Ballets Russes, the creation of a multi-genre space, the notion of highly trained dancers committed to modern movements and the rejection of naturalism, were extremely consequential for Group Theatre. In a useful phrase, given our questioning of the centrality of the written word, *Parade* exemplified a 'new language of choreography' (Crosland 1955, p. 50) and it was this dedication to a modern methodology of movement that marked the most noticeable connection between Group Theatre and the Ballets Russes.

Rhythms, beats and drumming

Within this inter-generic theatrical space, music became a vital element not just as incidental melody or simply as another entertaining medium, but as an important contributor to dramatic intention. This new connection of drama and music, again in some sense returning to an older method, gave music new roles. In many ways, music hall again provided a helpful precursor as a genre in which the songs, often socially aware if sentimental, stood alone, juxtaposed, though remaining distinct from the drama or acrobatics. With dance and movement at the fore of the theatrical aesthetic, it was perhaps inevitable that this most basic of musical elements, rhythm, would play a vital role in productions. Rhythm is in evidence initially in the very structure of the plays. As Meyerhold suggested, 'a director must be able to feel the time without looking at his watch. A performance of a play is an alteration of dynamic and static moments, as well as dynamic moments of different kinds. That is why the gift of rhythm seems to me one of the most important a director can have' (Schmidt, Levin and McGee 1996, p. 155).

Narrative rhythm was a dynamic aspect of British avant-garde theatre, leading to the frequent creation of fragmented works with particularly interesting tempos. Yet rhythm was not only a linguistic or text-based device; it was also an important motif in a theatre permeated by musical experimentation. In fact, the use of rhythmic percussive sounds seems to dominate a whole range of plays. In America, Eugene O'Neill's *Emperor Jones* (1920) is a prime example:

> *From the distant hills comes the faint, steady thumping of a tom-tom, low and vibrating. It starts at a rate exactly corresponding to normal pulse beat – seventy-two to the minute – and continues at a gradually accelerating rate from this point uninterruptedly to the very end of the play.*
>
> (O'Neill 1971, p. 250)

Beginning the beat by connecting it directly to the audience's own innate bodily rhythms is clearly an attempt to subliminally involve each spectator. By speeding up the rhythm throughout the play, the aim is to affect the pulse rates of the audience members. A similar effect is used by Toller in *Hoppla, We're Alive!* in which a heartbeat can be heard as the threat of war becomes ever more acute (2000, p. 273). In both cases the rhythms connect directly with the audience in a visceral way. In *Emperor Jones* drum rhythms are also suggestive of ever-increasing madness and threat, creating a parallel with the somewhat primeval undercurrent that was often seen in the avant-garde. This way of using rhythm is a recurring emblem that later reappeared in a number of plays including Yeats's *A Full Moon in March* (1935). Yeats's play, to a certain degree reminiscent of Kokoschka's *Murder Hope of Womankind*, is a direct agitational challenge to taste. Again, drumming is a sign of madness, danger and the primeval, with the Queen taking the severed head of the Swineherd and dancing 'with it to drum-taps, which grow quicker and quicker. As the drum-taps approach their climax, she presses her lips to the lips of the head. Her body shivers to very rapid drum-taps' (Yeats 1979, p. 182). Perhaps a connection could also be made to the 'Dance of the Seven Veils' in Oscar Wilde's *Salome* (1896, first performed in London in 1905). Like Yeats, Wilde had some difficulties in defining his vision behind the dance sequence, but there is the suggestion that, in its original conception anyway, the dance should have some sense of rhythmic abandonment (Wilde 1998, p. 330, n830). These sorts of rhythms can even be seen in Auden and Isherwood's *On the Frontier* where, on the outbreak of war, 'those horrible drums' (1966, p. 169), as Mrs Thorvald calls them, can be heard. While this is modern warfare, the drumming seems to hark back to previous traditions and the effect is remarkably similar to that in *Emperor Jones*. Eliot's *Sweeney Agonistes*, too, brings the rhythmic cadences of modern jazz and a continuous background drumbeat together to produce a piece that is both in keeping with its Greek myth origins and its modern feel. While all these plays have distinctly contemporary outlooks, discussing issues like war and challenging bourgeois taste, the practitioners seemed to be looking to more ancient forms. These plays could even be connected with the primitivist movement.[11]

In contrast, percussive sounds could also make a specific connection to the modern, industrialised landscape. One of the most vivid examples of the connections between rhythm and industry is in Slater's *New Way Wins*. Though supra-naturalistic in form, focusing on the plight of the Merthyr miners, Slater incorporated a powerful percussive element into his script:

> *A metronome set at largo is in the orchestra pit. A drum takes up the rhythm, various percussions die away into the sound of the metronome again.*

> (1937, p. 46)

It transpires that the noise is an air-lock in the pipes. In fact percussive pipes reappear again in MacColl's *The Other Animals* (1948) as the prisoners tap on the pipes to communicate to each other.

What role did that most basic of musical elements, the rhythmic beat have in British avant-garde theatre? There are a number of potential, interrelated answers to this question. Rhythmic sounds, like a language, are communicative. Yet, as was often the case within the British avant-garde, this was not universal. Returning to *The Dance of Death*, the *anti-communicative* function of percussion can be seen as the Dancer beats his drum in order to silence character 'α' who accuses the Dancer of stealing his/her clothes (Auden 1933, p. 13). Once again communication and intentional non-communication reside symbiotically. Rhythmic sounds could certainly be reconnected back to industry, where the modern individual becomes inextricably imbedded in his/her environment; so, like the characters in MacColl's *Landscape with Chimneys*, lives are defined by the rhythmic clatter of the machines in action (1951, pp. 28, 17, 30). Furthermore, in another connection with narrative structure, rhythmic sounds are a method of *creating* time in this industrial context. The metronome, a musical timing device, is the starting point for Slater's air-lock rhythm. Just as time and the questioning of linearity were central to the fragmented structure of the British theatrical avant-garde, so time and music (musical rhythms) were equally important.

'Incidental' theatrical music

Yet the British theatrical avant-garde moved beyond simple rhythms and music took on an important role in many of the plays. Indeed, it was a key aspect of the Diaghilevian 'total theatre' and, accordingly, Group Theatre's productions often contained musical episodes, particularly sung pieces. For *The Dance of Death*, the music was written by BBC Musical Director Herbert Murrill but, for later Group Theatre productions, Benjamin Britten wrote many of the musical scores and was an active member of the company[12] though, as we have seen, his connection with theatre was not restricted to Group Theatre but crossed over that poetic/political boundary. Britten's music was vitally important to the realisation of Auden and Isherwood's (and indeed MacNeice's) scripts; far from an optional extra, the music was at the very centre of the works, creating atmosphere and providing comment.

The songs in the Group Theatre plays do not exhibit the escapist sentimentality of the music hall pieces, but rather are vital components in the creation of politically engaged, linguistically witty performances. Certainly this is the case in *The Dance of Death* with a song like 'The Ship of England', which satirically presents the social instability of the English nation (Auden 1933, p. 19), but it is also perceptible in Auden's collaborations with Isherwood. Britten's music for *The Ascent of F6*, for example, is very much more than merely incidental. It contains, of course, the now well-known poem/song *Funeral Blues*, but it also includes a number of other pieces that prove vital to the overall structure and intention of the work. The contrast between these two particular pieces provides an insight into Auden, Isherwood and Britten's objective. The first is a satirical song played over the radio to Mr and Mrs A. The tune is played by a dance band while the Announcer sings, encouraging the couple to switch off the news, ignore current affairs, rather like the Doctor in *The Dance of Death*: 'don't enumer all the rumours of a war;/ Dance, John, dance!' (Auden and Isherwood 1966, p. 81). Yet the next full scene contains a markedly different musical number pointing to the threat of the Dragon (James Ransom) who has laid the land to waste: 'despair is in our faces' (Auden and Isherwood 1966, p. 86). James Ransom is emblematic of the hegemonic forces that are intent on national and economic prestige regardless of the cost to Britain's own population or indeed the citizens of other countries. These two examples illustrate Auden/Isherwood/Britten's musical intentions: to satirically assess the cultural products of the modern world and to challenge the actions of the hegemony. In many ways this was a theatrical rendering of the later ideas of a theorist like Louis Althusser with his analysis of ideological and repressive state apparatuses.

Music was an essential aspect of *The Ascent of F6* as a creator of mood and fabricator of a multi-generic work. However, the music of this play also had an obvious political aim. Interestingly, Britten's theatrical music can be directly connected to Weill's collaborations with Brecht, as the former was certainly influenced to some extent by the innovations of the latter (Mitchell 2000, p. 120). His music made an important satirical contribution to the plays, and revealed the political power of music that was seen, perhaps more readily, in the scores created by Weill and Eisler for Brecht's plays. Brecht made an active connection between music and politics, and, in keeping with his anti-Wagnerian method of juxtaposing genre, insisted that in order to retain its political potency, music had to preserve its independence and not become part of a 'total theatre' aesthetic; there must be a 'strict separation of music from all other elements of entertainment offered' (Brecht 2001, p. 85). This meant that music could make a unique contribution in the creation of a politically engaged work: it became a 'muck-raker, an informer, a nark' (ibid., p. 86).

The Group Theatre productions certainly demonstrated this concern with music as independent 'informer', but it is perhaps the plays of MacColl that reflected it most fully. In conjunction with *The Flying Doctor* with its Laban-infused movements, Theatre Workshop also presented the self-proclaimed 'ballad-opera' *Johnny Noble* (Goorney and MacColl 1986, p. 1). In performing such a piece, the company were once again returning to a very specific local musical genre.

The ballad had a vibrant history in British theatre from the eighteenth century onwards. John Gay's *The Beggar's Opera*, in particular, retained a central place in British theatrical genealogy, enjoying a celebrated revival by Nigel Playfair at the Lyric, Hammersmith (1920). In an interesting trans-Continental dialogue, Brecht was made aware of Playfair's production as he wrote *The Threepenny Opera* through Elisabeth Hauptmann's translation of the play (Esslin 1984, pp. 34–5). While Brecht's version differed considerably, it retained the ballad form. MacColl, like Brecht, returned to this vibrant, cross-generic tradition associated very specifically with the 'people' and with informing communities about their own history. Later, the ballad form became a vital model for MacColl who, in conjunction with Charles Parker and Peggy Seeger, wrote and performed the highly acclaimed 1960s *Radio Ballads*. In fact, the promotional material directly pointed to the connection between the *Radio Ballads* and MacColl's earlier theatre work (Topic n.d., p. 5). The theatrical influences for this later project came not just from his earlier reinterpretation of the ballad form, but also Theatre Workshop's innovations with Eisensteinian montage (Woods July 1973b, p. 7) and the Living Newspapers of the Federal Theatre Project (Watt 2003, p. 51).

As one might expect from a playwright who went on to be a leader in the 1960s folk music revival, in *Johnny Noble* the music is integral to the development of narrative. According to the musical cues, many of the tunes are traditional with only three specifically cited as newly penned by MacColl (Goorney and MacColl 1986, pp. 66–70). Again this adds to the sense of reconnecting drama with the people. This bond is further strengthened by the themes of the songs which largely examine the effects of industrial growth, unemployment and war on a young couple, Johnny and Mary. This provides a specific human image through which macro-narratives can be examined. Take, for example, the Second Narrator's song at Music Cue 8, which moves Johnny from the dying shipyards of Clydeside to the defunct mines of Durham in search of work:

> In Durham County it is the same,
> The pithead gear is standing still,
> And men are filled with a sense of shame
> For idle hands and wasted skill.

> (ibid., p. 46)

This is music, specifically the folk ballad, as a 'muck-raker', providing an insightful depiction of unemployment throughout Britain.

But MacColl's music did not just *present* actual working-class conditions, but actively attempted to change them. Brecht's term 'nark' suggests not only an informant but also denotes a sense of irritation and antagonism, and this was also crucial to MacColl's theatrical music. Nowhere is this clearer than in the final section of *Landscape with Chimneys*, another play which, like *Johnny Noble*, attempts to bring particular working-class experiences (of unemployment and the housing crisis, as well as war) to the stage. When Hugh and Clare's occupation of an empty property provokes a reaction from the police, all the characters unite in singing *Which Side are you On?*, a song that affirms the need for working-class unity:

> Don't listen to the landlords
> Don't listen to their lies
> There ain't no hope for us poor folks
> Unless we organise
> Which side are you on?

(MacColl 1951, p. 68)

This song was adapted from the original, written by Florence Reese in 1931 in response to the miners' strike in Kentucky. It was adopted by the politicised folk movement as a song of protest, and, in *Landscape With Chimneys* illustrated MacColl's move from using song as a narrative device able to present a sense of working-class truth on the stage, to music as agitational tactic. It invited the audience to react, participate and take its intentions from the theatre out on to the streets.

The creation of critical dialogues

So, with the advent of this multi-generic form, drama was no longer only the preserve of the written text. Given our earlier conclusions about verbal expression on the modern stage, such a turn is unsurprising. Terence Gray addressed this directly, saying that, at times, 'words become a strikingly inadequate medium for the expression of the emotion that they attempt to convey' (1926, p. 25). While language (in terms of linguistic signs) retained its important position, practitioners like Gray sought to create a cross-generic theatrical mode that could produce multi-faceted works, both formally experimental and thematically engaged. Often coming out of specific British variety traditions, and informed by the cross-generic models of Continental Europe, the examples in this chapter display a sense of artistic dialogues. In discussing Diaghilev's legacy, Massine reflected that, 'unless all the four sister arts [poetry/literature, painting, music, choreography] are on the same level the work will be on one leg' (Drummond 1998, p. 173). In Britain, with the development of the modern stage built on a plain platform, using light and colour, there was certainly a renewed interest in 'painting' in its broadest sense. And with the focus on interdisciplinarity and on creating new relationships between the other composite arts, came a vibrant canon of work, inflected with innovative music and experimental dance.

Conclusion: A British Theatrical Avant-Garde?

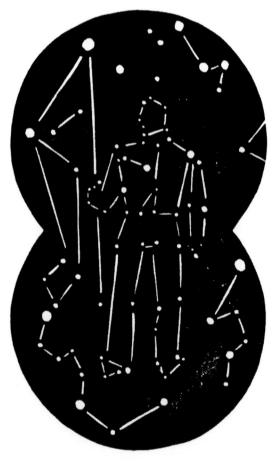

Figure 7   Hung in the sky of the mind (© the artist Beth Fletcher)

176

We began this book with *Sweeney Agonistes* and Virginia Woolf's reaction to it. In her posthumously published novel *Between the Acts* (1941),[1] she provides a useful description of the spectators' impression of the pageant that acts as a postscript:

> Still the play hung in the sky of the mind – moving, diminishing, but still there.
>
> (Woolf 1992, p. 191)[2]

The audience response could be applied just as pertinently to this consciously constructed British theatrical avant-garde. The movements and performances mentioned here existed for a time and made some impact, introducing fascinating (at times convoluted, at times remarkably effective) formal and thematic changes. And while the plays analysed are now largely unperformed, diminishing into the vaults of theatre history, the methods and examples still remain, residual but 'still there'.

Throughout this book we have been aware of the tensions and differences, but the similarities between companies and practitioners are, at times, striking. So while I have sought to maintain a sense of diversity, I have also attempted to create new or previously concealed dialogues, reassessing the relationship between the centre and periphery, between Continental Europe, America, Ireland and Britain, reading innovations in all these spaces through the lens of the avant-garde. While I hope the setting up of a British-defined, distinctly performance-based 'avant-garde' is a helpful way of bringing some semblance of unanimity to heterogeneous traditions, each of the major groups discussed here has been separately connected to the Continental avant-garde before. Donald Mitchell describes Group Theatre 'in its hey-day ... [as] a kind of English reflection of the experimental movement in the European theatre' (2000, p. 120) and Valentine Cunningham agrees that it 'did its best ... to import something of the avant-garde European stylization' (1989, p. 322). Derek Paget cites Theatre Workshop as 'the Trojan horse through which European radical theatre practices from the 1918–1939 period entered post-war Britain' (1995, p. 212) and connecting its project with similar productions in Russia and Germany, Raphael Samuel suggests that 'aesthetically, the Worker's Theatre Movement proclaimed itself modernist envisaging a total break with conventional dramaturgy' (Samuel, MacColl and Cosgrove 1985, p. 42). The WTM is a difficult case, at times purporting theatrical innovation while remaining doggedly committed to a fairly unsophisticated brand of agit-prop and later following the Russian turn towards Socialist Realism. Yet, even here, as Richard Stourac and Kathleen McCreery suggest, there were exceptions, particularly in its use of montage (1986, p. 265). And, as Colin Chambers confirms, while Unity Theatre never progressed its aesthetic as far as, say, Theatre Workshop, this collection of regional theatre groups did have a 'pioneering influence on beneficial developments in the theatrical life of Britain' (1989, p. 398). Other groups touched on in this book have also been understood through these ideas. Edith Craig's Pioneer Players, for example, have been described in similar terms to Theatre Workshop, as a 'Trojan horse, promising dramatic art, unexpectedly delivering feminism' (Cockin 2001, p. 41) and Terence Gray's Festival Theatre has been labelled 'the only experimental theatre of modern art in England' (Cornwall 2004, p. 262).

All these descriptions are infused with avant-garde ideas: practitioners as leading 'pioneers', a rejection of conventional forms, a commitment to experimentalism and a trans-national approach. The comments quoted illustrate the intricate workable connections across frontiers and barriers. But they also point to the universal commitment to change, both aesthetically and politically. Through this resolution to address the contemporary, the figures mentioned here also actively reached across another boundary: that of time and history. In seeking modern methods it is striking how often the practitioners looked to Britain's rich theatrical past, updating the techniques and reappropriating character, structure or theme. The definition of the British theatrical avant-garde that I posited in my introduction as 'leading, challenging and changing' can now be expanded upon when understood through the range of examples we have been considering. Dialogue and the disassembling (or at least crossing) of barriers are absolutely crucial to it.

Many of these plays have largely remained unperformed for many years and there are a number of reasons for this, many of which have been addressed in these pages: the perceived anti-performative bias, the complex language, the contemporaneous nature of theme and the ephemeral qualities of the plays. But perhaps it is also indicative of any avant-garde movement. In leading, challenging and changing, these plays, companies and playwrights placed themselves in a precarious position. It is a theme discussed in detail by Mabou Mines' artistic director, Ruth Maleczech, at a recent American Society for Theatre Research conference. She proclaimed that any avant-garde is always dominated by 'those who can afford to lose ... [by] those who go forth to be sacrificed' (Seattle 2010). Yet, returning to the military origins of the term, imagining these companies as a sort of Forlorn Hope, there will always be those who would come after to take up the mantle and continue on. While this seems a somewhat dramatic conclusion, the plays of the British avant-garde reflect this. In the later decades of the twentieth century and beyond there are practitioners that are emblematic of the avant-garde sensibility I posited in the introduction. While some remain on the cultural periphery, many have transported themselves firmly into mainstream theatrical consciousness, challenging the comfortable conventions of the modern stage.

Woolf's description of the theatrical experience suggests that something was 'still there' for those who came after, and the British avant-garde can be read as a continuing mode of theatre creation. Yet this is not at all straightforward. Dietrich Scheunemann in *Avant-Garde/Neo-Avant-Garde* negotiates that tricky transition between the historical avant-garde and that which came after, saying 'the neo-avant-garde can now be conceived as another bearer of the flame of hope, re-igniting it and passing it on after a period of darkness' (2005, p. 20). The idea of 're-igniting' a flame is a useful one in this British theatrical context. It suggests, as Scheunemann does later in the same volume, that there is not a clear genealogical connection between the historical avant-garde and later innovations (ibid., p. 44). Rather, there are breaks and ruptures, hence the *re*-ignition. I am certainly not claiming an uncritical neo-avant-garde in this British context, but there does seem to be a burgeoning avant-garde in the later decades of the twentieth century.[3] This movement is, as Scheunemann's image suggests, mostly a 're-ignition' rather than a direct linear evolution, but there are some useful connections to be made between the exciting, ephemeral plays of the British modernist avant-garde and the theatre of the 1960s, 1970s and onwards. As an example, there are prominent links between Theatre Workshop and the later politically engaged groups of the 1970s, particularly 7:84. John McGrath was quite clear in his admiration of *Oh What a Lovely War*, but his high regard was not just reserved for the Stratford company. Discussing Theatre Workshop's earlier tours of Scotland, he reflected, 'Joan and the company who worked with her had worked hard and learnt the cruel way about entertaining the working class' (McGrath 1996, p. 47). With *The Cheviot, the Stag and the Black, Black Oil* (1973), a play that comes directly out of a Living Newspaper tradition combined with local variety theatre and ceilidh forms (McGrath 1981), 7:84, like pre-Stratford East Theatre Workshop before them, took their form of theatre directly to their audience. Unity Theatre, too, inspired the new generation of theatre makers and its London base became a vibrant receiving house as the post-war period progressed, providing performance space for groups like CAST, Belt and Braces and 7:84 (England) (Chambers 1989, p. 385). While these cross-generational relationships were by no means without disagreements, they do mark a distinct genealogy.

Modern documentary theatre has also taken the lead (consciously or otherwise) from previous traditions. It is an issue taken up by Derek Paget in the recent collected edition, *Get Real*, in which he maintains 'the rhizomic nature of alternative forms allows for different kinds of flowerings – recoverable, like the past itself, by effort of will and circumstances of necessity' (Forsyth and Megson 2009, p. 224). Like Scheunemann's 'flame', Paget's 'flower' is '*re*-flowering'; it is an act of recovery. And certainly, with plays like Tricycle's *The Colour of Justice* (1999), the Royal Court's *My Name is Rachael Corrie* (2005) and the National Theatre of Scotland's *Black Watch* (2008), amongst countless other examples, the documentary theatre mode has had a remarkably fruitful resurgence.

In recent years there has also been a reappearance of a distinct Expressionistic tradition, with playwrights like Howard Barker and Sarah Kane. With their fragmented, tormented, in-flux characterisation, the central figures of plays like *Blasted* (1995) are at times remarkably similar to those in, say, Kokoschka's *Murderer Hope of Womankind*.[4] Even into the twenty-first century, movements like Expressionism continue to have an impact on the British stage. In his review of Simon McBurney's 2010 production of the Russian Opera, *A Dog's Heart* (based on Mikhail Bulgakov's 1925 work), Michael Billington reflected on the importance of revisiting avant-garde techniques as practitioners search for a theatrical medium to confront the modern world:

> The significant point is that British theatre, habitually accused of being wedded to realism, is far more experimental than we

acknowledge. And expressionism, which used to be greeted with a critical yawn as 'the kind of thing they did in Berlin in the 1920s', is alive and well and seems to chime with our own soul-searching, hysteria and sense of crisis.

(2010)

Interestingly, this piece narrates the story of a stray dog as he is turned into a man, a fascinating reminder of one of the British avant-garde's more radical plays, *The Dog Beneath the Skin*. In our modern world, conventions that look back to the historical avant-garde are once again appearing on the British stage, in an attempt to find a theatrical mode that is able to successfully cope with our complex world of financial meltdown, unpredictable wars with unknown enemies and overpowering consumerism.

One key feature of the modernist avant-garde was its decision to represent alternative views. These views were, at times, contradictory, but the performances discussed in this book are largely defined by antagonism and a commitment to making marginal voices audible. These marginal voices could be from different class backgrounds, ethnic identities or political interest groups and acted as a challenge to hegemonic perspectives. This is clear and unequivocal in the plays of WTM or Theatre Workshop, but can also be seen, despite the upbringing of many of its left-centre liberal members, in Group Theatre productions by Auden, Isherwood, MacNeice and Spender. Vocal challenges to prevailing views about identity, society and aesthetics can be seen throughout the British theatrical avant-garde, from Spender's Brother in *Trial of a Judge* to Robert Hanau in MacColl's *The Other Animals*, from the young couple searching for peace in Auden and Isherwood's *On the Frontier* to the passionate calls for international solidarity in a WTM sketch like *Meerut*.

While there are, therefore, some connections to be made between recent British theatre and the indigenous historical avant-garde there are surprisingly few definite links. Figures like Brecht and Meyerhold have had a great impact on modern theatre production, but the innovations of these British practitioners have largely disappeared. Their influence has really been astonishingly limited. Due to lack of available documentation and, mirroring the irrepressible impulse of the modernist theatrical avant-garde in Britain with its overwhelming need to confront the modern world in new ways, contemporary practitioners seem to have been in no position to place themselves within any particular genealogy (Kershaw 1992, p. 75). In the many books that examine post-war British theatre, the performances of the British historical avant-garde are almost entirely absent either as antecedents or as direct influences. A useful example of this absence can be seen in Aleks Sierz's excellent *In-Yer-Face Theatre* where he provides what he terms a 'brief history of provocation', pointing to figures such as Brecht, Jarry, Strindberg and Tzara. Britain is regarded as a place to be conquered by these foreign 'invaders' rather than a nation with a distinct experimental fringe of its own. He suggests, 'if British theatre guarded itself against shock, it soon found experimental theatre creeping in, despite the rigorous border controls' (Sierz 2001, p. 14). Again, here is the notion of overcoming borders, but any British precedents to these later innovations are conspicuously absent.[5]

Once again, reiterating my opening intention, I hope that this book provides a balanced reappraisal to be used by practitioners and scholars alike. While the performers, writers and directors of the British avant-garde did not always succeed in creating enduring, mature work, the plays and techniques are well worth re-exploring. Returning to that quotation from *Between the Acts*, the category of 'British avant-garde theatre' is one that is continuously 'moving'. As other performances are unearthed, rediscovered or reinvigorated, dialogues can expand and shift. The concept moves across contemporaneous borders of nation, class, genre and political intention. But the sensibility also moves across time, creating a perceptible if fractured line of descent which continues on into the twenty-first century.

Notes

Introduction: A British Theatrical Avant-Garde

1. The American Haillie Flanagan, later to become director of the Federal Theatre Project, had already given the premier of this play at Vassar College, New York on 6 May 1933 (Badenhausen 2004, p. 123).
2. 'Ottoline' refers to Lady Ottoline Morrell, the patroness who opened her home Garsington Manor for artists and pacifists during the war. 'Raymond' is almost certainly Raymond Bell Mortimer the critic and man of letters. He conducted his apprenticeship under Desmond MacCarthy who wrote a very favourable review of *Sweeney Agonistes*. 'Hope' is Hope Mirlees, the writer, whose poem, 'Paris' was amongst the first to be published by Hogarth Press. For these biographical descriptions I am indebted to the editors of Virginia Woolf's diaries.
3. Sidnell suggests that Brecht was at the final December production. However, in Ian Donaldson's edited edition, *Transformations in Modern Drama*, John Willett suggests that Brecht visited Group Theatre in 1935 (1983, p. 165). Whichever version Brecht saw, the consensus is that he was impressed by the play and by the company itself (Badenhausen 2004, p. 142).
4. This claim is substantiated by Matei Calinescu in *Five Faces of Modernity* (1987, p. 143).
5. Interesting examples of this recent turn can be found in books like Lucy Delap's *The Feminist Avant-Garde: Trans-Atlantic Encounters of the Early Twentieth Century*, Michael Saler's *The Avant-Garde in Interwar England*, Paul Peppis's *Literature, Politics and the English Avant-Garde and Edward Comentale's Modernism, Cultural Production and the British Avant-Garde*.
6. Actually this inadvertently mirrors Mike Sell's approach in his 2011 edited edition *Avant-Garde Performance and Material Exchange*. Rather than 'dialogues', he uses the term 'vectors of the radical'. Interestingly though, both Sell's 'vectors' and my own 'dialogues' are, appropriating Sell's description, 'a kind of thing that moves and interacts with the people and places it encounters' (2011, p. 1). Neither are fully realised or settled categories; they are imbued with a sense of movement in their very definition.
7. In this respect it takes up the mantle of Andrew Davies in *Other Theatres: The Development of Alternative and Experimental Theatre in Britain* who wrote that 'although the mainstream or commercial theatre is always likely to occupy the most prominent position, the other traditions deserve much greater attention from critics, historians, publishers and theatre-goers. *Other Theatres* is a small step in that direction' (1987, p. 11).

8. See, for example, Sascha Bru's *Democracy, Law and the Modernist Avant-Garde*.
9. The response from regional audiences seems to challenge the West End's suspicion of *Uranium 235*. In taped interviews MacColl recollected that 'they loved it, ordinary people. The response was fantastic' (Orr and O'Rourke 1985, Part Four).
10. As Luca Somigli puts it, 'it is precisely through manifestoes that avant-garde artists and writers confront their audience with the problem of the loss of the halo and attempt to articulate new strategies of legitimation of their activity' (2003, p. 20).
11. Christopher Isherwood, too, has become the focus of recent plays, films and television programmes. The interest begins with John van Druten's *I am a Camera* (1951) which, with Isherwood's *Berlin Stories,* was later an inspiration for Kander and Ebb's *Cabaret* (original Broadway production, 1966). More recently Isherwood's life and work has been reassessed through the Oscar-winning film adaptation of his novel *A Single Man* (2009), and the recent BBC series, *Christopher And His Kind* (2011).
12. Britten and MacColl worked on a piece entitled *The Chartists March* in 1938. Although MacColl's libretto was not entirely satisfactory to Britten, it did mark the beginning of a continuing relationship (Harker 2007, p. 163: Mitchell and Reed 1998, p. 555).
13. There are obvious, though not necessarily accurate, connections in company names here. 'The Red Megaphones' came from a distinct German tradition (Innes 1972, p. 55). Furthermore the titles, 'Theatre Union' and 'Theatre of Action' can be seen in American theatre of the period (Clurman 1957). Theatre Workshop used all these names during its early incarnations. Interestingly, while the Group Theatre in England was establishing itself as a foremost innovator in experimental theatre, an American theatre company with the same name appeared. There doesn't seem to be any direct link between these two companies, though both are attempting to create a new theatrical language. Unity, by contrast, did seem to consider a range of typical Continental European names before deciding on 'Unity' which 'summed up the prevailing political strategy of the moment' (Chambers 1989, p. 46).
14. See Chambers 1989, pp. 39–45 for details of this acrimonious split in the WTM.

1   Structure: The Fragmented and Episodic

1. Interestingly, though there is a distinct home-grown naturalist tradition, the British scene was greatly influenced by both local productions of naturalist plays and the visits of Continental companies. A play such as *Ghosts*, for instance, produced by Jacob Grein's Independent Theatre Society in 1891, caused such an outcry that 'the general playgoing public hereafter associated a naturalistic play, especially one from abroad, with

outrage and scandal in some form or other' (Styan 1997, p. 56). Visits from overseas were also extremely influential. The tour of the Saxe-Meiningen company, as an example, encouraged British practitioners to develop methods that enabled them to present accurate mimetic images (Schumacher 1996, pp. 384–5).

2. This latter episode marks an interesting parallel with Bertolt Brecht's *The Resistible Rise of Arturo Ui*, written in 1941, a year later than *Last Edition*. It too examines the history of Nazism using an American gangster scene.

3. Samuel Hynes also points to this parallel saying, 'while the climb in *F6* is a fable based on a 'thirties myth of heroism, it is also close to reportage' (Hynes 1976, p. 237).

4. It must be noted, however, that those involved with Group Theatre were anxious to partly disassociate themselves from Continental Expressionism. Group Theatre member Robert Medley addressed this, saying, 'neither were we, as some have thought, an English offshoot of the continental expressionist theatre, in spite of Rupert's association with Reinhardt and his admiration for the work of Kurt Jooss's (Medley 1983, p. 159). This seems to be an attempt to claim a local tradition, decidedly British and distinct from the innovations overseas.

5. Two other Toller plays were produced in Manchester during this pre-Second World War period: *The Blind Goddess* and *Pastor Hall* were performed by the Manchester Rep in 1935 and 1939 respectively. J. M. Ritchie suggests that 'it is perhaps permissible to conclude by complimenting Manchester on the part it had to play in helping to promote the work of expressionists in exile like Ernst Toller' (Behr, Fanning and Jarman 1993, p. 38). Breaking down the centre–periphery dialectic, it is interesting to note the importance of the Northern city in the development of a local tradition.

6. Ashley Dukes's name reappears in a range of contexts throughout the British avant-garde. He is affiliated to the ILP, as mentioned, but also set up the innovative Mercury Theatre in 1933. Later he worked closely with Group Theatre on productions like *The Ascent of F6:* 'Group Theatre operated "in association" with Ashley Dukes, who hired the actors, arranged for the scenery and costumes, paid a royalty to the authors, and managed performing rights' (Auden 1988, p. 502). He is an interesting and useful character transcending that barrier between the political and poetic traditions.

7. While being somewhat reluctant to claim an American historical avant-garde, Arnold Aronson does recognise the innovations of pre-1950s playwrights, citing both Eugene O'Neill and Elmer Rice, in addition to Federal Theatre (Aronson 2000, p. 2).

8. Important for our later discussion of critical naturalism, Priestley obviously held a certain admiration for O'Casey's work and particularly for the 'three Dublin plays', as he terms them in *Particular Pleasures* (1975, p. 146). Theatre Workshop too, admired O'Casey's work and performed *Juno and the Paycock* in its first season at Stratford East (Leach 2006,

p. 110). There is also the suggestion that O'Casey saw Ewan MacColl's play, *Uranium 235*, performed by Theatre Workshop in 1946 and 1952, and greatly enjoyed it (ibid., p. 77).

9. Kokoschka visited Britain in the 1920s and later, like a number of other artists from across Continental Europe, moved to Britain to escape fascism. See Hoffman's *Kokoschka: Life and Work* and Keegan's *The Eye of God: A Life of Oskar Kokoschka* for further information about these trips and his eventual residency in Britain. As he wrote in his 1945, *A Petition from a Foreign Artist to the Righteous People of Great Britain for a Secure and Present Peace*, 'Great Britain was the only country to admit me when, as a "degenerate artist", I had been deprived of civil rights in an Austria signed away to Hitler' (Hoffmann 1947, p. 246).

10. Richard Murphy confronts the central aims of this Expressionistic fragmentation:

> By contrast with the solidity of naturalist verisimilitude, what the expressionist text attempts to do is to undermine appearances in order firstly to shock the audience and undermine both the inherent conservatism and the sense of reassurance it derives from recognizing the familiar, and secondly to destroy the audience's comforting illusion of having a conceptually mastered or fixed reality.
>
> (1999, p. 71)

11. This play is mentioned in Stourac and McCreery's wonderful, comprehensive overview of European politically engaged theatre of the early twentieth century. They cite it as *Judges of All the Earth* and are unsure as to the author. I suggest that it is probably referring to Stephen Schofield's *The Judge of All the Earth*, produced first at Ruskin College, Oxford, in 1927 and later by London WTM.

12. In *The Other Animals*, the influence of Mahler can also be seen in MacColl's music choices. He writes in the stage directions, 'a simple childish theme is introduced but still in dance tempo rather like the "Henry Martin" theme in Mahler's First Symphony' (Littlewood 2003, p. 155). MacColl is probably referring to the slow movement commonly known as 'Frère Jacques'.

13. This is a theme taken up by Kevin McNeilly, who proposes that 'the "jazz" of *Sweeney Agonistes* engenders certain layers of indeterminacy, concentric strata that the poem itself, as it moves forward through its vestigial "plot" digs through and peels back in an apparent effort to make meaning, to exceed its fragments' (Cooper 2000, p. 25).

14. Although not the focus of the current study, it is interesting to note the connections between the British theatrical avant-garde and the burgeoning film movement. Of particular note is Auden's work for the General Post Office Film Unit with films like *Coal Face* (1935) and *Night Mail* (1935). For brief explanatory details of these films, see Mendelson's edited collection, *The Complete Works of W. H. Auden: Plays 1928–1938*, pp. 665–73. This also

marks another connecting point in the British avant-garde. In the GPO Film Unit Auden worked closely with Benjamin Britten, and Montagu Slater wrote 'the prose narration about coal mining' for *Coal Face* (Auden 1988, p. 665).

15. It is a key theme of Laura Marcus's recent book, *The Tenth Muse*, in which she analyses a range of literary examples through the conventions of the cinema. With its '"new" devices of the cinema, including flashbacks and tracking shots', Woolf's *Mrs Dalloway* is a key example of this filmic approach (Marcus 2007, p. 141).

16. Brecht and Eisenstein were, of course, well aware of one another and had met in Berlin in 1929 (Brecht 2001, p. 51n).

17. Brecht's relation to the modernist avant-garde has been the subject of many an analysis and it is not my intention to uncritically present Brecht as an avant-garde playwright. It is an issue taken up by Peter Bürger in his seminal *The Theory of the Avant-Garde* and, while I am consciously attempting to disconnect this book from the contentious debates about the historical avant-garde, his conclusions regarding Brecht are very useful. He suggested that, while not wanting to construct an artificial homogeneity, 'Brecht is avant-gardiste to the extent that the avant-garde work of art makes possible a new kind of political art because it frees the parts from their subordination to the whole' (Bürger 1999, p. 91). Usefully for our discussion here, Bürger suggests that Brecht can be read in parallel to the practitioners of the historical avant-garde because of his interest in fragmentation, whether that be montage or his non-Wagnerian juxtaposition of different art forms.

18. See, for example, Auden's translation of *The Caucasian Chalk Circle* (Brecht 1994, pp. 141–237).

19. For further information about this influence of Moussinac's text on the early incarnations of Theatre Workshop, see Derek Paget's 1995 article 'Theatre Workshop, Moussinac and the European Connection'.

20. Donald Mitchell is even more clear, saying, 'we know beyond any doubt that at least two works with texts by Brecht and music by Kurt Weill, *Die Dreigroschnoper* and *Aufsteig und Fall der Stadt Mahagonny*, directly influenced Auden and Isherwood when they were writing *The Dog Beneath the Skin*' (Mitchell 2000, p. 120).

21. Interestingly there is a marked similarity in subject matter with MacColl's *The Other Animals*, discussed earlier in this chapter. It too places the central character in a lunatic asylum and then transports him to a train which acts as a revelatory space, a moving arena in which issues are discussed and truths expounded. There is no clear evidence that MacColl was aware of the earlier play when he wrote *The Other Animals*, but the connection in imagery is an interesting one.

22. Varnedoe and Gopnik provide a thorough explanation of the relationship between high and low culture in the avant-garde. Their argument points to the difficulties of definition, particularly when it comes to low culture, and understands the high and the low as existing in a mutually

beneficial way. As they suggest, 'the exchange between high and low has not involved one-way ascents and descents along a ladder, but cycles in the turning of a wheel' (Varnedoe and Gopnik 1991, p. 406). Like the category 'British avant-garde theatre', the relationship between 'high' and 'low' culture is fluid and ever changing.

23. The only representative of the middle class is the character of the Professor who is, according to stage notes, 'the relic of a poor medical student who did a twelve month stretch for performing an abortion' (MacColl 1951, p. 10).

24. It seems that Strindberg never visited Britain, though he travelled extensively on the Continent. However, he influenced a number of British thinkers, mainly from the late Victorian era. For further information see Sven-Eric Liedman's 'Sweden and Victorian Britain'. Strindberg's plays, however, were performed in London, with *The Father,* for example, receiving its British premier in 1927. Shaw and Strindberg, too, had a rather uneasy relationship which began in 1908 when Shaw travelled over to Sweden (Bertolini 1993, pp. 9–24).

2   Staging: Platforms and Constructions

1. Simonson was a set designer for Guild Theatre, New York. Tyrone Guthrie had met him in 1935, saying, 'I saw most of Lee Simonson, who was designing the sets, and found him wonderfully glamorous and stimulating. He did nothing by halves. Everything was extreme' (Guthrie 1961, p. 152). Simonson's set designs for Ernst Toller's *Masses Man* are also included in Leon Moussinac's *The New Movement in Theatre,* the book that so influenced Theatre Workshop in its early incarnations (1931, plates 112 and 113).

2. See Melvin's *The Art of Theatre Workshop* (2006) for a detailed description and pictures of the company's 1936 version of Lope de Vega's *Fuente Ovejuna* which point to the contributions of Barbara Niven, fellow artist Ernest Brooks and even L. S. Lowry. It is an example of early Theatre Workshop's commitment to producing visual sets (2006, pp. 24–6).

3. For further information about the connections between Eliot, Yeats, Granville-Barker, Craig and the Cambridge Ritualists, see Taxidou's *Modernism and Performance: Jarry to Brecht* (2007), pp. 150–62.

4. There are a number of moments when the British theatrical avant-garde and the ancient traditions of the Mummers seem to connect. Auden and Isherwood's *Paid on Both Sides* (1928), for example, is grounded in a distinct Mummers tradition, while Theatre Workshop clamed the Mummers as an influence early on, maintaining that, 'almost without knowing it we stumbled upon a form which wasn't really so different from that of the old Mumming plays' (MacColl 1973, p. 58). While this impacted set choices, the influence of Mummers can be seen even more clearly in the characters that populate the stage. Interestingly for the argument here,

Cambridge Ritualist Francis Cornford points to a number of connections between the British Mummers tradition and the ancient Hellenic stage, particularly through dance and stock characterisation (Cornford 1934, pp. 61, 147).

5. See Samuel, MacColl and Cosgrove for a number of examples of political speeches as performative events; in particular, the funeral speech for Keir Hardie given by Ramsey MacDonald in 1916 (1985, pp. 4–7).

6. While Dorn's quotation is extremely useful as a way of creating a definable movement of pre-avant garde innovators, it should be acknowledged that these figures had very different intentions and aesthetic projects. For example, Poel wanted a return to a pre-naturalistic Elizabethan stage. Craig, by contrast, was looking for a contemporary method.

7. Terence Gray had a good number of dealings with the Lord Chamberlain's office over the years. Shellard and Nicholson suggest that 'Toller's *Hoppla!*, Wilde's *Salome*, Strindberg's *Miss Julie*, Tretiakov's *Roar China!* and Lenormand's *Man and His Phantoms* were among the plays which Gray was prevented from staging in Cambridge' (2004, p. 106).

8. MacColl suggests that this play was adapted from a fairly unimaginative WTM play called *Hammer* (Goorney and MacColl 1986, p. xxxv). However, Len Jones, in a 1974 paper 'The Worker's Theatre in the Thirties', mentions a play entitled *Slickers Ltd*, written in October 1935 by a certain John Hammer. His description of the play is extremely similar to the narrative of *John Bullion* (1974, p. 278).

9. It must be remembered, of course, that there were a number of different 'Gordon Craigs'. Most likely, MacColl's 'Gordon Craig' was taken from the pages of *On the Art of Theatre*.

10. This was a story taken up by MacColl in this British context. He suggests that 'both Joan and I had read Hasek's [sic] novel some years before [the Theatre Workshop production of Hašek's story] and had fallen in love with it' (Goorney and MacColl 1986, p. xlii). He wrote his own theatrical version of this novel in 1938.

11. Norman Marshall wrote the preface for the later 1928 version. I suggest that this is largely due to Dean's focus on amateur theatre in his introduction. The later publication illustrates Ridge's desire to move towards a more professional theatre.

12. It must be noted at this stage that Spender's play was not uniformly accepted by the audience. In fact, many Unity Theatre members rejected it 'for what they considered to be his liberal retreat into symbolism and mysticism' (Chambers 1989, p. 147). Chambers goes on to suggest, 'it seems to have been a clash of temperament and style of work as well as a clash of politics' (ibid.). It is a prime example of the differences between companies and the potential friction they could cause, as well as a stark confirmation of the contrasts between various groups of the British avant-garde. However, in the Unity Theatre weekly bulletin of 9 February 1938, the excitement about this collaboration was palpable: 'the importance of this [production] can be gauged from the fact that this will be

the first professional group of actors to perform in our Workers' Theatre' (Unity, 1936–1940). Certainly there were tensions, but this piece still remains an important example of a fruitful artistic dialogue.

13. This motif is just as obvious in the prose and poetic writing outside the theatre. See Chapter 4, 'In the Cages', in Valentine Cunningham's *British Writers of the Thirties* (1989).

14. *Machinal* was performed in London as *The Life Machine* in 1931. It was not performed under its original title in Britain until 1993 when Fiona Shaw took the lead role at the Royal National Theatre. See the introduction to Nick Hern's 2003 version of the play.

15. It must be noted that Toller was dissatisfied with Piscator's designs, 'feeling that the technical effects had often eclipsed the play itself' (Dove 1993, p. 169).

16. This play is of real importance in a British context as it was performed by the 'Masses Stage and Film Guild' in 1930 (Samuel, MacColl and Cosgrove 1985, p. 22). It is also a likely influence for Ewan MacColl's *The Other Animals* (Leach 2006, p. 52).

17. Eugene O'Neill, too, was an important playwright for the British avant-garde. Seemingly the first British production of *The Hairy Ape* was performed at the Festival Theatre, Cambridge, in 1928 (Cornwall 2004, p. 162). His plays were also popular with Unity Theatre and with the various WTM groups (Samuel, MacColl and Cosgrove 1985, p. 20).

3 Language: Disturbing Words

1. Guthrie is a fascinating connecting character for the British avant-garde. He worked with the Scottish National Theatre Society before moving to the Festival Theatre, Cambridge, where Terence Gray had created one of the foremost experimental companies in Britain. Yet, he also worked closely with Group Theatre, assisting Rupert Doone in the direction of *The Dance of Death* (1933) (Medley 1983, p. 135). Furthermore, he supported Unity Theatre as a member of the company's 1937 Management Committee (Chambers 1989, p. 107).

2. This was an extremely long project lasting most of the 1950s until the publication of the unfinished manuscript in *Plays: 11* in 1959 (Brecht 2001, p. 265).

3. Komisarjevsky trained in Russia and moved to England in 1919 (Hartnoll 1968, p. 444).

4. As well as Shakespeare, there are references to a number of other figures of this period in the companies' play lists. Ben Jonson's satirical approach was particularly popular in Theatre Workshop with performances of *The Alchemist* (1953) and *Volpone* (1955). MacColl also based his play, *Hell is What You Make It* (performed in 1950 at Unity Theatre) on Ben Jonson's *The Devil is as Ass*. Furthermore, at the Maddermarket Theatre in Norwich, Nugent Monck had created 'the only Elizabethan playhouse in Britain' (Dukes 1942, p. 79). As well as running the influential Maddermarket,

Monck directed Group Theatre's 1935 version of *Timon of Athens* (Sidnell 1984, p. 286).

5. Just as with the growth in film, there are myriad links between the British theatrical avant-garde and radio work. An exemplary figure would be the BBC producer, John Pudney. Pudney produced the 1937 *Hadrian's Wall*, for which Auden wrote the text while Benjamin Britten was commissioned to write the incidental music (Auden 1988b, p. 675). Pudney also worked with MacColl on *The Chartists March* (also 1937), for which, despite some artistic differences, Britten wrote the score (Harker 2007, pp. 53–4). Radio later became a central medium for MacColl who, along with Peggy Seeger and Charles Parker, created the influential 1960s *Radio Ballads*.

6. Although Lewis's play first appeared in 1914, all citations here are from the published 1932 version, reproduced in Lewis 2003.

7. Patrick McGuiness reflects that 'Maeterlinck's plays abound in repetitions, unfinished sentences, inarticulacies, and unanswered questions [showing the] inadequacy and provisionality of language' (McGuinness 2002, p. 249).

8. There are a number of different endings and there were immediate concerns about this finale as 'during rehearsals the published version of the final scene proved difficult to stage' (Auden 1988, p. 586).

4   Character: The Screaming Man and the Talking Feet

1. Yeats's understanding of Noh theatre rests on this relationship between puppetry and movement: 'the players all wear masks and found their movements upon those of puppets' (Yeats 1961, p. 231).

2. There are a few plays that made some impression in Britain that focused on female experience. Sophie Treadwell's *Machinal* is an obvious example but Toller's *Masses Man* is another play that places a woman, Sonia Irene L., at its centre.

3. In her book, *Poetic Drama*, Glenda Leeming makes another connection between Sorge's play and the British avant-garde, suggesting that 'Sorge, in *The Beggar* (1912), for instance, used tableaux and choral group scenes to make a social comment, and some of these, such as his row of newspaper readers, are very similar to scenes in Auden's *On the Frontier*' (1989, p. 14).

4. Lyndall Gordon suggests, 'the lack of visible action is often seen to be a flaw in Eliot's play, but interior action can be dramatic in its own way. In his 1935 revival Rupert Doone made all the characters projections of Sweeney's mind: they were his bogeys on a darkened stage' (1998, p. 289).

5. Certainly, both did associate themselves with their central characters in other plays. In MacColl's *Landscape with Chimneys,* for example, the character of Ginger is remarkably similar to MacColl himself in terms of his romanticised outlook and political fervour. For Eliot it is the character

of Harry in *The Family Reunion* that seems to most resemble the poet-playwright.

6. It must be recognised that these Auden/Isherwood collaborations often have a number of endings. For further information, see Mendelson's edited edition, *The Complete Works of W. H. Auden: Plays 1928–1938*.

7. In *Theatre Workshop: Joan Littlewood and the Making of Modern British Theatre*, Robert Leach says that the way MacColl encouraged his audience to make sense of the on-stage events was exemplified by his 'use of meta-theatre, derived perhaps from Thornton Wilder … [which helped to] demystify his processes' (2006, p. 73).

8. In another British perspective, Unity Theatre's Jack Lindsay maintained 'from his early days Tzara steadily fought out his poetic positions. From Dada in Zurich till his later poetry he was engaged in a strenuous struggle to understand the place of the poet in the modern world and to find a valid ground on which to base his activity. No other poet of the twentieth century has carried on so consistent, so deepgoing, so passionate a quest; and for this reason I believe that Tzara has a place all his own in the literary history of the first half of that century' (1968, p. 216).

9. Auden and Isherwood had explored this idea in their earlier *Enemies of the Bishop* (1929). In this play the Spectre presents Robert Bicknell with a '*beautiful milliner's wax figure of a woman*' and, adopting a falsetto voice, creates a fabricated image of Julia Stagg (Auden 1988, p. 52). The similarity with the Alan–Miss Vipond relationship is not a coincidence. *The Enemies of the Bishop* was never published and, in many ways, like Auden's 1930 solo effort, *The Fronny*, it feels like an early experiment, preparing the way for plays like *The Dog Beneath the Skin* and *The Ascent of F6* (ibid., pp. xviii–xix).

10. Edwards refers to Radius's speech as a serious impediment to the revolutionary potential of this play. He also maintains that the end is disappointing as there is no real revolutionary model (Samuel, MacColl and Cosgrove 1985, p. 187).

11. Reassessing *R.U.R.*, Kara Reilly has recently read it alongside other earlier examples of automatons in the theatre in her 2011 *Automata and Mimesis on the Stage of Theatre History*.

12. For further information about Theatre Workshop's interest in Spanish theatre, see Gwynne Edwards, 'Theatre Workshop and the Spanish Drama'.

5   Crossing Genres: Movement and Music

1. This is evidently a highly complex idea that Wagner modified and developed during his career. Dieter Borchmeyer even goes as far as saying that 'Wagner's concept of the "total work of art", at least to the extent that it aims to combine *all* the arts, is merely an ideological construct which he soon abandoned and which had no significance in terms of his dramaturgical praxis' (1991, p. 68). However, it has remained a highly influential

position and it would be difficult to make a claim for new dialogues between genres without at least pointing to his theory.

2. For a full explanation of the connections between the Auden generation and Futurism, see Bergonzi's *Reading the Thirties* (1978, p. 90).

3. The body is a key element in avant-garde aesthetics. For further information on the body as a site of modernist discourse, see Taxidou's *Modernism and Performance: Jarry to Brecht* (2007) and Puchner's *Stage Fright: Modernism, Anti-Theatricality and Drama* (2006).

4. This quotation referred specifically to the theme of his choreographed dance *The Night*. After this production Laban concluded that 'I must have succeeded in portraying our time, or else the audience would not have reacted with such indignation' (1975, p. 45).

5. Looking at Newlove's 'Basic Effort Actions' table, the identity of this movement becomes clearer. Thrusting is '*strong/sudden/direct*' while a dabbing is '*light/sudden/direct*' (Newlove 2003, p. 164). So, they are very similar movements albeit with different intensities. The dab-thrust must retain the '*sudden/direct*' characteristic while changing the intensity.

6. Charlie Mann, a leading figure in WTM group Red Players was an admirer of ballet and 'believes he was influenced by it' (Stourac and McCreery 1986, p. 217) and, of course, MacColl termed his play *Uranium 235* a 'nuclear fission ballet' and includes an 'Atom Ballet' scene (Goorney 1981, p. 52). However, neither group was so profoundly influenced by Continental European ballet as Group Theatre.

7. Surely Yeats meant to write of Fuller's *Japanese* dancers here (Garelick 2009, pp. 103–6).

8. I am indebted to Michael Sidnell's *Dances of Death* for the original idea here (1984, p. 74).

9. Jooss worked closely with Laban until 1924 and remained highly influenced by Laban's theories. Indeed in 1938 the dance was set into Labanotation (Jooss 2003, p. 4). Like Laban, Jooss also fled Nazi Germany and, in 1934, reopened the Jooss-Leeder School of Dance in Dartington Hall, Devon (ibid., p. 15). He therefore marks not only another connection with Laban, but also another link with the British historical avant-garde.

10. Diaghilev and the Ballet Russes have obviously had tremendous influence over dance in Britain. While I acknowledge his impact on figures such as Ninette de Valois, founder of Sadler's Wells Ballet; Anton Dolin, who later directed London Festival Ballet; and Alicia Markova, the first British Principal Ballerina, for brevity this monograph focuses only on the instances when Diaghilev's ideas directly impact upon the theatre. These individuals all discuss their opinions of Diaghilev's work in Drummond's *Speaking of Diaghilev*.

11. Modern critiques of primitivism have challenged the movement's innate exoticism of other cultures and the profoundly problematic sexual politics. In fact, similar accusations could be levelled at the plays mentioned in this section.

12. There is the suggestion that Britten took over the Musical Directorship of Group Theatre alongside Brian Easdale in 1937 (Sidnell 1984, p. 179). Medley insists that, although Britten was offered the directorship, he did not take it, preferring not to get involved with the executive (1983, p. 163). Whichever of these readings is correct, it is sufficient to say that Britten was well regarded by the company and played a vital role in a number of productions.

Conclusion: A British Theatrical Avant-Garde?

1. There is, of course, a direct connection between Woolf's novel and the British avant-garde as Miss La Trobe is based on Edith Craig, the director of the Pioneer Players.
2. While it may initially seem odd to begin and end this book with reference to Woolf, traditionally seen as a doyen of high Modernism, recent reinterpretations have placed the Bloomsbury Group within the context of the avant-garde. See Froula's *Virginia Woolf and the Bloomsbury Avant-Garde*. Chapter 9 of Froula's book is devoted to *Between the Acts*, presenting both the novel and the pageant within it as fine examples of an avant-garde aesthetic.
3. For further information about this more modern British avant-garde, see John Bull's *New British Political Dramatists*. Interestingly, rather like this book, Bull discusses the two strands of British alternative theatre: he refers to them as the 'avant-garde' and the 'agit-prop' traditions. Although he presents them as separate, sometimes antagonistic methods, he does suggest that 'it would be misleading to suggest that, in practice, the division has been absolute. The relationship has been symbiotic, the *avant-garde* being increasingly infused with a didactic seriousness as the seventies advanced, and the agit-prop groupings readily borrowing techniques from fringe and alternative theatre' (1984, p. 25). It is fascinating that this idea is just as applicable, if not more so, in the modernist avant-garde I lay out here.
4. For a more detailed study of 'neo-Expressionism', see Gritzner's '(Post)Modern Subjectivity and the New Expressionism'.
5. Sierz's most recent book *Rewriting the Nation* places writers like Martin Crimp, Sarah Kane and Mark Ravenhill in an avant-garde tradition saying, 'in writers such as these, the streams of European absurdism, surrealism and modernism wash through the British theatre' (2011, p. 25). Again, the historical theatrical avant-garde in Britain represents an ongoing absence.

Bibliography

Ackerman, Robert (2002) *The Myth and Ritual School: J. G. Frazer and the Cambridge Ritualists*, London: Routledge.

Ackroyd, Peter (1993) *T. S. Eliot*, London: Penguin.

Adorno, Theodor (1981) *In Search of Wagner*, trans. Rodney Livingstone, London: Verso.

Agate, James (1944) *Red Letter Nights*, London: Jonathan Cape.

Anderson, Alexandra and Carol Saltus (eds) (1984) *Jean Cocteau and the French Scene*, New York: Abbeville.

Andrews, Geoff, Nina Fishman and Kevin Morgan (eds) (1999) *Opening the Books: Essays on the Social and Cultural History of British Communism*, London: Pluto.

Anon (2002) 'Everyman', in G. A. Lester (ed.), *Three Late Medieval Morality Plays*, London: A&C Black.

Anon (1938) 'Living Newspaper: Unity Theatre's Unique Production', Unity Theatre Archive, V&A, THM/9/4/5/6.

Appia, Adolphe (1975) *Work of Living Art and Man is the Measure of All Things*, ed. H. D Albright and Barnard Hewitt, Miami, FL: Miami University Press.

—— (1962) *Music and the Art of Theatre*, ed. Robert W. Corrigan and Mary Douglas Dirks, Miami, FL: Miami University Press.

Aragay, Mireia, Hidegard Klein, Enric Monforte and Pilar Zozaya (eds) (2007) *British Theatre of the 1990s*, Basingstoke: Palgrave Macmillan.

Aristotle (1969) *Poetics*, London: Everyman.

Aronson, Arnold (2000) *American Avant-Garde Theatre*, London: Routledge.

Artaud, Antonin (2010) *Theatre and its Double*, Surrey: Oneworld.

Auden, W. H., (2007) *Collected Poems*, ed. Edward Mendelson, London: Faber & Faber.

—— (2000) *Lectures on Shakespeare*, ed. Arthur Kirsch, Princeton, NJ: Princeton University Press.

—— (1988a) *Paul Bunyan: The Libretto of the Opera by Benjamin Britten*, London: Faber & Faber.

—— (1988b) *The Complete Works of W. H. Auden: Plays 1928–1938*, ed. Edward Mendelson, Princeton, NJ: Princeton University Press.

—— (1986) *The English Auden: Poems, Essays and Dramatic Writings 1927–1939*, ed. Edward Mendelson, London: Faber & Faber.

—— (1979) *Selected Poems*, ed. Edward Mendelson, London: Faber & Faber.

—— (1933) *The Dance of Death*, London: Faber & Faber.

Auden, W. H. and Christopher Isherwood (1968) *The Dog Beneath the Skin*, London: Faber & Faber.

—— (1966) *'The Ascent of F6' and 'On The Frontier'*, London: Faber & Faber.

Badenhausen, Richard (2004) *T. S. Eliot and the Art of Collaboration*, Cambridge: Cambridge University Press.

Baer, Nancy von Norman (1991) *Theatre in Revolution: Russian Avant-Garde Stage Design 1913–1935*, London: Thames & Hudson.

Barker, Clive and Maggie B. Gale (eds) (2000) *British Theatre Between the Wars 1918–1939*, Cambridge: Cambridge University Press.

Baskerville, Stephen and Ralph Willett (eds) (1985) *Nothing to Fear: New Perspectives on America in the Thirties*, Manchester: Manchester University Press.

Behr, Shulamith, David Fanning and Douglas Jarman (1993) *Expressionism Reassessed*, Manchester: Manchester University Press.

Belden, K. D (1965) *The Story of Westminster Theatre*, London: Westminster Productions.

Bengal, Ben (1939) *Plant in the Sun*, Unity Theatre Archive, V&A, THM/9/7/73.

Berghaus, Günter, (2005) *Theatre, Performance and the Historical Avant-Garde*, Basingstoke: Palgrave Macmillan.

Berghaus, Günter (ed.) (2000) *International Futurism in Arts and Literature*, Berlin: de Gruyter.

Bergonzi, Bernard (1978) *Reading the Thirties*, London: Macmillan.

Bertolini, John (1993) *Shaw and other Playwrights*: Volume 13, University Park, PA: Penn State University Press.

Billingham, Peter (2002) *Theatres of Conscience 1939–53*, London: Routledge.

Billington, Michael (2010) 'The great expressionist experiment: Theatre seizes the essence of life', The *Guardian*, 25 November.

—— (2007) *State of the Nation*, London: Faber & Faber.

Bodek, Richard (1997) *Proletarian Performance in Weimar Berlin: Agitprop, Chorus and Brecht*, Columbia: Camden House.

Booth, Michael (1991) *Theatre in the Victorian Age*, Cambridge: Cambridge University Press.

—— (1981) *Victorian Spectacular Theatre: 1850–1910*, London: Routledge & Kegan Paul.

Booth, Michael R. and Joel H. Kaplan (eds) (1996) *The Edwardian Theatre: Essays on Performance and the Stage*, Cambridge: Cambridge University Press.

Borchmeyer, Dieter (1991) *Richard Wagner: Theory and Theatre*, trans. Stewart Spencer, Oxford: Clarendon.

Bradbury, Malcolm and James McFarlane (1991) *Modernism: A Guide to European Literature 1890–1930*, London: Penguin.

Brecht, Bertolt (2003) *Brecht on Art and Politics*, ed. Tom Kuhn and Steve Giles, London: Methuen.

—— (2002) *The Messingkauf Dialogues*, trans. John Willett, London: Methuen.

—— (2001) *Brecht on Theatre: The Development of an Aesthetic*, ed. John Willett, London: Methuen.

—— (1994) *Collected Plays*: 7, ed. John Willett and Ralph Manheim, London: Methuen.

—— (1993) *Journals 1934–1955*, London: Methuen.
—— (1979) *Collected Plays*: 2, part 3, ed. John Willett and Ralph Manheim, London: Methuen.
—— (1956) *The Threepenny Opera*, dir. Sam Wanamaker, Aldwych Theatre, London, 21 March.
Breton, Andrè, (1972) *Manifestoes of Surrealism*, trans. Richard Seaver and Helen R. Lane, Ann Arbor, MI: Michigan University Press.
Brighouse, Harold (1964) *Hobson's Choice*, London: Heinemann.
Brook, Peter (1968) *The Empty Space*, London: MacGibbon & Kee.
Brooker, Peter and Andrew Thacker (eds) (2009) *The Oxford Critical and Cultural History of Modernist Magazines*: Volume 1 *Britain and Ireland 1880–1955*, Oxford: Oxford University Press.
Brown, Terence, (2001) *The Life of W. B. Yeats*, Oxford: Blackwell.
Bru, Sascha (2009) *Democracy, Law and the Modernist Avant-Garde*, Edinburgh: Edinburgh University Press.
Bru, Sascha and Gunther Martens (2006) *The Invention of Politics in the European Avant-Garde (1906–1940)*, New York: Rodopi.
Büchner, Georg (1979) *Woyzeck*, London: Methuen.
Bull, John (1984) *New British Political Dramatists*, London: Macmillan.
Bürger, Peter (1999) *Theory of the Avant-Garde*, trans. Michael Shaw, Minneapolis, MN: Minnesota University Press.
Butler, Judith (1999) *Gender Trouble*, London: Routledge.
Calinescu, Matei (1987) *Five Faces of Modernity*, Durham, NC: Duke University Press.
Čapek Brothers (1966) *'R.U.R.' and 'The Insect Play'*, Oxford: Oxford University Press.
Čapek, Karel (2004) *Letters from England*, London: Continuum.
Carter, Huntly (1929) *A New Spirit in the Russian Theatre 1917–28*, London: Brentano's.
—— (1925) *The New Spirit in the European Theatre 1914–1924: A Comparative Study of the Changes Effected by War and Revolution*, London: Ernst Benn.
—— (1914) *The Theatre of Max Reinhardt*, London: Frank and Cecil Palmer.
Cass, Eddie and Steve Roud (2002) *An Introduction to the English Mummers' Play*, London: English Folk Dance and Song Society.
Chambers, Colin (1989) *The Story of Unity Theatre*, London: Lawrence & Wishart.
Chlumberg, Hans (1932) *Miracle at Verdun*, London: Victor Gollancz.
Christie, Ian and Richard Taylor (eds) (1993) *Eisenstein Rediscovered*, London: Routledge.
Clayton, J. Douglas (1993) *Pierrot in Petrograd: The Commedia dell'Arte/Balagan in Twentieth-Century Russian Theatre and Drama*, Montreal: McGill – Queens University Press.
Clurman, Harold (1957) *The Fervent Years: The Story of Group Theatre and the Thirties*, New York: Hill & Wang.
Cockin, Katharine (2001) *Women and Theatre in the Age of Suffrage: The Pioneer Players, 1911–1925*, Basingstoke: Palgrave Macmillan.

Cocteau, Jean (1963) *The Infernal Machine and Other Plays*, New York: New Directions.

Comentale, Edward (2004) *Modernism, Cultural Production and the British Avant-Garde*, Cambridge: Cambridge University Press.

Cooper, John Xiros (ed.) (2000) *T. S. Eliot's Orchestra: Critical Essays on Poetry and Music*, New York: Garland.

Copeau, Jacques, (1990) *Texts on Theatre*, ed. John Rudlin and Norman H. Paul, London: Routledge.

Cornford, Francis MacDonald (1934) *The Origin of Attic Comedy*, Cambridge: Cambridge University Press.

Cornwall, Peter (2004) *Only by Failure: The Many Faces of the Impossible Life of Terence Gray*, Cambridge: Salt.

Corrie, Joe (1985) *Plays, Poems and Theatre Writings*, ed. Linda MacKenney, Edinburgh: 7:84 Publications.

Craig, Edward Gordon (1983) *Craig on Theatre*, ed. J. Michael Walton, London: Methuen.

Croft, Andy (2003) *Comrade Heart: A Life of Randall Swingler*, Manchester: Manchester University Press.

Crosland, Margaret (1955) *Jean Cocteau*, London: Peter Nevill.

Cunningham, Valentine (1989) *British Writers of the Thirties*, Oxford: Oxford University Press.

Dalcroze, Emile-Jacques (1917) *The Eurythmics of Jacques-Dalcroze*, London: Constable.

Davidson, John (n.d.) *Four Proletarian Dialogues, Labour History Archive*, John Rylands Library Manchester 372.4.

Davies, Andrew (1987) *Other Theatres: The Development of Alternative and Experimental Theatre in Britain*, Basingstoke: Palgrave Macmillan.

Davies, Andrew and Steven Fielding (eds) (1992) *Workers Worlds: Cultures and Communities in Manchester and Salford, 1880–1939*, Manchester: Manchester University Press.

Davis, Tracy C. (2000) *Economics of the British Stage 1800–1914*, Cambridge: Cambridge University Press.

Dawson, Gary Fisher (1999) *Documentary Theatre in the United States: An Historical Survey and Analysis of its Content, Form and Stagecraft*, Westport, CT: Greenwood.

Dawson, Jerry (1985) *Left Theatre: Merseyside Unity Theatre: A Documentary Record*, Liverpool: Merseyside Writers.

Dean, Basil (1948) 'Letters from Maurice Maeterlinck', Basil Dean Archive, John Rylands Library, 2/7/12–2/7/27.

—— (1938) 'Letters to and from Benjamin Britten', Basil Dean Archive, John Rylands Library, 2/37/11. 2/37/60–2/37/64.

—— (1928) 'Letters to and from Terence Gray', Basil Dean Archive, John Rylands Library, 2/32/141–2/32/146, 2/32/494–2/32/498.

—— (c.1926) 'Address to the English Playgoers Club', Basil Dean Archive, John Rylands Library, 12/1/28.

—— (c.1926) 'The Machine Artists: Notes on a recent visit to the Russian Theatre', Basil Dean Archive, John Rylands Library, 12/1/35.

—— (1926) 'Roast Beef and Caviare: Reflections upon the Theatre in England and Russia', in *The Soviet Union Monthly*, pp. 90–1.

—— (1925) 'Foreword' from Harold Ridge, *Stage Lighting for Little Theatres*, Basil Dean Archive, John Rylands Library, 12/1/26.

—— (1923) '*R.U.R.* by Karel Čapek', John Rylands Library, 2/57/1–2.

Dean, Basil and Louis MacNeice (1943) *Salute to the Red Army*, Basil Dean Archive, John Rylands Library 5/4/2.

Delap, Lucy (2007) *The Feminist Avant-Garde: Trans-Atlantic Encounters of the Early Twentieth Century*, Cambridge: Cambridge University Press.

Donald, James, Anne Friedberg and Laura Marcus (eds) (1998) *Close Up 1927–1933: Cinema and Modernism*, London: Cassell.

Donaldson, Ian (ed.) (1983) *Transformations in Modern Drama*, Canberra: Australian National University.

Dorn, Karen (1984) *Players and the Painted Stage*, Sussex: Harvester.

Dove, Richard (1993) *He Was a German: A Biography of Ernst Toller*, London: Libris.

Drama Societies (1938) 'English Parallel to U.S. Stage Experiments', 26 April, Unity Theatre Archive, V&A, THM/9/4/5/6.

Drummond, John (1998) *Speaking of Diaghilev*, London: Faber & Faber.

Dukes, Ashley (1942) *The Scene is Changed*, London: Macmillan.

Dunne, J. W. (1981) *An Experiment with Time*, London: Macmillan.

Eagleton, Terry (1986) *William Shakespeare*, Oxford: Basil Blackwell.

Edwards, Gwynne (2007) 'Theatre Workshop and the Spanish Drama', *New Theatre Quarterly* 23 (November), pp. 304–16.

Edwards, Ness (1930) *The Workers' Theatre*, Caerdydd: Cymric Federation.

Eliot, T. S. (1969) *The Complete Poems and Plays*, London: Faber & Faber.

—— (1966) *Selected Essays*, London: Faber & Faber.

—— (1951) *Poetry and Drama*, London: Faber & Faber.

—— (1928) 'Dialogue on Poetic Drama', in *John Dryden, Of Dramatick Poesie*, London: Frederick Etchells and Hugh MacDonald.

Esslin, Martin (1984) *Brecht: A Choice of Evils*, London: Methuen.

Evans, John (ed.) (2009) *Journeying By: The Diaries of the Young Benjamin Britten 1928–1938*, London: Faber & Faber.

Evelein, Johannes (ed.) (2009) *Exiles Travelling: Exploring Displacement, Crossing Boundaries in German Exile Arts and Writings 1933–1945*, Amsterdam: Rodopi.

Evreinov, Nikolai (1915) *The Theatre of the Soul*, London: Hendersons.

Findley, Bill (2008) *Scottish People's Theatre: Plays by Glasgow Unity Writers*, Glasgow: ASLS.

Fischer-Lichte, Erika (2008) *The Transformative Power of Performance: A New Aesthetics*, London: Routledge.

Flannery, James W. (1976) *W. B. Yeats and the Idea of a Theatre*, New Haven, CT: Yale University Press.

Fletcher, Anne (2009) *Rediscovering Mordecai Gorelik: Scene Design and the American Theatre*, Carbondale, IL: Southern Illinois University Press.

Forsyth, Alison and Chris Megson (eds) (2009) *Get Real: Documentary Theatre Past and Present*, Basingstoke: Palgrave Macmillan.

Frattarola, Angela (2009) 'The Modernist "Microphone Play"', *Modern Drama* 52:1 (Winter), pp. 449–68.

Freshwater, Helen (2009) *Theatre Censorship in Britain: Silencing, Censure and Suppression*, Basingstoke: Palgrave Macmillan.

Freud, Sigmund (1991) *Introductory Lectures on Psychoanalysis*, trans. James Strachey, London: Penguin.

—— (1960) 'Psychopathic Characters on the Stage', *The Tulane Drama Review* 4:3 (March), pp. 144–8.

Froula, Christina (2005) *Virginia Woolf and the Bloomsbury Avant-Garde*, New York: Columbia University Press.

Fuchs, Elinor (1996) *The Death of Character: Perspectives on Theater after Modernism*, Bloomington, IN: Indiana University Press.

Gale, Maggie (2008) *J. B. Priestley*, London: Routledge.

Galsworthy, John (1999) *Five Plays*, London: Methuen.

Garafola, Lynn (1989) *Diaghilev's Ballets Russes*, Oxford: Oxford University Press.

Garelick, Rhonda (2009) *Electric Salome: Loie Fuller's Performance of Modernism*, Princeton, NJ: Princeton University Press.

Garten, H. F. (1959) *Modern German Drama*, London: Methuen.

Gasset. Ortega Y. (1948) *The Dehumanization of Art and Notes on the Novel*, trans. Helene Weyl, Princeton, NJ: Princeton University Press.

Gay, John (1986) *The Beggar's Opera*, London: Penguin.

Gladkov, Aleksandr (1997) *Meyerhold Speaks, Meyerhold Rehearses*, ed. Alma Law, Amsterdam: Overseas Publishers Association.

Goorney, Howard (1981) *The Theatre Workshop Story*, London: Eyre Methuen.

Goorney, Howard, and Ewan MacColl (1986) *Agit-Prop to Theatre Workshop: Political Playscripts 1930–50*, Manchester: Manchester University Press.

Gordon, Lyndall (1998) *T. S. Eliot: An Imperfect Life*, London: Vintage.

Gordon, Mel (1975) 'German Expressionist Acting', *Drama Review* 19:3 (September), pp. 34–46.

—— (1974) 'Meyerhold's Biomechanics', *Drama Review* 18.3 (September), pp. 73–88.

Gorelik, Mordecai (1947) *New Theatres for Old*, London: Dennis Dobson.

Grant, Michael (ed.) (1982) *T. S. Eliot: The Critical Heritage*, London: Routledge.

Granville-Barker, Harley (1994) *The Collected Plays*: Volume 2, London: Methuen.

—— (1993) *The Collected Plays*: Volume 1, London: Methuen.

—— (1931) *On Dramatic Method*, London: Sidgwick & Jackson.

Gray, Terence (1926) *Dance-Drama: Experiments in the Art of Theatre*, Cambridge: Heffer & Sons.

Greenwood, Walter (1966) 'Love on the Dole', in *Plays of the Thirties*: Volume 1, London: Pan.

Gritzner, Karoline (2008) '(Post)Modern Subjectivity and the New Expressionism', *Contemporary Theatre Review* 18:3, pp. 328–40.

Groys, Boris (1992) *The Total Art of Stalinism: Avant-Garde, Aesthetic, Dictatorship and Beyond*, Princeton, NJ: Princeton University Press.

Guthrie, Tyrone (1961) *A Life in Theatre*, London: Hamish Hamilton.

Haffenden, John (ed.) (1983) *W. H. Auden: The Critical Heritage*, London: Routledge.

Harding, James (ed.) (2000) *Contours of the Theatrical Avant-Garde: Performance and Textuality*, Ann Arbor, MI: Michigan University Press.

Harding, James and John Rouse (2006) *Not the Other Avant-Garde: The Transnational Foundations of Avant-Garde Performance*, Ann Arbor, MI: Michigan University Press.

Harker, Ben (2007) *Class Act: The Cultural and Political Life of Ewan MacColl*, London: Pluto.

Harrison, Jane (1927) *Themis: A Study of the Social Origins of Greek Religion*, Cambridge: Cambridge University Press.

Hartnoll, Phyllis (1968) *A Concise History of the Theatre*, London: Thames & Hudson.

Hauptmann, Gerhart (1980) *The Weavers*, trans. Frank Marcus, London: Methuen.

Helm, Alex (1981) *The English Mummer's Play*, Woodbridge, Suffolk: Folklore Society, Boydell & Brewer.

Hickey, William (1938) 'Busmen', 25 April, Unity Theatre Archive, V&A THM/9/4/5/6.

Hill, John (n.d.) 'Towards a Scottish Peoples' Theatre: The Rise and Fall of Glasgow Unity', Unity Theatre Archive, V&A, THM/9/6/1/2.

Hodge, Alison (ed.) (1999) *Twentieth Century Actor Training*, London: Routledge.

Hodge, Herbert (1936/7) *Cannibal Carnival*, Unity Theatre Archive, V&A, THM/9/7/26.

Hoffman, Edith (1947) *Kokoschka: Life and Work*, London: Faber & Faber.

Hoggart, Richard (1960 [1957]) *The Uses of Literacy*, London: Penguin.

Holdsworth, Nadine (2006) *Joan Littlewood*, London: Routledge.

Houghton, Stanley (2009) *Hindle Wakes: A Play in Three Acts*, London: BiblioBazaar.

Howarth, Herbert (1965) *Notes on Some Figures Behind T. S. Eliot*, London: Chatto & Windus.

Huelsenbeck, Richard (1969) *Memoirs of a Dada Drummer*, ed. Hans J. Kleinschmidt and Joachim Neugroschel, New York: Viking Press.

Hughes, Glen (1972) *Imagism and the Imagists*, New York: Biblo & Tannen.

Hynes, Samuel (1976) *The Auden Generation: Literature and Politics in England in the 1930s*, London: Bodly Head.

Innes, Christopher (1998) *Edward Gordon Craig: A Vision of Theatre*, London: Routledge.

—— (1993) *Avant Garde Theatre: 1892–1992*, London: Routledge.

—— (1972) *Erwin Piscator's Political Theatre: The Development of Modern German Drama*, Cambridge: Cambridge University Press.

Ionesco, Eugène (1978) *Rhinoceros*, London: Penguin.

Isherwood, Christopher (1977) *Christopher and His Friends*, London: Eyre Methuen.

Jameson, Frederic (ed.) (2007) *Aesthetics and Politics*, London: Verso.

Jarry, Alfred (1965) *Selected Works*, London: Eyre Methuen.

Jones, Len (1974) 'The Workers' Theatre in the Thirties', *Marxism Today* 18:9 (September), pp. 271–8.

Jooss, Kurt (2003) *The Green Table: The Labanotion Score, Text, Photographs and Music*, ed. Anna Markard and Ann Hutchinson Guest, London: Routledge.

Kandinsky, Wassily and Franz Marc (eds) (1974) *The 'Blaue Reiter' Almanac*, ed. Klaus Lankheit, London: Thames & Hudson.

Kantor, Tadeusz (1993) *A Journey through Other Spaces: Essays and Manifestos, 1944–1990*, ed. Michael Kobialka, Berkeley, CA: California University Press.

Keegan, Susanne (1999) *The Eye of God: A Life of Oskar Kokoschka*, London: Bloomsbury.

Kermode, Frank (1957) *Romantic Image*, London: Routledge & Kegan Paul.

Kershaw, Baz (1992) *The Politics of Performance: Radical Theatre as Cultural Intervention*, London: Routledge.

Kift, Dagmar (1996) *The Victorian Music Hall: Class, Culture and Conflict*, trans. Roy Kift, Cambridge: Cambridge University Press.

Kleberg, Lars (1993) *Theatre as Action: Soviet Russian Avant-Garde Aesthetics*, trans. Charles Rougle, London: Macmillan.

Kolocotroni, Vassiliki, Jane Goldman and Olga Taxidou (eds) (1998) *Modernism: An Anthology of Sources and Documents*, Edinburgh: Edinburgh University Press.

Krause, David (ed.) (1975) *The Letters of Sean O'Casey*: Volume 1, *1910–1941*, London: Cassell.

Laban, Rudolf (1975) *A Life for Dance*, trans. Lisa Ullmann, London: MacDonald & Evans.

—— (1971) *The Mastery of Movement*, London: MacDonald & Evans.

—— (1966) *Choreutics*, ed. Lisa Ullmann, London: MacDonald & Evans.

Lamont Stewart, Ena (1983) *Men Should Weep*, London: Samuel French.

Law, Alma, (1982) 'Meyerhold's "The Magnanimous Cuckold"', *Drama Review* 26:1 (Spring), pp. 61–86.

Law, Alma and Mel Gordon (1996) *Meyerhold, Eisenstein and Biomechanics: Actor Training in Revolutionary Russia*, North Carolina: McFarland.

Lawrence, D. H. (1965) *Complete Plays*, London: Heinemann.

Leach, Robert (2006) *Theatre Workshop: Joan Littlewood and the Making of Modern British Theatre*, Exeter: Exeter University Press.

—— (1994) *Revolutionary Theatre*, London: Routledge.

Leeming, Glenda (1989) *Poetic Drama*, London: Macmillan.

Levitas, Ben (2002) *The Theatre of Nation: Irish Drama and Cultural Nationalism 1890–1916*, Oxford: Oxford University Press.

Lewis, Wyndham (2003) *Collected Poems and Plays*, London: Routledge.

—— (1975) *Enemy Salvoes*, ed. C. J. Fox, London: Vision.

Lewis, Wyndham (ed.) (1914) *BLAST*, London: John Lane.

Liedman, Sven-Eric (1999) 'Sweden and Victorian Britain', *The European Legacy: Toward New Paradigms* (December), pp. 72–84.

Lindsay, Jack (1968*) Meetings with Poets*, London: Frederick Muller.

—— (1939) *England, My England*, London: Fore.

—— (1937) *On Guard for Spain*, Unity Theatre Archive, V&A, THM/9/7/44.

Littlewood, Joan (2003) *Joan's Book: The Autobiography of Joan Littlewood*, London: Methuen.

Lodder, Christina (1990) *Russian Constructivism*, New Haven, CT: Yale University Press.

Lorca, Federico García (1970) *Five Plays*, London: Faber & Faber.

MacColl, Ewan (1990) *Journeyman*, London: Sidgwick & Jackson.

—— (1973) 'The Grassroots of Theatre Workshop', *Theatre Quarterly* 3:9 (January–March), pp. 58–68.

—— (1951) *Landscape with Chimneys*, Ewan MacColl and Peggy Seeger Archive, Ruskin College Oxford.

—— (1950) *Hell is What You Make It*, 7:84 Scotland Archive, National Library of Scotland, ACC 10893/216.

—— (1945) *The Flying Doctor*, 7:84, Scotland Archive, National Library of Scotland, ACC10893/214.

—— (*c*.1940) *The Damnable Town*, Ewan MacColl and Peggy Seeger Archive, Ruskin College Oxford.

MacNeice, Louis (1944) *Christopher Columbus: A Radio Play*, London: Faber & Faber.

—— (1937) *Out of the Picture*, London: Faber & Faber.

—— (1936) *The Agamemnon of Aeschylus*, London: Faber & Faber.

Maeterlinck, Maurice (1912) *The Intruder*, New York: Dodd, Mead.

Maleczech, Ruth (2010) American Society for Theatre Research Conference, Seattle.

Marcus, Laura (2007) *The Tenth Muse: Writing about Cinema in the Modernist Period*, Oxford: Oxford University Press.

Marinetti, F. T. (2008) *Critical Writings*, ed. Günter Berghaus, Basingstoke: Palgrave Macmillan.

—— (1972) *Selected Writings*, trans. R. W. Flint and Arthur Cappotelli, London: Secker & Warburg.

Marshall, Norman (1975) *The Producer and the Play*, London: Davis-Poynter.

Marshall, Vance, (1938) *A.R.P.*, 2nd draft with revisions, Unity Theatre Archive, V&A, THM/9/7/11.

Marx, Karl and Friedrich Engels (1987) *The Communist Manifesto*, Harmondsworth: Penguin.

Mayakovsky, Vladimir (1995) *Plays*, trans. Guy Daniels, Evanston, IL: Northwestern University Press.

McDonald, Jan (1986) *The 'New Drama' 1900–1914*, London: Macmillan.

McGrath, John (2002) *Naked Thoughts That Roam About*, London: Nick Hern.

—— (1996) *A Good Night Out: Popular Theatre, Audience, Class and Form*, London: Nick Hern.

—— (1981) *The Cheviot, the Stag and the Black, Black Oil*, London: Eyre Methuen.

McGuinness, Patrick (2002) *Maurice Maeterlinck and the Making of Modern Theatre*, Oxford: Oxford University Press.

Medley, Robert (1983) *Drawn from a Life*, London: Faber & Faber.

—— (1966) *Rupert Doone Remembered*, London: n.p.

Melvin, Murray (2006) *The Art of Theatre Workshop*, London: Oberon.

Melzer, Annabelle (1994) *Dada and Surrealist Performance*, Baltimore, MD: Johns Hopkins University Press.

Mester, Terri A. (1997) *Movement and Modernism*, Fayetteville, AR: Arkansas University Press.

Mitchell, Donald (2000) *Britten and Auden in the Thirties*, Woodbridge: Boydell.

Mitchell, Donald and Hans Keller (eds) (1952) *Benjamin Britten: A Commentary on his Works from a Group of Specialists*, London: Rockliff.

Mitchell, Donald and Philip Reed (eds) (1998) *Letters from a Life*, Volume 1, London: Faber & Faber.

Morley, Sheridan (1977) *Sybil Thorndike: A Life in Theatre*, London: Weidenfeld & Nicholson.

Moussinac, Léon (1931) *The New Movement in Theatre*, New York: B. Blom.

Murphy, Richard (1999) *Theorizing the Avant-Garde: Modernism, Expressionism and the Problem of Postmodernity*, Cambridge: Cambridge University Press.

Murchie, Guy (1981) *The Seven Mysteries of life: An Exploration in Science and Philosophy*, Orlando, FL: Houghton Mifflin Harcourt.

Newlove, Jean (2003) *Laban for All*, London: Nick Hern.

—— (1993) *Laban for Actors and Dancers*, London: Routledge.

Nicolson, Steve (1999) *British Theatre and the Red Peril: The Portrayal of Communism 1917–1945*, Exeter: Exeter University Press.

O'Casey, Sean (1985) *Seven Plays*, London: Macmillan.

—— (1981) *Autobiographies 2*, London: Macmillan.

—— (1950) *Collected Plays*: Volume 2, London: Macmillan.

O'Connor, John and Lorraine Brown (eds) (1980) *The Federal Theatre Project: Free, Adult, Uncensored*, London: Eyre Methuen.

O'Neill, Eugene (1971) *Penguin Collected Plays*, ed. Martin Browne, Penguin: Middlesex.

Obey, André (1965) *Noah*, trans. Arthur Wilmurt, London: Heinemann.

Odets, Clifford (1979) *Six Plays*, New York: Grove Publishing.

Orr, Mary, and Michael O'Rourke (1985) *Parsley, Sage and Politics: The Lives of Peggy Seeger and Ewan MacColl*, taped interviews.

Osborne, John, (1978) *Look Back in Anger*, London: Faber & Faber.

Osbourne, Charles (1980) *W. H. Auden: The Life of a Poet*, London: Eyre Methuen.

Osbourne, Peter (1996) *Politics of Time: Modernity and Avant-Garde*, London: Verso.

Paget, Derek (1995) 'Theatre Workshop, Moussinac and the European Connection', *New Theatre Quarterly* 11:43, pp. 211–24.

—— (1993) 'Oh What a Lovely War: The Texts and Their Context', *New Theatre Quarterly* 6:23, pp. 244–60.

—— (1990) *True Stories? Documentary Drama on Radio, Screen and Stage*, Manchester: Manchester University Press.

Peacock, Keith D (2007) *Changing Performance: Culture and Performance in the British Theatre since 1945*, London: Peter Lang.

Peppis, Paul (2000) *Literature, Politics and the English Avant-Garde*, Cambridge: Cambridge University Press.

Perdigao, Lisa and Mark Pizzato (2010) *Death in American Texts and Performances*, London: Ashgate.

Piper, John (1955) *Paintings, Drawings and Theatre Designs 1932–1954*, London: Faber & Faber.

Piscator, Erwin (1980) *The Political Theatre*, trans. Hugh Rorrison, London: Eyre Methuen.

Poggioli, Renato (1968) *The Theory of the Avant-Garde*, Cambridge, MA: Harvard University Press.

Pogson, Rex (1952) *Miss Hornimann and the Gaiety Theatre Manchester*, London: Rockliff.

Preston-Dunlop, Valerie (1998) *Rudolf Laban: An Extraordinary Life*, London: Dance Books.

—— (1969) *Practical Kinetography Laban*, London: MacDonald & Evans.

Priestley, J. B. (1987) *Time and the Conways and Other Plays*, London: Penguin.

—— (1975) *Particular Pleasures*, London: Heinemann.

—— (1964) *Man and Time*, London: Aldus.

—— (1939) *Johnson Over Jordan*, prompt copy, Basil Dean archive, John Rylands Library.

Puchner, Martin (2006) *Poetry of the Revolution: Marx, Manifestos, and the Avant-Gardes*, Princeton, NJ: Princeton University Press.

—— (2002) *Stage Fright: Modernism, Anti-Theatricality and Drama*, Baltimore, MD: Johns Hopkins University Press.

Rainey, Lawrence (2005) *Modernism: An Anthology*, Oxford: Blackwell.

Rambert, Marie (1972) *Quicksilver*, London: Macmillan.

Rees, Roland (1992) *Fringe First: Pioneers of Fringe Theatre on the Record*, London: Oberon.

Reilly, Kara (2011) *Automata and Mimesis on the Stage of Theatre History*, Basingstoke: Palgrave Macmillan.

Reinelt, Janelle (1994) *After Brecht: British Epic Theater*, Ann Arbor, MI: Michigan University Press.

Remy, Michel (1999) *Surrealism in Britain*, Aldershot: Ashgate.

Rice, Elmer (1997) *Three Plays*, New York: Hill & Wang.

Ridge, C. Harold and F. S. Aldred (1935) *Stage Lighting: Principles and Practice*, London: Pitman.

Ritchie, J. M. (1976) *German Expressionist Drama*, Boston, MA: Twayne.

Ritchie, J. M., and H. F. Garten (eds) (1968) *Seven Expressionist Plays: Kokoschka to Barlach*, London: John Calder.

Roose-Evans, James (1989) *Experimental Theatre: From Stanislavsky to Peter Brook*, London: Routledge.

Russell, Ian, and David Atkinson (2004) *Folk Song: Tradition, Revival and Re-Creation*, Elphinstone Institute: University of Aberdeen.

Saint-Simon, Henri Comte de (1952) *Selected Writings*, ed. F. M. H. Markham, Oxford: Blackwell.

Saler, Michael (1999) *The Avant-Garde in Interwar England*, Oxford: Oxford University Press.

Samuel, Raphael, Ewan MacColl and Stuart Cosgrove (1985) *Theatres of the Left 1880–1935: Workers' Theatre Movements in Britain and America*, London: Routledge & Kegan Paul.

Saussure, Ferdinand de (1983) *Course in General Linguistics*, London: Duckworth.

Scheunemann, Dietrich (ed.) (2005) *Avant Garde/Neo-Avant-Garde*, New York: Rodopi.

—— (2000) *European Avant-Garde New Perspectives*, Amsterdam: Rodopi.

Schmidt, Paul, Ilya Levin and Vern McGee (1996) *Meyerhold at Work*, New York: Applause.

Schofield, Stephen (1927) *The Judge of All the Earth*, London: Labour Publishing Company.

Schumacher, Claude (ed.) (1996) *Naturalism and Symbolism in European Theatre 1850–1918*, Cambridge: Cambridge University Press.

Scullion, Adrienne (2002) 'Glasgow Unity Theatre', *20th Century British History* 13:3, pp. 215–52.

Segal, Harold B. (1995) *Pinocchio's Progeny: Puppets, Marionettes, Automatons and Robots in Modernist and Avant-Garde Drama*, Baltimore, MD: Johns Hopkins University Press.

Sell, Mike (ed.) (2011) *Avant-Garde Performance and Material Exchange: Vectors of the Radical*, Basingstoke: Palgrave Macmillan.

Shakespeare, William (1967) *Macbeth*, London: Penguin.

Shaw, Irwin (1936) *Bury the Dead*, New York: Dramatists Play Service.

Shellard, Dominic (1999) *British Theatre since the War*, New Haven, CT:Yale University Press.

Shellard, Dominic and Steve Nicholson with Miriam Handley (2004) *The Lord Chamberlain Regrets …: A History of British Theatre Censorship*, London: British Library.

Sidnell, Michael (1984) *Dances of Death: The Group Theatre of London in the Thirties*, London: Faber & Faber.

Sierz, Aleks (2011) *Rewriting the Nation*, London: Methuen.

—— (2001) *In-Yer-Face Theatre*, London: Faber & Faber.

Simmons, James (1993) *Sean O'Casey*, London: Macmillan.

Simonson, Lee (1932) *The Stage is Set*, New York: Harcourt & Brace.

Sinclair, Upton (1924) *Singing Jailbirds*, California: n.p.

Slater, Montagu (1937) *New Way Wins*, London: Lawrence & Wishart.

Sokel, Walter H. (1959) *The Writer is Extremis: Expressionism in Twentieth-Century German Literature*, Stanford, CA: Stanford University Press.

Sokel, Walter (ed.) (1963) *An Anthology of German Expressionist Drama: A Prelude to the Absurd*, New York: Anchor.

Somigli, Luca (2003) *Legitimizing the Artist: Manifesto Writing and European Modernism, 1885–1915*, Toronto: Toronto University Press.

Southern, Richard (1953) *The Open Stage*, London: Faber & Faber.

Spalding, Frances (2009) *John Piper, Myfanwy Piper: Lives in Art*, Oxford: Oxford University Press.

Spender, Stephen (1985) *Collected Poems 1928–1985*, London: Faber & Faber.

—— (1980) *Letters to Christopher*, ed. Lee Bartlett, Santa Barbara, CA: Black Sparrow.

—— (1978) *The Thirties and After*, London: Macmillan.

—— (1963) *The Struggle of the Modern*, London: Hamish Hamilton.

—— (1938) *Trial of a Judge*, London: Faber & Faber.

Stallworthy, Jon (1995) *Louis MacNeice*, London: Faber & Faber.

Stott, William (1973) *Documentary Expression and Thirties America*, Oxford: Oxford University Press.

Stourac, Richard and Kathleen McCreery (1986) *Theatre as a Weapon: Workers' Theatre in the Soviet Union, Germany and Britain, 1917–1934*, London: Routledge & Kegan Paul.

Strindberg, August (1982) *Plays Two*, trans. Michael Meyer, London: Methuen.

—— (1991) *Plays Three*, trans. Michael Meyer, London: Methuen.

Styan, J. L. (1997) *Modern Drama in Theory and Practice 1: Realism and Naturalism*, Cambridge: Cambridge University Press.

—— (1982) *Max Reinhardt*, Cambridge: Cambridge University Press.

Symons, James M. (1971) *Meyerhold's Theatre of the Grotesque: The Post-Revolutionary Productions, 1920–1932*, Miami, FL: Miami University Press.

Taxidou, Olga (2007) *Modernism and Performance: Jarry to Brecht*, Basingstoke: Palgrave Macmillan.

—— (1998) *The Mask: A Periodical Performance by Edward Gordon Craig*, London: Harwood.

Timms, Edward and Peter Collier (1988) *Visions and Blueprints: Avant-Garde Culture and Radical Politics in Early Twentieth-Century Europe*, Manchester: Manchester University Press.

Thomas, Tom (1936) *The Ragged Trousered Philanthropists*, London: Richards.

Toller, Ernst (2000) *Plays One*, trans. Alan Pearlman, London: Oberon.

—— (1939) *Pastor Hall*, trans. Stephen Spender, London: John Lane.

—— (1936) *Letters from Prison*, trans. R. Ellis Roberts, London: John Lane.

Topic Records (n.d.) 'Pamphlet: The Radio Ballads'.

Treadwell, Sophie (2003) *Machinal*, London: Nick Hern.

Tuckett, Angela (1980) *The People's Theatre in Bristol 1930–45*, Bristol: Bristol Unit Players.

Tzara, Tristan (1977) *Seven Dada Manifestos and Lampisteries*, trans. Barbara Wright, London: Calder.

—— (1921) *The Gas Heart*, Online: http://www.english.emory.edu/DRAMA/TzaraGas.html (accessed 3 August 2010).

Unity Theatre (1984) *Busmen*, Nottingham: Nottingham Drama Texts.

—— (1942–1946) *Newsletters*, Unity Theatre Archive, V&A, THM/9/4/1/2.

—— (1942) *Get Cracking*, Unity Theatre Archive, V&A, THM/9/7/110.

—— (1936–1940) *Newsletters*, Unity Theatre Archive, V&A, THM/9/4/6/1.

—— (1936/7) *The Fall of the House of Slusher*, Unity Theatre Archive, V&A, THM/9/7/100.

Van Druten, John (1954) *I am a Camera*, London: Victor Gollancz.

Varnedoe, Kirk and Adam Gopnik (1991) *High and Low: Modern Art and Popular Culture*, New York: MOMA.

Veitch, Norman (1950) *The People's: Being a History of The People's Theatre, Newcastle upon Tyne 1911–1939*, Gateshead: Northumberland Press.

Volbach, Walter R (1968) *Adolphe Appia: Prophet of the Modern Theatre*, Middletown, CT: Wesleyan University Press.

Wagner, Richard (1970) *Wagner on Music and Drama*, ed. Albert Goldman, Evert Sprinchorn and H. Ashton Ellis, London: Victor Gollancz.

Walker, Julia (2005) *Expressionism and Modernism in the American Theatre*, Cambridge: Cambridge University Press.

Warden, Claire (2007) 'The Shadows and the Rush of Light: Ewan MacColl and Expressionist Drama', *New Theatre Quarterly* 23:4, pp. 317–25.

Watt, David (2003) '"The Maker and The Tool": Charles Parker, Documentary Performance, and the Search for a Popular Culture', *New Theatre Quarterly* 19:1, pp. 41–66.

Webber, Andrew J. (2004) *The European Avant-Garde 1900–1940*, Cambridge: Polity.

Wedekind, Frank (1972) *The Lulu Plays and Six Other Sex Tragedies*, trans. Stephen Spender, London: Calder & Boyars.

Wees, William C. (1972) *Vorticism and the English Avant-Garde*, Manchester: Manchester University Press.

Weisstein, Ulrich (1973) *Expressionism as an International Literary Phenomenon*, Paris: Didier.

Wesker, Arnold (2001) *Plays 1*, London: Methuen.

White, Eric Walter (1983) *Benjamin Britten: His Life and Operas*, London: Faber & Faber.

—— (1973) 'Britten in the Theatre: A Provisional Catalogue', *Tempo* 107, pp. 2–10.

Wilde, Oscar (1998) *The Importance of Being Earnest and Other Plays*, Oxford: Oxford University Press.

Wilder, Thornton (1938) *Our Town*, New York: Coward McGann.

—— (1931) *Pullman Car Hiawatha*, London: Samuel French.

Willett, John (1978) *The Theatre of Erwin Piscator: Half a Century of Politics in the Theatre*, London: Eyre Methuen.

Williams, James S. (2006) *Jean Cocteau*, Manchester: Manchester University Press.

Williams, Raymond (1993) *Drama from Ibsen to Brecht*, London: Hogarth.

—— (1989) *The Politics of Modernism: Against the New Conformists*, London: Verso.

Williams, Tennessee (2000) *A Streetcar Named Desire and Other Plays*, London: Penguin.

Witham, Barry (2003) *The Federal Theatre Project: A Case Study*, Cambridge: Cambridge University Press.

Wood, Paul (ed.) (1999) *The Challenge of the Avant-Garde*, New Haven, CT: Yale University Press.

Woods, Fred (1973a) 'And So We Sang', *Folk Review* (May), pp. 4–7.

—— (1973b) 'And So We Sang', *Folk Review* (July), pp. 4–8.

Woolf, Virginia (1992) *Between the Acts*, Oxford: Oxford University Press.

—— (1982) *The Diary of Virginia Woolf*: Volume 4, *1931–35*, ed. Anne Oliver Bell, London: Penguin.

'Workers' Theatre Movement Monthly Bulletin (1932) December, Unity Theatre Archive, V&A, THM/9/6/2/1.

'Workers' Theatre Movement Monthly Bulletin (1934) March, Unity Theatre Archive, V&A, THM/9/6/2/1.

www.nationalarchives.gov.uk, Ewan MacColl MI5 file KV/2/2175 (accessed 18 May 2007).

Yeats, W. B. (1979) *Selected Plays*, London: Pan.

—— (1961) *Essays and Introductions*, London: Macmillan.

—— (1921) *Four Plays for Dancers*, London: Macmillan.

Index

7:84, 179–80

Adorno, Theodor, 152
Appia, Adolphe, 72–4, 80, 150
Aragon, Louis, 137
Aristotle, 23, 68, 135
Aristotelian, 23–4, 38, 42, 46, 53,
   149
Artaud, Antonin, 110–11
Auden, W.H., 12–13, 15, 36, 43, 75,
   86, 88, 90, 96, 116, 133, 141–2,
   149, 153, 167, 186n, 187n
   The Dance of Death, 2–3, 89, 108,
   118, 132–3, 162–6, 170–2, 190n
   The Fronny, 192n
Auden-Isherwood collaborations:
   The Ascent of F6, 11–14, 30–2, 36,
   45, 91, 101–2, 122, 128, 130,
   140, 155, 171–2, 185n, 192n
   The Dog Beneath the Skin, 44–6, 63,
   96–7, 108, 111–12, 117–19, 120,
   136–8, 145, 181, 187n, 192n
   On the Frontier, 31, 35–8, 45, 80–1,
   91, 103, 133, 169, 181, 191n
   Paid on Both Sides, 188n
   see also Group Theatre
Austen, J.L., 6

Ball, Hugo, 109
   see also Dadaism
Ballets Russes, 151, 162–3, 193n
   connection with Marie Rambert,
   155
   influence on Group Theatre, 19,
   166–8
   see also Cocteau, Jean; Copeau,
   Jacques; Diaghilev, Sergei
Belt and Braces, 180
Bennett, Alan, 13
Biomechanics, 155–6, 159

Theatre Workshop's use of, 157,
   162
   see also Meyerhold, Vsevolod
Bloomsbury, 194n
   connection with Group Theatre,
   93
Blue Blouse, 25, 60–1
Brecht, Bertolt, 3, 53–4, 63, 83, 87,
   165, 100, 152, 172, 174, 181–2,
   187n
   influence on Auden and Group
   Theatre, 2, 43, 183n, 187n
   influence on Ewan MacColl and
   Theatre Workshop, 43–4, 161,
   185n
   influence on Unity, 18, 44, 105,
   141; *The Caucasian Chalk Circle*,
   187n; *The Messingkauf Diaries*,
   42; *Señora Carrar's Rifles*, 44,
   141; *The Seven Deadly Sins of
   the Petty Bourgeoisie*, 45; *The
   Threepenny Opera*, 44, 173
Breton, Andrè, 109
Brighouse, Harold, 23, 48
Britten, Benjamin, 2–3, 118, 184n,
   194n
   The Ascent of F6 (with Auden and
   Isherwood), 171–2
   Coal Face (with Auden and Slater),
   187n
   Hadrian's Wall (with Auden),
   191n
   Johnson Over Jordan (with
   Priestley), 133
   New Way Wins (with Slater), 13
Brook, Peter, 58, 154
Bryher, 42
Büchner, Georg, 78
Bulgakov, Mikhail, 180
Butler, Judith, 6, 59

Cambridge Ritualists, 57, 124, 188n, 189n
Čapek Karel, 139
  R.U.R., 117, 139
Carter, Huntly, 40, 42, 73, 68–9, 155–6
Casson, Lewis, 88
CAST, 180
Chekhov, Anton, 48, 135
  The Cherry Orchard, 148
Chlumberg, Hans,
  Miracle at Verdun, 131–2
Close Up, 41–2
Cocteau, Jean:
  influence on Group Theatre, 162, 167
  The Eiffel Tower Wedding Party, 138–9
Commedia dell'arte, 116, 118, 120, 160
CPGB (Communist Party of Great Britain), 98
Copeau, Jacques, 8, 64, 72, 151–2, 166–7
  influence on Festival Theatre, 65, 150
  influence on Group Theatre, 162, 166
Cornford, Frances, 57, 189n
  see also Cambridge Ritualists
Corrie, Joe, 48
Craig, Edith, 13, 178, 194n, 121
  see also Pioneer Players
Craig, Edward Gordon, 62–3, 67, 72, 117–18, 138, 188n, 189n
  connection with Yeats, 65, 120
  influence on Festival Theatre, 65
  influence on Theatre Workshop, 68
Crommelynk, Ferdnand, 69
  The Magnanimous Cuckold, 56, 69, 82

Dadaism, 7, 12, 92, 109
  see also Ball, Hugo; Tzara, Tristan
Dalcroze, Emile-Jacques:
  influence on Theatre Workshop, 154–5
Davidson, John, 97

Dean, Basil, 3, 13, 69, 73, 110, 139, 189n
  Johnson Over Jordan
    (with Priestley), 133
  Salute to the Red Army
    (with MacNeice), 142–4
Delaney, Shelagh, 49
Diaghilev, Sergei, 3, 152, 163, 175, 193n
  influence on Rupert Doone and Group Theatre, 151, 162, 166–7, 171
  see also Ballets Russes
Doone, Rupert, 2–3, 19, 32, 37, 43, 61, 191n
  connection with Ballets Russes, 166–7
  connection with Bloomsbury and Fry, 93
  connection with Festival Theatre, 66, 190n
  in *The Dance of Death*, 164
  see also Group Theatre
Dunne, J.W., 52
Dukes, Ashley, 14, 32, 40, 73, 83, 101, 122, 155, 164, 185n
  see also Mercury Theatre

Eden, Anthony, 143
Edinburgh Festival, 37
Edwards, Ness, 139–40
Eisenstein, Sergei, 41–3, 54
  influence on Theatre Workshop, 173
  influence on WTM, 155
Eisler, Hanns, 44, 172
Eliot, T.S., 9, 41, 47, 57, 86, 91, 97, 104, 113, 140, 149
  connection with Cambridge Ritualists, 58, 124, 188n
  connection with Group Theatre, 19; *The Family Reunion*, 129; *Murder in the Cathedral*, 100–1, 145; *Sweeney Agonistes*, 2–3, 37, 39, 54, 118, 123–5, 170, 191n; *The Waste Land*, 108

Engels, Friedrich, 145, 158
Evreinov, Nikolai:
  The Theatre of the Soul, 121–2

Federal Theatre Project, 25, 135,
  173, 183n, 185n
  One Third of a Nation, 18, 25
Festival Theatre, Cambridge, 19, 32,
  59, 65–6, 73, 151, 178, 190n
  see also Gray, Terence
Freud, Sigmund, 120–1, 124
Fry, Roger, 93
  see also Bloomsbury
Fuller, Loie, 163, 193n

Gaiety Theatre (Manchester), 13,
  23, 48
Galsworthy, John, 23, 50, 48
Gate Theatre, 10, 32
Gay, John, 173
Gielgud, John, 142
Goorney, Howard, 12, 48, 107,
  160
  see also Theatre Workshop
Gorelik, Mordecai, 49–50
Granville-Barker, Harley, 57, 62–3,
  86, 188n
Gray, Terence, 3, 65–6, 73, 113–14,
  151, 153, 174–5, 178, 189n,
  190n
  see also Festival Theatre
Greenwood, Walter, 48, 107
Gropius, Walter, 8, 56
Grosz, George, 71
Group Theatre, 2–3, 12, 17, 19, 43,
  57–8, 61, 80, 86, 112–13, 118,
  133, 140–1, 155, 163, 166–7,
  171–2, 177, 181, 162, 168,
  183n, 185n, 193n, 194n
  and Expressionism, 32, 37, 185n
  and film, 41
  connection with Ballets Russes,
  151
  connection with Festival Theatre,
  73, 66
  connection with Wyndham Lewis,
  93

see also Auden, W.H.; Britten,
  Benjamin; Copeau, Jacques;
  Doone, Rupert; Eliot, T.S;
  Isherwood, Christopher;
  MacNeice, Louis; Medley,
  Robert; Monck, Nugent;
  Spender, Stephen
Group Theatre (American), 144
Guthrie, Tyrone, 62, 86–7, 116,
  188n, 190n
  and Festival Theatre, 66
Gyseghem, Andre van:
  and Embassy Theatre, 131
  and Rebel Players, 18
  and Unity Theatre, 13, 26, 130

Hackney Peoples' Players, 18, 60
  see also Thomas, Tom; WTM
Hammer and Sickle Group
  (London):
  Meerut, 79–80
  see also WTM
Harrison, Jane, 57
  see also Cambridge Ritualists
Hatch Andrews, Donald, 161
Hauptmann, Elisabeth, 173
Hauptmann, Gerhart, 50
Hoggart, Richard, 29
Houghton, Stanley, 23, 48

Ibsen, Henrik, 23
  A Doll's House, 148
  Peer Gynt, 45
Illingworth, Nelson, 98–9, 108
ILP (Independent Labour Party), 14,
  32, 48, 143, 155, 185n
Ionesco, Eugène, 136
Isherwood, Christopher, 3, 19, 166,
  184n
  see also Auden-Isherwood
  Collaborations

Jarry, Alfred, 182
  Ubu Roi, 119
Jooss, Kurt, 3, 8, 185n, 193n
  The Green Table, 165
Jonson, Ben, 125–6, 190n

Kaiser, Georg, 40
Kandinsky, Wassily, 38
   The Yellow Sound, 34
Kane, Sarah, 180, 194n
Kantor, Tadeusz, 138
Kokoschka, Oskar, 186n
   Murderer Hope of Womankind, 34,
      76–8, 169, 180
Komisarjevsky, Theodor, 190n
   Macbeth, 87

Laban, Rudolf, 8, 162, 193n
   influence on Theatre Workshop,
      158–61, 172
Laboratory Theatre (New York), 26
   Newsboy, 27, 54, 135, 154
Lamont Stewart, Ena, 49
Lawrence, D.H., 48, 107
Left Theatre, 13
Lewis, Wyndham, 99, 101, 140
   connection with Group Theatre,
      93
   BLAST, 5, 12, 89
   Enemy of the Stars, 92, 94–5,
      191n
   One Way Song, 95
Library Theatre, Manchester, 37
Lindsay, Jack, 140, 192n
   On Guard for Spain, 104–5, 141
Littlewood, Joan, 9, 18–19, 28, 37,
      39, 44, 46–7, 58, 88, 97–8,
      154–5, 158–60
   see also MacColl, Ewan; Theatre of
      Action; Theatre Union; Theatre
      Workshop
Lloyd, Marie, 149
Lorca, Federico García, 141
Lukács, Georg, 4, 35

Mabou Mines, 179
MacColl, Ewan, 12–14, 18–19, 26,
      28, 32, 36, 44, 46, 53, 57, 60,
      68, 72, 82–3, 88, 90, 97, 105,
      140, 150, 154, 158–9, 173,
      189n, 191n, 192n
   The Damnable Town, 51
   The Flying Doctor, 160, 172

Hell is What You Make It, 125–7,
   190n
Johnny Noble, 107, 131, 143, 160,
   172
Landscape with Chimneys, 49–52,
   64, 132, 137–8, 157, 164,
   174
The Other Animals, 35–7, 38–9, 75,
   80, 89, 99–101, 111, 123, 143–4,
   170, 181, 187
Uranium, 235, 29, 129, 134–5,
   161–2, 184n, 186n, 193n
   see also Littlewood, Joan; Red
      Megaphones; Theatre of
      Action; Theatre Union; Theatre
      Workshop
MacDiarmid, Hugh, 88
MacNeice, Louis, 3, 19, 86, 90, 97,
   100, 141, 166, 171, 181
   The Agamemnon of Aeschylus, 13
   Christopher Columbus, 104
   Out of the Picture, 23–4, 90–1, 135
   Salute to the Red Army (with Basil
      Dean), 142–4
Maddermarket Theatre (Norwich),
   14, 190n
   see also Monck, Nugent
Maeterlinck, Maurice, 110, 191n
Mahler, Gustav, 39, 186n
Maleczech, Ruth, 179
Malleson, Miles, 13, 48
Mann, Charlie, 79, 193n
Mann, Heinrich, 137
Marinetti, F.T., 11, 46, 94, 109, 149,
   153
Marshall, Herbert (Bert), 26, 71, 99
Marshall, Norman, 189n
Marshall, Vance, 107
Marx, Karl, 145, 158, 164
Massine, Léonide, 151, 167, 175
   see also Ballets Russes
Mayakovsky, Vladimir:
   Mystery-Bouffe, 125–7
   The Bedbug, 78–9
McGrath, John, 179–80
   see also 7:84
McLeish, Robert, 113

Medley, Robert, 2, 19, 57, 73, 112, 167, 185n
connection with Bloomsbury, 93
see also Group Theatre
Mercury Theatre, 14, 19, 101, 155, 185n
see also Dukes, Ashley
Meyerhold, Vsevolod, 70–1, 75, 81, 87, 116–17, 155–6, 159, 162, 166, 168, 181
influence on Theatre Workshop, 68, 80, 157
The Magnanimous Cuckold, 56, 69
Moholy-Nagy, László, 56
Monck, Nugent, 14, 190n, 191n
Moussinac, Léon, 43, 68, 70, 187n, 188n
Mummers play, 58, 116, 188n 189n
Munch, Edvard, 111
Murray, Gilbert, 57–8
see also Cambridge Ritualists
Murrill, Herbert, 171
Music Hall, 8, 47, 89, 149–50, 157, 168

Neruda, Pablo, 137
Newlove, Jean, 158, 160–1, 193n
see also Theatre Workshop
Niven, Barbara, 57, 188n

O'Casey, Sean, 13, 16, 33, 36, 103, 185n, 186n
O'Neill, Eugene, 32, 66, 77–9, 157, 169, 185n, 190n
Obey, André, 125–6
Odets, Clifford, 18, 117, 144
Olivier, Laurence, 142
Osborne, John, 49

Parker, Charles, 173, 191n
People's Theatre, the (Newcastle), 32, 77, 139
Piper, John, 57, 81
Pioneer Players, 13, 19, 121, 178, 194n
Pirandello, Luigi, 66, 116

Piscator, Erwin, 26, 43, 56, 68, 70–1, 76, 80–1, 83, 190n
Playfair, Nigel, 173
Poel, William, 62–3, 86–7, 189n
Pogodin, Nikolai, 71, 99
Popova, Lyubov, 56, 69
Pound, Ezra, 101
Priestley, J.B., 53, 185n
Johnson Over Jordan, 133–4
Time and the Conways, 49–52

Rambert, Marie, 155
Rebel Players, 18
see also WTM
Red Megaphones, 10, 19, 32, 60, 80, 106, 144, 156, 184n
see also MacColl, Ewan; Theatre of Action; Theatre Union; Theatre Workshop
Rice, Elmer, 32, 78, 128, 185n
Ridge, Harold, 73
Robeson, Paul, 13

Saint-Denis, Michel, 126–7
Saint-Simon, Henri, 4–5, 7
Saussure, Ferdinand de, 109–10
Schofield, Stephen:
The Judge of All the Earth, 18, 35, 67, 186
Scott, Benedick, 74
Seeger, Peggy, 173, 191n
Shakespeare, William, 58, 62, 86–7, 89, 96
Coriolanus, 87
Hamlet, 89–90, 121
Macbeth, 87–8, 101–2
Shaw, George Bernard, 23, 48, 188n
Shaw, Irwin:
Bury the Dead, 130, 132
Slater, Montagu, 3, 187n
New Way Wins (Stay Down Miner), 13, 49, 51
Simonson, Lee, 56, 188n
Sinclair, Upton, 79
Prince Hagen, 56
Singing Jailbirds, 77, 143–4

Sorge, Reinhard:
   The Beggar, 75, 122, 191n
Spanish Civil War, 27–8, 60, 104,
   137, 140–1
Spender, Stephen, 3, 8, 14–15, 19,
   86, 91, 93, 95–6, 101, 105, 113,
   141, 153, 166, 189n
   Trial of a Judge, 74, 80–1, 102, 127,
   145, 181
St John, Christopher, 121
   see also Pioneer Players
Stage Society, 14, 78
Stravinsky, Igor, 39
   The Rite of Spring, 155
Strindberg, August, 182, 188n
   A Dream Play, 134
   Miss Julie, 189n
   The Father, 53
   To Damascus, 125
Swingler, Randall, 13
Surrealism, 7, 194n

Theatre of Action, 19, 184n
   John Bullion, 67–8, 91, 117, 189n
   see also MacColl, Ewan; Red
     Megaphones; Theatre Union;
     Theatre Workshop
Theatre Union, 12, 19, 141, 158,
   184n
   Last Edition, 27–8, 31, 46, 129–30,
   149, 185n
   see also MacColl, Ewan; Red
     Megaphones; Theatre of Action;
     Theatre Workshop
Theatre Workshop, 3, 9, 12, 17, 19,
   60, 86, 88, 97, 105, 107–8, 140,
   162, 177–81, 184n, 188n, 190n
   and Adolphe Appia, 72, 80
   and Expressionism, 32, 40
   and Gaiety Theatre, 48
   and Greek Theatre, 58
   and Leon Moussinac, 43, 68, 187n
   and Living Newspaper, 25–6,
     29–31, 142–3, 173
   connection with Barbara Niven, 57
   connection with Nelson
     Illingworth, 98–9

and Sean O'Casey, 185
audience, 113
influence of Wagner, 150
influence of Piscator, 70
movement, 154, 157, 159
Oh What a Lovely War!, 47, 150,
   179
see also Littlewood, Joan; Red
   Megaphones; Theatre of Action;
   Theatre Union
for specific plays see MacColl, Ewan
Thomas, Tom, 18, 60, 68, 80
   *The Ragged Trousered
   Philanthropists*, 48
   see also Hackney People's Players
Toller, Ernst, 3, 8, 14, 35, 40, 48,
   66, 79
   Draw the Fires, 32
   Hoppla, We're Alive, 52, 70–1, 76,
   83, 169, 189n
   The Machine Wreckers, 14, 155
   Masses Man, 13, 35, 77, 124–5,
   127–8, 188n, 191n
   Pastor Hall, 15, 185
   Transformation, 36, 38, 54, 111,
   128
Thorndike, Sybil, 13, 88, 142
Treadwell, Sophie:
   Machinal, 76–7, 127, 191
Tretiakov, Sergei, 43, 66, 189n
Tricycle Theatre (London), 180
Tzara, Tristan, 109, 182, 192n
   The Gas Heart, 137

Unity Theatre, 3, 10, 12, 13, 17–18,
   33, 44, 48, 57, 86, 97–9, 105,
   108, 125, 130, 140, 142, 144,
   149, 178, 180, 184n, 189n
   and Expressionism, 14, 32, 40,
     74, 81
   and Living Newspapers, 26–7, 29,
     30–1, 112
   and Piscator, 70
   Busmen, 25–8, 42, 66–7
   Cannibal Carnival, 117
   The Fall of the House of Slusher, 117
   Get Cracking, 47, 89

Unity Theatre – *continued*
  Trial of a Judge (with Stephen
    Spender), 189
  see also Lindsay, Jack; Marshall,
    Herbert; Marshall, Vance
Unity Theatre (Bristol), 141
Unity Theatre (Glasgow), 74, 113
Unity Theatre (Liverpool,
  Merseyside), 46

Van, Druten, John:
  I am a Camera, 184n
Vega, Lope de:
  The Sheep's Well, 141, 188n
Vorticism, 12, 87
  see also Lewis, Wyndham

Wagner, Richard, 150–2, 167, 172,
  192n
Weill, Kurt, 172, 187n
Wesker, Arnold, 49
Wilde, Oscar, 66
  Salome, 169, 189n
Wilder, Thornton, 192n
  Our Town, 131–2
  Pullman Car Hiawatha, 52
Woolf, Virginia, 2–3, 12, 187n
  Between the Acts, 177, 179, 194n

Workers' Film Movement, 41
WTM (Workers' Theatre Movement),
  18, 59–60, 66, 86, 105, 108,
  143, 178, 181, 184n, 190n
  and agit-prop, 61, 82
  and Expressionism, 32–3, 35
  and music hall, 149
  audience, 113
  influence of Meyerhold, 67–8
  movement, 155, 162, 193n
  Art is a Weapon, 117
  Their Theatre and Ours, 107,
    156–7
  see also Hammer and Sickle
    Group; Red Megaphones;
    Schofield, Stephen

Yeats, W.B., 2, 16, 57, 63–4, 66,
  91, 99, 116, 118, 163–4, 188n,
  191n, 193n
  The Dreaming of the Bones, 65, 67,
    129
  A Full Moon in March, 169
  The Only Jealousy of Emer, 120

Zola, Emile, 23, 53